EAMONN ANDREWS

His Life

Also by Gus Smith and published by W.H. Allen

WOGAN

EAMONN ANDREWS

His Life

Gus Smith

W H ALLEN · LONDON
1988

Printed and bound in Great Britain by
Mackays of Chatham Plc, Lordswood, Chatham, Kent
for the Publishers, W.H. Allen & Co. Plc
44 Hill Street, London W1X 8LB

ISBN 0 491 03088 6

6790P

CONTENTS

Author's acknowledgements

Producing a book like this raised the difficult question – which people to leave out? For Eamonn Andrews, in presenting hundreds of *This Is Your Life* programmes made many lasting friendships; he also worked with different BBC and Thames Television production teams, who remember him with esteem. So I was obliged to exercise careful selectivity. Inevitably some people will be disappointed. In the course of my research, which I began almost a year before Eamonn died, I talked to people who influenced his career more than others, or knew him more closely; a few people, for reasons I can only respect, wished not to be identified, though their contributions were extremely useful to the story. Happily, I was able to use my own interviews with Eamonn over a span of twenty years.

I wish to acknowledge the following people who helped me piece together the life of a truly legendary broadcaster and remarkable man. They include:

T. Leslie Jackson, Malcolm Morris, Brian Tesler, Maurice Leonard, Terry Yarwood, Joe Loss, Mildred Loss, Group Captain Leonard Cheshire, Lady Ryder of Warsaw, Terry Wogan, Henry Cooper, Val Doonican, Richard Harris, Jimmy Savile, Barbara Kelly, Frankie Vaughan, James Gilbert, Danny Blanchflower, Bill (Liam) Nolan, Max Boyce, Micheal O hAodha, Joe Kearns, Dermot Doolan, Joan O'Hara, Jack O'Connor, Fred O'Donovan, Bernadette Greevy, J.J. Finegan, Philip O'Flynn.

I am indebted to Dublin photographer, Pat Maxwell, a longtime friend of Eamonn Andrews, for a number of special studies of the broadcaster.

I am grateful to the RTE, BBC and Thames Television library staffs for their valuable assistance, as well as to the following sources of information: *Radio Times, TV Times, The Listener, The Observer, Sunday Times, Sunday Express, Sunday Independent, Sunday Tribune, The Times, Irish Independent, Irish Press, Irish Times, Daily Mail, Daily Mirror, Evening Standard*; and the following books: *This Is My Life* by Eamonn Andrews (MacDonald & Co. Publishers, 1963), *The Special Years* by Val Doonican (Elm Tree Books, 1980), *Surprise of Your Life* by Eamonn Andrews & Jack Crawshaw (Everest Books Ltd., 1978), *Gilbert Harding by his friends*, edited by Stephen Grenfell (Andrew Deutsch, 1961), *Master of None* by Gilbert Harding (Putnam, 1958), *Forty Years of Irish Broadcasting* by Maurice Gorham (Radio Telefis Eireann, 1961), *Wogan* by Gus Smith (W.H. Allen & Co., 1987), *Mountbatten* by Philip Ziegler (Collins & Co. Ltd., 1985), *Freedom at Midnight* by Larry Collins & Dominique Lapierre (Collins & Co. Ltd., 1975), *James Joyce* by Herbert Gorman (The Bodley Head, 1941), *Sean O'Casey – The Man I Knew* by Gabriel Fallon (Routledge & Kegan Paul, Ltd., 1965).

Gus Smith
February 1988

INTRODUCTION

A large photograph of Eamonn Andrews greets you in one of the winding corridors of Thames Television Studios in Teddington, Middlesex. The smile, relaxed and genial, dominates the broad, handsome face and reaches, it seems, to the granite-like jaw. It is a smile that for years inspired loyalty and friendship and was first seen way back in those flickering, snow-storming black-and-white TV days. By the middle of the 1980s Eamonn was the only survivor of that pioneering era.

As chairman of the popular middle-brow entertainment, *What's My Line?* he became a national celebrity. As one critic commented, 'He neither patronised nor hectored his audience; he never upstaged or bullied his guests, and he eschewed the vitriolic. And his friendly smile was invariably accompanied by a soft, classless Irish brogue.'

Eamonn remembered those days with affection: 'The first time I was recognised was at the old Kensington air-station. You know in those days the first people who seemed to buy sets were taxi-drivers, in fact there was a strange sort of snobbery at first about not having watched any telly at all. For years I was being greeted on the social scene by "Oh, yes, you're the chap who does that thing, what do you call it?"'

In a way the ambitious young Andrews looked an unlikely candidate for stardom in the tough television jungle. Polite and innately shy, he projected ordinariness and charm as opposed to the brashness of some of his colleagues. Later, those trying to draw a distinction between his public and private images found it difficult to reconcile the two. For off-screen he was a devout Catholic and a happy family man who was singularly lacking pretension. Nonetheless, in a relatively few years he was to become in broadcasting terms a colossus, despite his life-long nervousness before a camera. Undeniably his professional skill and friendly face made him a success, though his versatility as a performer was another powerful asset in his favour. He was known to broadcast a world heavyweight title fight from America and return the next day to resume his presentation of *What's My Line?* and *This Is Your Life.*

The big man took it all in his stride. His genuine interest in people made it easy for his audience to identify with him. His success in Britain was all the more remarkable when you consider he was the first Irishman to break into the British media. It was this unique achievement that tended to attract Terry Wogan's attention. Discussing Eamonn's career with me in his dressing-room in the BBC Theatre in Shepherd's Bush on a November afternoon in 1987, Terry remarked, 'It is Eamonn's record as a broadcaster that impresses me. No one will ever equal it, certainly not me.' Someone else said, 'Eamonn ended up the benign "Godfather" of a whole "Murphia" of Irish broadcasters who followed him onto the mail-boat and have benefited similarly.'

However, his insistence on perfection tended to exasperate not a few producers, who occasionally found his over-methodical approach old-fashioned, yet in time they were compelled to admire his sheer consistency. Whatever he did was done with energy, gusto and a deep devotion to the difficult art he practised. In a lengthy career it can be said that Eamonn enjoyed more success than failure. In addition, his dexterity in combining two careers – businessman and showman – almost paid off, save for some bad luck in his Irish enterprises.

Presumably, he was attracted to the world of big business

because of the money and security it offered. Coming from humble origins, he was occasionally assailed by a feeling of insecurity; it was one of the reasons why, his friends say, he never stopped working, even when he reached millionaire status. Eamonn enjoyed working. His own definition of success was: 'Success to me has meant deriving the maximum enjoyment from my work. The older I get the more I realise what a bonus this is. Since most of one's life is spent working, isn't it marvellous to be able to enjoy every moment of one's working days? If people could achieve this enjoyment from work they would be halfway to a more relaxed and happy life.'

As a broadcaster he coped extremely well with the vicissitudes and at crucial moments in his career, when it seemed his star was on the wane, his resilience stood him well and he bounced back to achieve more success. He identified completely with *This Is Your Life;* in time it became a fetish with him. As one critic put it, 'Banal it may have been at times, but it was Eamonn's lucrative meal ticket and it earned its place in media history.'

Like life itself, which he viewed with an optimist's eye, he never once lost faith in *Life*. Perhaps he is after all irreplaceable as its presenter.

PART ONE

Dublin

I sometimes think I must have come from the shyest family in Ireland.

Eamonn Andrews

1 *The Plotters*

AT ABOUT THE same time that Eamonn Andrews was arriving at Dublin Airport on Thursday evening, October 15, 1987, Richard Harris was ensconced in an armchair in his seventh floor hotel suite six miles away. Eamonn was on his way to his home in Portmarnock to join his wife, Grainne, and their children, Emma, Fergal and Niamh, while Harris was spending a short vacation in Ireland.

The previous evening he had watched the *This Is Your Life* show with an uneasy feeling. For twice, he would tell friends, Eamonn and the Thames *Life* team had tried to 'target him' but without success.

Early in the 1980s, when he was starring in *Camelot* in a West End theatre they had tried. He remembers: 'My brother Dermot and a business associate John McMichael were first approached. They sat in at a meeting with the *Life* team, but Dermot told them, "You can spend all the money you like, assemble all the Hollywood stars you want, but if Richard doesn't want to do the show, that's that". I think they planned to have my two ex-wives on the show. Funnily, they would both have been in London at the same time.'

It was proposed to surprise Harris in the theatre. 'I think that Eamonn would have got a terrible shock,' he says today. 'I would have walked off, I certainly would. I had severed connections with my second wife and didn't want her paraded before me in *This Is Your Life*. I think she would have gloried in it.'

Eighteen months later the *Life* team were on his trail again. He had rented a house in Stroud and staying with him was his brother Dermot, and his own first wife, Elizabeth and their children. Harris had a habit of writing on bits of paper and sticking the notes on walls and chairs or mirrors. One morning, in the bathroom, he noticed a note stuck on the wall in which was scribbled 'Andrews, Life' and a telephone number. By now Dermot had acquired the same habit to remind him of dates and events. When he came down to breakfast, Richard asked him if the note was his.

'Oh, yeah,' Dermot said casually.

'What does it mean?'

'Well,' Dermot said, 'while you were out yesterday John McMichael called and told me that Eamonn Andrews was after you again.'

'Tell them forget it. I'm not going through with it.'

Dermot gave a wry smile. 'I knew all along you wouldn't. They'll probably come after you again.'

'You know what to say to them.'

Richard Harris wasn't sure if his brother had meant to keep the *Life* secret from him. 'Dermot regarded me as mercurial and didn't know for sure whether I'd say yes. But I could always trust him.'

It was Eamonn's suggestion in the first place. Remembering Harris's hellraising days in London in the fifties, he knew he would make a lively subject for *This Is Your Life* and had always been eager to get him. He also knew the stage and screen star could be difficult.

Today, Richard Harris says, 'I've no objection to anyone who wants to go on the show. Because it's running so long, one must assume that people like it. I do believe, though, that half an hour is too short a duration in which to tell a worthwhile story.'

That December, his stay in Stroud was, on his own admission, made miserable. 'I was terrified. Every time I went for a walk I kept looking around the park benches for fear of seeing Eamonn Andrews pop out on me with his red book. Even when I went to do my shopping for Christmas I dared not look at Santa Claus in case he was Eamonn in disguise. The fact that someone is trying to get you can be very unnerving, despite my years in show-business.'

Harris's genuine apprehension underlined not only the powerful affect the show could have on certain stars but also the show business pinnacle Eamonn Andrews had now reached. Obviously, to some people, he had become a kind of super sleuth ready to pounce on his victim, and someone to be avoided at any cost. To the majority of the British population, though, he was – after completing nearly 900 *Life* shows – still a big, amiable television presenter who wasn't trying to discover skeletons in anybody's cupboard but rather provide a happy party show.

The famous unchanged format which had survived for decades continued to be popular with millions of viewers, though it provided fuel for detractors who found it much too gentle and affectionate; a show that admitted no malice or scandal, its brief biographies being more panegyrics than profiles. The show's title, *This Is Your Life*, hinted at more than it delivered, yet the durability of the show remained unquestionable, and made a mockery of those who asked, 'How long more can it survive?'

Richard Harris was not alone in trying to avoid Eamonn. There were others. Eamonn had suggested at a Thames conference that Maureen O'Hara would make an ideal subject for *Life*. His researchers began to work on her Irish and Hollywood backgrounds and when it seemed they could go ahead and surprise her eventually at her holiday home in West Cork, they ran into a snag.

'We discovered,' Eamonn confided later to a friend, 'that her family felt it would not be appropriate to do the show at that particular time, but our file isn't closed for good on Maureen.'

He had greatly enjoyed her starring role in John Ford's film,

The Quiet Man, which was shot on location in the West of Ireland, with John Wayne as her co-star. For her *Life*, he had intended parading on screen some legendary Hollywood stars.

Eamonn was also disappointed when the team ran into snags after initial research on the life of distinguished Irish actor Cyril Cusack. As in the case of Maureen O'Hara, the Cusack family did not think that Cyril 'would be keen to appear in the show'. Parading on screen famous theatrical families strongly appealed to Eamonn – and the Cusack dynasty was by now among the best known in the business. Cusack had filmed with the Burtons, Sir Alec Guinness and a host of stars, and he was one of the greatest Abbey Theatre actors of his generation.

Such disappointments were a source of real frustration to Eamonn – and the *Life* team generally. Brian Klein, associate producer of the programme remarked, 'I feel like jumping off window ledges when the secrets go prematurely public. All that work, all that intrigue, all for nothing.'

How did a secret get blown? Sometimes it stemmed from jealousy – a 'why should they be on the show?' attitude of a subject's colleague. Sometimes it was because a friend or relative felt that a potential subject would not enjoy all the emotion that went with appearing on the show.

'It's difficult to positively identify the wrecker,' Eamonn once remarked. 'The person who has spilled the beans, but it's maddening, heartbreaking and also very expensive.'

Occasionally the luck was with *Life*. Des O'Connor's *This Is Your Life* came from the London Palladium where he was doing a season. Just before his stage show he had walked out of the theatre for a breath of air and half thought he had seen a coach full of old friends and relatives. He reckoned he was dreaming and forgot all about it.

But Eamonn could laugh also when things went wrong. Ronnie Barker opened a drawer at his wife's dressing table and found a man's business card tucked among the underwear. He phoned the number on it, and ended up talking to another *This Is Your Life* researcher and rubbing out the work of weeks. The

[6]

bizarre also happened in the case of entertainer Bernard Braden. His wife, Barbara Kelly, was the 'link' as plans went ahead for the show. The production team chirped away about the arrangements while a young nephew, aged four, played in the house. Only days before recording, Bernard happened to be talking about his plans for the week with Barbara and was discussing a particular night. 'We're not doing anything that night anyway,' he told his wife. Suddenly the little relative interjected, 'Oh yes you are, you're on *This Is Your Life*'. The show was immediately scrapped after Bernard phoned the production team to inform them that the secret was out.

Eamonn was prepared to do almost anything to ensure the success of the show. Using fancy disguises did not embarrass him. To surprise Arthur Askey, he became a giant Easter egg. Astronomer Patrick Moore proved a challenge. 'I wore a spacesuit,' recalled Eamonn. 'The trouble was that it was a real astronaut's suit, with heavy gravity boots, and Patrick moves quickly.'

He enjoyed catching two Londoners well known for their quick wits. He was a newspaper seller outside a Fleet Street restaurant to confront former Fleet Street editor Derek Jameson. 'I had a muffler and a cap and I actually sold a few papers while I was waiting for him.' They mocked up a front page which said 'Derek Jameson in Trouble Again', so he naturally stopped and bought one. To pick up Fred Housego, the cabby who won *Mastermind*, Eamonn became a very old man, hard of hearing, whom he had to collect from Waterloo. Nor was it unusual for him to travel abroad to surprise his subjects. Katie Boyle proved to be one of the most dramatic targets. Eamonn flew to Rome for the pick-up. He dressed as an Italian policeman, directing traffic round the Coliseum. Presently Katie appeared driving towards him in a pony and trap. She believed she was being filmed. As the carriage appeared in front of him, he put up his hand to stop it. What he hadn't bargained for was the fact that Katie is an Italian contessa and fluent in the language.

'She let fly in colourful Italian at the driver,' he said later, 'telling him to ignore me and drive on. I had to leap up and grab the reins shouting "This Is Your Life"!'

The *Life* team knew that Eamonn lived for such exciting moments. It was no surprise therefore that his faith in the programme never once wavered. 'I've always felt it was the best television idea I've come across. It's always different, you never know what is going to happen, and there's always – for me – the knowledge and the feeling that you are going out there to talk to twenty million people.' He recognised that it was *This Is Your Life* that had made him a superstar. He was absolutely convinced that despite the criticisms and the sneers it was first-class television. He came to love the show and was never completely satisfied. At the *Life* conferences he would ask, 'There's someone in Nigeria who'd make a good subject; should we try for him?' Or: 'Why not try again to capture that war hero in Devon?'

Secretly, Eamonn had thought of the Queen Mother as a potential subject. If he succeeded he knew he would have the greatest Royal show of the lot. However, when a *Life* researcher made an approach the answer was not unexpected. 'The time was not appropriate.'

The closest he had come to the Queen Mother was Lord Mountbatten, when he surprised him on a Wednesday evening in April 1977. As producer Jack Crawshaw would remark, 'It's taken us eight years to get any member of the Royal Family and it seemed most fitting in the Jubilee Year to try to approach Lord Mountbatten. We knew that he had a sense of humour and his family seemed to agree that the idea of doing the programme would appeal.' Eamonn was in no doubt about the merits of his first Royal programme: 'It was most exciting for me and the team. In fact, the best *This Is Your Life* we ever did. For me, it was personally a night of many golden memories – and one of course of intense relief. I know my heart stopped when I revealed the *Life* book to Lord

Mountbatten.'

He was himself the subject of *Life* on two different occasions. On each occasion he found the experience 'shattering'. He was also able to see the humorous side, as when his mother Margaret nearly caused an upset:

When they flew her and the family over from Dublin, they booked her into an hotel on the south side of Hyde Park. I was living on the north side. My mother became assailed by doubts as to whether she was doing the right thing. She didn't know all these strange people who were arranging all these incredible things. The only one she did know was producer Leslie Jackson, who kept on assuring her that everything was alright. Even so, she told me afterwards, her hand strayed towards the telephone in the hotel time and time again. 'I must ring Eamonn and ask him if it's all right'. Fortunately she never did. Or bang would have gone another *This Is Your Life*.

Joe Loss, the popular dance band leader, was also the recipient of the red book on two occasions from Eamonn. Afterwards, he would say, 'It was an unforgettable experience'. Now, as he sat at his desk on the fourth floor of Morley House in Regent Street, he recalled their friendship spanning nearly forty years. When Eamonn first handed him the red book back in the sixties he said he was 'stunned'. 'I think most people in my position go through the same experience – we can't call it anything else. We never think it can happen to us and when it does happen we never expect it. We are shattered.'

On the second occasion, in the early eighties, he reckoned the experience was even more profound. Mildred, his wife, was in on the secret on both occasions and found it increasingly hard to keep it to herself. 'When you've been open with your husband for so long, it's not easy to carry around secrets from him.'

After Terry Wogan was surprised in the late seventies,

during his morning radio programme in Broadcasting House, he told himself he was not nearly as perceptive as he'd reckoned he was. 'I mean my producer, my wife, relatives and friends – even my children – were all in on the plot and yet I never sensed a thing. It showed me that I was as sensitive as a toilet seat.' To Terry, the only thing wrong with the show was that it was done five years too early. He hadn't presented *Blankety Blank* or the Wogan chat show; otherwise, he enjoyed the experience. 'I never considered it an intrusion. I now know that I reacted in startled fashion when confronted by Eamonn but I think that was understandable in the circumstances. I was glad in another way that it happened to me then, for my father was alive to enjoy it; that was an enormous advantage – he was thrilled.'

Eamonn went to extremes to ensure that secrecy was maintained. He even expected the *Life* team to dine together – and keep to themselves. So obsessed had he become about keeping the guests a surprise that he did not even let Grainne in on the secret. As he explained, 'I was a clam – but I kept it from her because I liked her to be able to judge the programme objectively. And I'd never tell anyone else because then if it *did* leak out they could be blamed. Sometimes, however, I wondered if the celebrity knew and was pretending not to. But I usually looked them right in the eye and it was seldom I had a doubt. Some people reacted very low key and sat there in shock, others were very excited. If you heard some of the speeches after the programme you'd be moved.'

The secrecy surrounding the show is maintained at Thames by the use of codenames. Bob Geldof, for example, was known as 'Mice' because of his connection with the Boomtown Rats. Even Eamonn himself had a codename when he was the subject. 'I was told later that my codename was "Miracle", meaning it is a miracle, if they could pull it off without my finding out,' he later recalled. 'And they nearly didn't. I came into my office unexpectedly one day, and in the very next room

[10]

they were planning my programme, with photographs of me laid out all over the desk.'

There is further evidence of this strict secrecy on the second floor of Thames Television in Teddington. A dozen members of the *Life* team work there while in the adjacent room, much smaller and divided by a glass partition, sits Malcolm Morris, a longtime producer of the show. Dark-haired, affable and of medium height, he is proud to recall that he had accompanied Eamonn Andrews on innumerable programme pick-ups in Britain and overseas. 'It's always exciting, sometimes even quite breathtaking,' he says. Behind his desk can be seen more than a dozen photographs of Eamonn with the celebrities he surprised, including Lord Mountbatten. But the most significant object on the wall is a large board on which is written words such as 'Stump', 'Chart' and 'Copter'. They are the code words used for *Life* subjects and only Morris and a few of his team can decode them. He is of the view that most people secretly wish to be surprised by Eamonn Andrews. As he explains, 'Wives have told me that despite their husbands' repeated warnings to them not to plot with us for their appearance on the show, they really felt that their husbands would jump at the chance of being handed the red book. I believe that – and Eamonn shared with me that view also.'

Eamonn, like his producers, always placed great value on the surprise element in *Life*: 'The big surprise is important, indeed it is everything.'

Producer Jack Crawshaw agreed: 'So important is the surprise that if we thought for one moment our chosen guest of honour knew our plans we would cancel the presentation. Why is it so important? First of all, it is more fun for the guest. Secondly, it protects him – or her – from any accusation of immodesty in accepting tributes.'

For that reason Richard Harris had no cause for worry as he prepared to leave his hotel suite for dinner in the ground floor dining-room. Nonetheless he felt that the *Life* team would try again. 'I know they will', he said.

★

It was a fact that Eamonn did not easily accept failure. From boyhood, determination was a strong characteristic, a powerful motivating force, even if it was often masked by a beaming smile. Malcolm Morris would say that Eamonn was prepared to go to the moon to achieve a successful *Life* pick-up. When the *This Is Your Life* team pointed out hurdles or obstacles in getting someone's story, he immediately wanted to know how quickly they could be surmounted.

When David Frost's name came up for discussion at the weekly Thames production conference, it was stated that it would be very difficult to surprise him because he was rarely in the country. Frost was by now a jet-setter and an international TV personality. Eamonn admired the way he had made it in America, as well as his talent and industry. He described him then as 'a young man in a hurry'.

But how was he going to surprise him? He pondered the question for days. The only hope was at Frost's favourite restaurant – in this case, Quaglino's, where he had once worked in cabaret. Mona Frost, his mother, agreed to assist the *Life* team but because she was close to her son found the secret 'terribly hard to keep'.

That evening, Eamonn waited nervously for the Frosts to arrive at the restaurant, wondering if David would after all refuse to take the table chosen for him rather than his own. Eamonn would say later, 'Fortunately David succumbed to the charms of the invincible combination of mother and Maitre d'. And while they tucked into sumptuous dinners I waited, mouth watering, until a decent interval had passed before interrupting, as the coffee was about to be served, with my own addition to the menu.'

Like the Romeo who counts his conquests, Eamonn also derived personal satisfaction in making what seemed difficult *Life* conquests. Surprising David Frost afforded him genuine pleasure, in the same way as when he handed the red book to the elusive Jimmy Savile, who for months had led Thames a merry dance before they finally caught up with him. As he would joke, 'They spent a small fortune trying to make a present to me of a book'.

Again, Eamonn showed his rare determination. Failure on the first occasion in no way deterred him; if anything, it acted as a spur. The *Life* team enticed Savile to a Royal Marines camp in Exeter where he was supposed to be inspecting a commando unit. To everyone's surprise, he didn't suspect a thing. Now, as he began to inspect the Marines, accompanied by an officer, Eamonn, dressed in uniform, suddenly broke rank and said, 'Jimmy Savile, This Is Your Life!' At that moment the disc-jockey fumed. 'You bloody Irish potato.'

Eamonn, who on his own admission was as nervous as a kitten at all *Life* pick-ups, quickly left the feeling behind him after he had succeeded in netting his 'victim'. The satisfaction showed in his victorious smile, indeed in his whole demeanour. He was like a young newspaperman after his first scoop. 'It's a wonderful sensation,' Eamonn would admit. 'It's hard really to describe in detail'.

2 The Quarry

IF RICHARD HARRIS had been living in fear that the *Life* team would eventually catch up with him, it was nothing to Eamonn Andrews' own fear that when he came face to face with the person he had just surprised with the words, 'This Is Your Life', they would just turn away and refuse to go through with the show.

This only happened on two occasions. One of those who refused was Richard Gordon, author of the *Doctor* stories which become very successful comedy films. The other was soccer personality, Danny Blanchflower. Gordon however relented and the show went ahead a week later.

Always Eamonn tried to avoid looking back on life. 'It's only because I'm such a sentimental person I can't afford to look back.' On the particular October evening when he made that remark he was in relaxed mood; he was back in the house he called his 'real home'. Years before he had bought it as a holiday home but decided to ask his friend, Dublin architect Sam Stephenson, to plan an extension and convert it into permanent living quarters. The result was impressive. The house is set in about three acres of gardens which Stephenson transformed from a disused quarry. It is luxurious and meets the description of 'a scene from a James Bond film'. Surrounded by trees, shaven lawns, rockeries, shrubs and flowers, it appears more attractive than Wogan Towers which is hidden away in leafy Buckinghamshire; no one ever dared to draw a comparison between the mansions.

To Eamonn, who sought privacy, it was the realisation of a personal ambition. He saw it as mirroring his own achievements in life rather than an actual status symbol, such as a Rolls Royce. Privately he was proud of the house. Sometimes he was reluctant, though, to be photographed by the heated swimming-pool. 'I don't want to give the impression we live in some Hollywood-style place – the Dublin Riviera – although I know it's difficult to stop people talking.'

The Quarry, as the house was called, provided the perfect retreat from the excitement of *This Is Your Life* and the hassle of travel. It possesses charm and elegance, though Eamonn was sometimes amused to read what visiting journalists wrote. He felt they exaggerated the 'exotic side', yet there was no disguising the truth – it *was* an unusual mansion, despite the fact that it was set in rather ordinary surroundings by the sea in Portmarnock, about eight miles from Dublin. To the visitor, there is a tremendous feeling of spaciousness and light throughout, enhanced by numerous mirrors giving it an air of perpetual summer, though in winter the log fires must bring a seasonable glow, and there is something unexpected to be found in every corner. White dominates. Even the dining room has a white fitted carpet. In this room there is a little bar with a huge mirror at the back of it, with glass shelves covered with crystal glasses, and a white marble counter. Eamonn and Grainne's bedroom is on this floor. Here also the theme is white, apart from the patchwork bedspread and lamp in varying shades of red. Another interesting touch is the sunken marble bath with golden taps. Everything is spotless and in perfect order.

'When you walk into the house,' remarked a young woman journalist, 'it is like entering a peaceful undersea world, lying somewhere off a Pacific island.' She found the walls 'rich with paintings and etchings and unobtrusive shelves carry beautiful pieces of ladro and china. An open house. A bright house.'

Usually Eamonn relaxed in his study, where the balloon

windows overlooked the swimming pool and a waterfall which cascaded over the rock at the back of the house. Here he liked to read for an hour or two, maybe do some writing, or talk to a visiting journalist. On Sundays, about noon, he and Grainne invited some friends round for drinks. Eamonn would stand around and casually talk to them about broadcasting, golf, or even politics. Good jokes amused him.

During the summer months he would have as house guests a few of the Thames *Life* team, including Malcolm Morris, his friend for over twenty years. 'Eamonn was great company,' he recalled, 'We'd play golf, dine out occasionally, or take in a play in town. I once accompanied him to the Gate Theatre to see Sean O'Casey's *Juno and the Paycock* and he was most knowledgeable about the playwright.'

Another welcome visitor to The Quarry was Reg Gutteridge, the boxing commentator for ITV. Eamonn and Reg had first met during the days of BBC's *Sports Report*, and later in the sixties when they worked together again on *World of Sport*. To Reg, Eamonn had been an outstanding commentator because he could convey the passion and appeal of boxing. As they played golf they recalled some boxing memories going back thirty years. Reg Gutteridge had been in New York with Eamonn in the fifties for the Floyd Patterson and Ingmar Johannson world heavyweight fight. 'He revelled in the boxing atmosphere,' he recalls. 'The excitement got to him.' At The Quarry, he found Eamonn a generous host. He wondered why he hadn't written more, for the pieces he did for boxing magazine annuals were superb. Their paths had also crossed in *This Is Your Life*. 'I've done my walk-on bits eight times,' said Reg.

Often Eamonn strolled the sandy beach at Portmarnock alone. 'It's a magnificent walk,' he would say, 'lovely for the dogs, but I only go down there in the winter when it's quiet. In my business, you tend to avoid crowds, or you're trapped. Talking of crowds, I went for a walk the other day in Howth with Gay Byrne and although it was quite crowded with people I found that Gay was stopped more often than I was. I didn't get a second look from some of them. It didn't bother me.'

At other times people greeted him in the street with a 'Hello', which once prompted him to explain: 'They don't treat me as a star in Ireland, just someone who turns up in their homes from time to time.' Surprisingly, he said he was rarely troubled by having such a famous face. On the contrary, he found it flattering that people were still interested in him.

Grainne Andrews found plenty to do around the house. The Quarry, as her husband would say, owed all its attractiveness to her imaginative taste. She never allowed its elegance to fade. At times she read more books than Eamonn, but now, with her innate talent for design, she had ventured into the wedding business. Reviving old skills with a needle and thread, and applying a flair for the ornate, she was specialising in handmade head-dresses for the bride who wanted a romantic, fairytale wedding.

As Grainne explained, 'My original idea was to make wedding dresses and ball gowns. Then I went out to buy a head-dress to match a gown I'd made. I eventually found one but it was terribly expensive, and the choice seemed very limited. I brought it home, sat down and had a good look at it, and decided I would have a go at making them myself.' Her work soon graced the covers of Irish magazines, and was being sold through leading Dublin shops. But her biggest coup came with the sale of a collection at Harrods in London, 'I was in the bridal department there when they mounted one of my head-dresses. It was a marvellous moment.'

Although Eamonn encouraged her, she had no particular ambition to expand the business. 'I took him out to lunch once – and that's the extent of my ambitions. But they are selling well.' With the approach of autumn, 1987, she was now more concerned about Eamonn's poor health. She decided to accompany him as often as possible on his weekly flights to London for his presentation of *This Is Your Life*.

*

At sixty-four, Eamonn appeared at the zenith of his television achievements. Earlier that summer he had accepted a new contract from Thames Television which provided for a £60,000-a-year pay rise. At the same time Thames dismissed rumours that Eamonn was thinking of quitting *This Is Your Life*; the channel's chiefs were at this time more concerned about his state of health.

He had been advised by his doctors to slow down. Since January he had stopped smoking cigars. It wasn't an easy decision for him. 'I still love them – but I don't smoke them any more.' He used to smoke three king size cigars a day and they became a symbol of his success, but he decided to stop smoking after he had surprised Bob Geldof in *This Is Your Life*. 'My throat felt groppy,' he recalled. 'Maybe it was a warning. I decided I was smoking too much. I haven't touched a cigar but I miss them.'

It was announced that his new series of *What's My Line?* had been shelved so that he could concentrate on *This Is Your Life*. His loss of weight made him look drawn and haggard. But he did not try to evade questions from newspaper columnists. At a function in a Dublin art gallery, he admitted to an evening paper columnist, 'I was drawing on my reserves for too long. Suddenly it was all too much of an effort. I knew I was sick and couldn't cope any more. I was hammering myself into the ground. *This Is Your Life* is enough to be going on with. It's very tense and there's a lot of stress involved. As well as commuting between Dublin and London, I also took two trips to Los Angeles. Finally I cracked with this virus that has been going the rounds in the office.'

As his friends continued to worry about him, he emphasised that he had no plans to give up his television career. 'I love every second of what I do. I now try to pace myself better. I've learned to say no.'

Was it enough? Those who knew him well believed he was still taking too much on. Headlines in the press, which Eamonn described as 'wild', annoyed him. They hinted he had

[18]

cancer but he insisted he was in good health. 'Touch wood and thank God.'

The health scares surfaced in Britain and the Fleet Street papers wondered how much longer Eamonn would be able to carry on. He faced a gruelling twenty-six weeks of hard slog as presenter of *This Is Your Life*. 'Too punishing' was the general verdict by those who saw the big man beginning to look only a shadow of himself. Grainne admitted that her husband needed 'more care'.

By now in Dublin some people were inclined to link the cause of Eamonn Andrews' ill health partly to the stress caused to him by the collapse a few years before of his company's £1 million business empire. It was mere speculation, though it was accepted at the time that it hurt his pride and sensitivity. For twenty years on the Irish business scene he had been regarded as one of that rare breed – the showman with the entrepreneurial flair and the man with the Midas touch. Now his enterprises were in disarray and for the first time in his business career he appeared vulnerable. Ironically, what was causing him to 'sink' was his own idea – a floating night club on the River Liffey in the centre of Dublin.

The club, the *MV Arran*, a converted Scottish ferry-boat, had been opened less than six months before in 1984. Eamonn and Grainne Andrews had been photographed at the official opening. 'I'm excited by the project', he told friends. 'It's something new for Dublin.' People who had invested sums of money in the enterprise joined in the celebrations on board.

Behind the scenes, however, serious doubts were being expressed. No one seemed to be sure what market was being aimed at, or what section of the population was expected to patronise the club. Furthermore, it was felt the boat was berthed in the wrong place. Parking facilities were poor, the threat of vandalism ever present. Perhaps the most puzzling aspect was that the *MV Arran* itself did not seem ready to provide the necessary night club amenities.

As Jack O'Connor, a public relations consultant with the Andrews' companies, explained, 'I was unhappy about the lack of space for cabaret and dining. I knew that Eamonn Andrews was excited by the project, but I felt that we should have postponed the opening to allow for more in-depth marketing and time to complete the conversion of the *Arran*.'

It was soon evident by the poor public response that Eamonn's idea might be better suited to the Thames. Security at the club was costing considerable money, and the lack of car parking facilities was, as feared, a serious drawback. It came as no surprise when the *MV Arran* eventually ran into rough waters and a liquidator was appointed. Already losses ran at IR£736,000, with assets of only IR£202. It was an embarrassing time for Eamonn as well as the people who had invested in the enterprise. 'Scuttled hopes' was one evening paper headline that seemed to sum up the disaster.

But worse was to follow. That collapse affected Eamonn Andrews Studios, owners of a discotheque and a recording studio complex, and the Receiver moved in. But what was to hurt Eamonn most of all was the loss of Dublin's finest theatre – the 100-year-old Gaiety Theatre which Eamonn Andrews Productions had run successfully for nearly twenty years. Peter Ustinov, Spike Milligan and Joan Sutherland had graced its stage. In the sixties, Eamonn's company had first leased the theatre from millionaire, Irish-born builder Joe Murphy and in subsequent years made considerable profits. As Joe Kearns, manager of the Gaiety would confirm, 'In very good years we'd probably make a profit of £40,000.'

Now the theatre needed to be refurbished. Kearns some times was embarrassed when he escorted Ireland's President Hillery and Mrs Maeve Hillery along worn carpets to the Presidential Box in the Grand Circle. Later, he complained to his directors that the theatre needed new carpeting. But he was told there was no money available. Eamonn and his directors held a press conference to appeal for public funding to carry out 'urgent maintenance to the theatre'. Eamonn smoked a king size cigar and looked unhappy.

The loss of the Gaiety was the final blow in the sad saga. For a while, Eamonn kept silent about the affair, but clearly it haunted him. Redundant workers in his companies expressed anger at the outcome of events, but time in Ireland is a marvellous healer. Joe Murphy, who was by now living in Jersey, found a new company to lease the Gaiety Theatre and hundreds of thousands of pounds was spent in refurbishing it.

When he eventually broke his silence, Eamonn said, 'The recession in Ireland had a lot to do with compounding my companies' problems. The whole affair was a great shock and a great embarrassment to me really, and, indeed I lost a lot of money. In the case of the Gaiety Theatre, the 23 per cent government Value Added Tax was a crippling blow to us. But I agree that the Gaiety was almost a tragedy.' He was reputed to have incurred personal losses of £500,000 in the ventures, but the figure was never confirmed. However, he emerged from the whole sorry business still a wealthy man, even though he had learned some salutary lessons. As he admitted, 'I know that this long distance involvement doesn't really work. I don't think it need have happened but it was a domino situation. Once it started, that was it.'

The denting of his business reputation in Ireland had no effect whatsoever on his show business image in Britain. Was it that the majority of the British people found his involvement in Irish business affairs totally puzzling? When he walked the corridors of Thames Television, there was scarcely a mention by his colleagues of what had become known as 'Eamonn's Irish disasters'.

A close colleague said, 'Eamonn can't do any wrong over here. He is one of the most popular men in television and is regarded as a high calibre professional by all of his colleagues. Nobody has a bad word about him and he just goes from strength to strength.'

Now, in 1987, when questioned about the crash, he shrugged off the question: 'I think it's yesterday's story'.

[21]

Therefore it would probably be an exaggeration to presume that the collapse of his business empire affected his health in any serious way. Smoking had probably a bigger effect, or his periodic attacks of bronchitis, or even his punishing work schedule. Yet some of his loyal Irish friends, who saw Eamonn as a very sensitive individual, felt his illness stemmed from the time of the crash.

The Andrews' own paradise, The Quarry, remained intact throughout the business collapse. There was never any likelihood that they would put it on the market and perhaps return to London where they had lived until 1970. To Eamonn, the house still represented security and stability. He had no intention of taking up roots.

Gradually most of those people who had been hurt by the business crash forgot about it, as Eamonn himself endeavoured to do. What was of paramount importance to him now was the family – and his marriage. He was nearly thirty-six years married, a little longer than the span of *This Is Your Life*, and the partnership had been just as rewarding. As he liked to say, 'I don't think there is a secret for a happy marriage – I've just been very, very lucky. Grainne is very tolerant. I suppose you have to take care of a relationship but I just say hallelujah and thank God.'

If he had cared, on this October evening, to look back further into his eventful life he'd probably have wondered how a once gangling Dublin youth could have arrived in such style at The Quarry.

3   *Nuns and Brothers*

DRIVING HIS MERCEDES at speed to The Quarry, or being chauffeur-driven across the streets of London to ambush his next unsuspecting victim of *This Is Your Life*, afforded Eamonn Andrews scant time for nostalgia. In fact, during his lengthy, and glamorous television career, he had talked little about his early days growing up in Dublin. He could be excused for forgetting the more drab moments.

The city into which he was born on Tuesday, 19 December, 1922 was smaller and more compact than modern Dublin. Big, sprawling suburban housing schemes were conspicuous by their absence. Instead, many poor and working class people lived in tall tenements where disease was rampant and deprivation the norm. In a few years these tenements would, in a theatrical sense, form the backdrop for Sean O'Casey's greatest tragi-comedies.

To visitors, however, Dublin had its attractions, such as riding in the street trams, climbing to the top of Nelson's Pillar in O'Connell Street, or watching the canal barges cruise by on the River Liffey. Politically, Eamonn Andrews was born into a new Ireland. The country had its own parliament and members that week were debating the passing of new bills.

His parents, Willie and Margaret Andrews, lived in humble circumstances, paying eighteen shillings a week for a top room flat in Synge Street – Bernard Shaw had been born at the other end of the street. It was a good deal of money for a carpenter but Mrs Andrews, astute and hard-working, stretched to the limit every penny of her husband's wages. Soon, to her delight, they were able to move into a small Corporation house in St Thomas' Street where they paid a few shillings a week less rent, and the house had a bathroom, a luxury in those days.

Willie Andrews, whom Eamonn would remember as 'slight, quiet and sensitive with grey hair', cycled to work to Ringsend and on his return in the evening his wife had the main meal of the day ready for him. She frowned on alcohol and was relieved that her husband drank little, though he smoked cigarettes. He had ample hobbies, including a love of amateur dramatics; he often talked about Henry Irving and other leading actors of the day.

By now, young Eamonn was attending convent school and making a good impression on the Holy Faith nuns. They prepared him zealously for his First Holy Communion and his mother dressed him out in a new suit. The occasion was considered a milestone in Dublin; even the poor people in the tenements managed to celebrate the day, which was regarded as a sign that a child was no longer an infant, and that its babyhood had gone for ever.

This may have been so, but the shy young Andrews was scarcely prepared for his next educational venture – enrolment at Synge Street Christian Brothers' School. The Brothers enjoyed an excellent reputation as teachers but at the same time demanded strict discipline from pupils, as Eamonn would learn. Occasionally, when he felt bored during class his eyes strayed to a book or comic and when this caused him to miss the teacher's words he was rapped on the knuckles with a leather strap until it pained. He grew to fear such punishment.

He was amused to find that boys at Synge Street were called 'Canaries' because of the pronunciation of the school name. Special school occasions appealed to his sense of excitement. In 1932, when he was ten years of age, his mother bought him new white flannel trousers and a white shirt to take part with the other boys at the Eucharist Congress in the Phoenix Park. Marching like a young soldier to the Park thrilled him and he was to remember for years afterwards the huge throng of people present and particularly seeing them all stand in silence for the singing by John McCormack and the choir.

To Mrs Andrews, her son promised to be a tall, shy and thin boy. He caused her little or no trouble. But the family's circumstances had not improved appreciably and making ends meet was still a struggle. Eamonn had by now two little sisters. He recalled, 'My parents were frightened of debts, and I seldom remember ever getting anything "on the book". Always we paid cash. There were times, towards the end of the week, when there was no butter to put on the bread, only dripping from the previous Sunday's joints. The Sunday dinner was, in fact, the only big dinner of the week. Everyone looked forward to it, and we all sat round the table for that.'

Unlike better off families, the Andrews could not afford to take their children on holidays; instead, in summer months Eamonn took day adventure trips to Bray and Howth. He loved the hot sunshine and the 'marvellous picnics on the beach at Killiney'. It was a happy family and he was proud of the sacrifices made by his parents.

Eamonn found he was closer to his mother than his father, but this was not unusual in Irish families of the time for the mother was the dominant figure in the home. He did however accompany his father after Mass on Sundays to drama rehearsals at St Teresa's Hall in Clarendon Street. To the other actors, his father was known as 'Will' Andrews. As he listened to him give a speech in a loud, melodic voice he sometimes felt embarrassment as it sounded strange. But his father never once suggested that he take up acting. Eamonn wasn't interested. As he recalled, 'Secretly I wanted to get back into the billiards rooms and leave the actors to themselves.'

Although he was tall for his age, he soon discovered that size alone was not enough if he was to protect himself adequately from school bullies or get the better of school fights. He decided, on a pal's advice, to join a boxing club to learn how to defend himself. St Andrew's Club in York Street had a fine reputation, and though it was located in a shabby area of the city, he had no fears about going there for practice.

He had always hated fighting but in the club it was different. Gloves were worn, it was skilful, and he was quickly learning defensive skills. There were nights when Jimmy Ingle, one of the big names of boxing, came in and took on the juveniles. 'He never bashed us about,' remembered Eamonn, 'but it was good exercise for Jimmy as well as being magnificent experience for us to see how a champion boxer defended himself against our impulsiveness.'

Mrs Andrews wasn't keen on the idea of her son frequenting the boxing club. In her mind it wasn't 'quite respectable'. But Eamonn convinced her that it was a useful exercise because he was now able to defend himself. When he went home one evening and told his mother that he had been selected to box in the County Dublin Championships she did not know what to say. In her eyes, Eamonn was a good boy, an altar boy, and she trusted him to do the right thing. Her only real concern was that boxing might interfere with his schoolwork.

Soon her fears were confirmed by his poor first year examination results. While Willie Andrews was also upset by his son's performance he agreed with his wife that Eamonn should continue with his schooling. They had faith in his ability to do better. The results shattered Eamonn and he vowed to 'make it up to his parents'. He was now in a scholarship class which meant that the bright boys had a good chance of winning enough money to take care of the rest of their education. To Eamonn, who was fourteen, it was a great incentive and he was excited about the prospect of winning. The house now seemed full, as the Andrews family had grown to five children, three girls and two boys, the youngest being called Noel.

Eventually when the examination results came through Eamonn couldn't believe he had won a scholarship. As he recalled, 'It was incredible. Surely there was a mistake? But no, there was no mistake. Somehow I had got through; and in the matter of getting results, Brother Madden had proved himself a brilliant teacher.'

The boys had nicknamed Brother Madden 'The Badger' and Eamonn regarded his mathematics teacher as 'fantastic' but someone who taught by fear. 'It seemed to us that his range of punishments was enormous.' But he quickly forgot about the experience when the cheque for the first scholarship instalment arrived at his home, made payable to himself. 'For the first time in my life I went inside the doors of a bank. My mother was with me – but the feeling of importance belonged to me when I had to sign my name on the back of the cheque and was paid out a whole twenty pounds by the remote, God-like cashier from behind the grille.'

Despite his interest in boxing, and his growing success at the sport, Eamonn was a studious pupil. After school, he read as many books as he could, including the works of O. Henry, Chesterton and Conrad. At the Abbey Theatre he enjoyed plays by O'Casey and Shaw, and not far away at the Gate Theatre, which was founded in the late twenties by Micheal MacLiammoir and Hilton Edwards, he was fascinated by the contrasting styles of Shakespeare and Wilde. At Christmas time he laughed at the pantomime and the Dublin humour of comedian Jimmy O'Dea, a little man with 'great gift of the gab'.

He envied the self-confidence shown by actors, in particular when he thought of his own shyness and how embarrassed he could be on occasions. He was not certain, though, that he wanted to be an actor; the precarious nature of their existence in Dublin tended to put him off. Broadcasting appealed to him, but as yet he didn't know much about it, except what he heard on the radio – and that consisted mostly of drama and music.

He decided he wanted to write more than anything else. His essays were always regarded as among the best in his English class and his pals knew that he'd like to be a journalist. He saved up enough money to buy a secondhand typewriter, and it was on this machine that he slowly wrote a piece entitled, 'How to Train for a Fight' and submitted it to the Sports Editor of an evening paper. To his utter surprise, it was published under his byline and he was paid a guinea.

Young Andrews felt he was going places. By now he had won a juvenile boxing title, had had a poem published in the school magazine, and soon he would be leaving school altogether. Job opportunities, however, were scarce. He answered an advertisement and was called for an interview to the Hibernian Insurance Company in Dame Street. Although he would have preferred to start work in a newspaper, he was relieved when he was offered the job at £60 a year. His parents were pleased; they both regarded insurance work as secure and respectable. Mrs Andrews was fond of her eldest son. 'Eamonn's such a kind boy,' she would tell neighbours. 'D'you know he saved all his pennies to buy me a kitchen knife for Christmas?'

The air of formality he found in the insurance office came as a surprise to him, and he was overawed by 'the millions of files' he was told to look after. 'I seemed to be at the mercy of all these people who wanted files in a hurry,' he would complain to his friends. But he found the staff friendly and they took an interest in his boxing career. When he turned in with a black eye, the girls showed sympathy, and he felt flattered when a girl joked, 'Eamonn, stop boxing or you'll have no good looks left.'

At times, though, he found the office work unrewarding, and as if to fire his imagination he would sometimes go home in the evening and type out poems.

Back in the insurance office, Eamonn was bored by people commanding, 'Mr Andrews, get this file for me.' In desperation, he wrote to Radio Eireann for a job as a part-time boxing commentator – and got it; but the money from this irregular work was not enough to survive on, so he decided to stay on in the insurance office. For light relief, he formed an amateur dramatic company. This pleased his father who saw his son perhaps one day as an actor or a playwright. The new company, Blue White Productions, included a number of Eamonn's co-workers.

One of the plays presented was the thriller, *Night Must Fall*, with Eamonn playing the part of Danny. Shortly afterwards he told the company he was going to write a play. For a while his interest in boxing took second place to his literary pursuits. On summer evenings he joined his friends, including Dermot Doolan and Jack MacGowran at a hut in Howth. The hut had no light and no water, and any cooking had to be done on an iron stove burning sticks and coal. Water had to be fetched from a well in the vicinity. The hut, which was made of wood, was infested with earwigs in the late summer.

Coming from a strict home, Eamonn enjoyed the freedom. He was popular with his pals, who regarded him as a writer – he was at this time contributing articles to a boxing magazine. Recalled Dermot Doolan: 'One time in Howth Eamonn brought along a Brother Carew who had taught him in Synge Street on a visit and wined and dined him. He felt it was his duty to show his appreciation to his teacher for all he had done for him. The rest of us thought it quite astonishing; it was as if a prisoner on his release from jail had taken out the Governor to dinner. When we spoke about it he was quite sincere. This was a typical gesture of Eamonn's. He was never afraid and he never lacked moral courage. He had strong views about many things and wasn't afraid to express them.'

Once, when a friend of his returned home on a visit, Eamonn was appalled to learn that he would not be staying with his parents in the old home; instead his friend booked himself into a Dublin hotel. To Eamonn, the inference was that this fellow could not be seen, in his position, staying in his old neighbourhood. Eamonn just couldn't understand it.

By now he was carrying a card with the words, 'Eamonn Andrews, Commentator and Journalist'. In between his

[29]

boxing commentaries, he finished his play *The Moon is Black* and booked the one-hundred-seater Peacock Theatre for the premiere. In the cast was Jack MacGowran, who would shortly join the Abbey Theatre Company; but when Noel de Chenu, in the leading role, was forced to withdraw because of objections by the Dean at the University ('It's either study, or plays, De Chenu, not both') Eamonn reluctantly stepped in. He felt he was miscast because the part was that of a weak consumptive and he was, he told himself, a muscular boxer. Some time before he had won the Irish junior middleweight title while at the same time astonishing everyone by rushing from the ringside into the control box to commentate on other fights.

Eamonn's first venture into dramatic writing wasn't a success. The critics did not spare him – or the production. Gabriel Fallon, a friend of Sean O'Casey's and one of the city's leading theatre critics, wrote: 'Most of us get the measles at some time or other. Andrews has now had his literary measles. Let's hope he's got it out of his system and maybe next time will write a *good* play.'

Eamonn's friends were upset by the critics. As one recalled, 'We wrote to the newspapers and damned them for savaging Eamonn and his play. But wisely they didn't print our letters.' To Dermot Doolan, Eamonn was mature for his years and always had a great sense of responsibility. 'I remember he once arrived at the hut in Howth with a black eye he had received in a boxing match at the National Stadium. He became an immediate hero with us. I was over the moon when he asked me to write for a boxing magazine he was editing. To all of us, Eamonn was a leader, an innovator, and we liked to be with him. He was always in command. And he was certain that his future lay in the entertainment business in some form.'

Although Eamonn had by now won promotion at the Hibernian Insurance Company, his heart wasn't in the work. He wanted something more exciting and creative. To achieve his goal, he was prepared to try his hand at any sport, even if, as

[30]

in the case of soccer, he knew very little about the game. He was engaged to broadcast a commentary on a big game at Dalymount Park, Dublin, involving the English League, but was worried because he didn't know enough about the teams. Since the English League's first match was in Belfast, the previous Saturday, he decided to travel to Belfast. He got his sister to ring the insurance office and say that he was ill.

On the following Wednesday he was sharing the broadcast with Brian Durnin from Dalymount Park and during the interval he asked Durnin what he thought of the game so far. His reply made Eamonn wince: 'Well, Eamonn, I think you'll agree this English side is not playing quite so well as when *we* watched them on Saturday in Belfast....'

The General Manager of the Hibernian Insurance Company happened to be listening to the broadcast and next day summoned Eamonn to his office. Eamonn recalled the scene: 'There wasn't much to be said. It was too late for bluff. I was glad of the twinkle in his eye at loggerheads with the frown on his face, when he opined that the time for parting had come. He did give me the choice but comforted me by saying I was doing the right if risky thing when I said I'd quit.'

When he tried to explain what had happened to his parents that evening, his father asked sternly, 'Why are you leaving insurance?'

'Because I'm going to be a full-time broadcaster,' said Eamonn, trying to reassure him.

4 *Dreams Evaporate*

EAMONN BOMBARDED THE BBC with begging letters but the replies he got back from Portland Place, though polite, invariably were the same, 'Sorry... but...'. Undeterred, he kept applying. Later, he would joke, 'If anyone ever analyses the BBC's archives of files, I am sure that under the section headed Unsolicited Correspondence, they will find more letters from E. Andrews of Dublin than from any other pair of individuals.'

As a last resort, he had tapes made of his boxing commentaries and sent them along, but he soon discovered that no one was interested in the unknown Eamonn Andrews. He did not allow the BBC's apathy, however, to shatter his romantic dreams about broadcasting; he was more determined than ever to achieve his goal. He turned in earnest to Radio Eireann. After months of pestering the station his luck at last seemed to be in. Certain doors were opened to him.

But his dreams soon evaporated as he sauntered through the stuffy corridors of the General Post Office, which housed Radio Eireann in O'Connell Street. Years later he wrote: 'Unmarked doors with frosted glass panes punctuated white tiles stretching from one end of the corridor to another. It was a vision that persuaded one producer to describe Radio Eireann as "the largest public lavatory" in the world'.

It was obvious to him that the civil servants who controlled the station felt that broadcasting was too important to be trusted to broadcasters. Before long, he concluded that the system was born out of the British establishment and the BBC and thrived on secrecy and the Old Boy network. As he regularly applied for new programmes, he came up against a stone wall. 'I knew that many of the more sombre and settled characters on steady wage packets at the GPO interpreted my unceasing desire to broadcast as greed rather than ambition.'

There were exceptions. He found he could talk naturally to young producer Micheal O hAodha. One afternoon, as they walked together in Henry Street, he asked him directly if he thought he could make a success of broadcasting. 'Why not?' O hAodha replied. 'You've got the voice and you're versatile.'

The young producer had heard Eamonn's commentaries and felt he was exceptionally good at conveying to listeners the excitement of boxing. 'I began to regard him as quietly ambitious and a young man in search of outlets for his talent. He was the reliable type – and that was important in radio – and he didn't concern himself much with alcohol.'

Eamonn's breakthrough arrived in an unusual way. Joe Linnane was compère of Radio Eireann's most popular light entertainment show, *Question Time*. But each summer he took a rest when the show was presented at holiday resorts around the country under the auspices of the Irish Tourist Association, with Noel Hartnett, a barrister and a political *éminence-grise*, the usual compère. He continued his legal work and appeared as junior counsel, with Sean MacBride as his senior, on behalf of the next-of-kin at an inquest on an IRA prisoner who had died in Portlaoise Prison.

A few nights afterwards, Hartnett spoke at a public protest meeting in O'Connell Street, Dublin, and was reported as describing the government as 'Belsen-camp gaolers'. Next day the Minister for Posts and Telegraphs, P.J. Little, sent for the Director of Broadcasting and told him that in view of Hartnett's provocative speech he could no longer go on air. Radio Eireann's chiefs tried to argue that Hartnett was employed by the Irish Tourist Association, not the radio station, but the Minister was adamant. He must go.

Eamonn Andrews was approached to take over as compère of *Question Time*, and he accepted on the spot. On the following Sunday evening he arrived at the quiet County Dublin seaside resort of Rush to present the programme. Recalled Micheal O hAodha, 'Many Special Branch officers were among the audience in case of any protest or disturbance, but the live broadcast went off without incident. It is very likely that Eamonn Andrews was blissfully unaware of the contentious background as he seemed in those days to be that *rara avis*, an apolitical Irishman, with an eye to the main opportunity.'

O hAodha was better able to appraise Eamonn's talent when he produced *Microphone Parade*, with Eamonn sharing the presentation with an army officer, Terry O'Sullivan. Between them, they interviewed visiting celebrities and well-known Dublin personalities. To O hAodha, O'Sullivan possessed the greater flair and charm, but when it came to timekeeping and sheer professionalism Eamonn 'won hands down'.

'I recall his interview with heavyweight boxer Joe Baksi, which he handled very well, and on the occasion his enthusiasm for the sport shone through. But he was floored several times in a no contest interview with artist Jack Yeats, who resisted all of Eamonn's blandishments to get him to say anything about painting – his own or anyone else's.'

In his search for celebrities, Eamonn continued to make the rounds of the city's hotels. Sometimes his persistence was rewarded, as when Gene Tunney, one of his boxing heroes, granted him an interview. He was also lucky with Jose Iturbi and Charlie Kunz. To his embarrassment, Radio Eireann didn't provide for payment to the interviewees and this made his task all the harder. 'On the day that Charlie Kunz came along, I actually had the nerve to ask him if he would play a few tunes on the piano for listeners of *Microphone Parade*, and he obliged.'

Trying to crack the Radio Eireann system was proving more difficult than he had anticipated. His lack of fluent Irish was a drawback, for the 'in' people seemed to talk between themselves in the Gaelic language. Something else amused him: 'No one ever said, "What a good idea." Instead, they made you feel you were raiding the larder after dark. I kept at it anyway. I wrote scripts. I did everything I could to make a few extra pounds. I appeared in plays with talented actors like Dan O'Herlihy, Seamus Forde and Pegg Monahan.

Miss Monahan was an outstanding actress with the Radio Eireann Players. Young and attractive, she called Eamonn 'Andy' and soon they were seeing a lot of each other. But the dull corridors of Radio Eireann seemed alien to romance and colleagues were not sure of what to make of the affair. 'I think Eamonn was serious about Pegg,' recalled one actor, 'but he always seemed more committed to his career.'

Standing at 6ft 1in. Eamonn cut an impressive figure, and his reputation as a boxer enhanced his image. By now, he had shed some of the shyness that had dogged him for years. As Dermot Doolan recalled, 'He would be the first person up to do a turn at a party, or the first to speak at a meeting. He would be nervous – indeed I once saw his hands shake – but he would feel it important to fight any such fear. It was, in his eyes, a hurdle to be overcome. He was a member of the League of Health and Beauty, a type of physical fitness club usually associated with women, yet he paraded on stage in the Mansion House as a male model when most men would have been ashamed to appear.'

To improve his speech and movement, Eamonn joined the Gaiety Theatre School of Acting, which was run by well known actress Miss Ria Mooney. When his old pals at the hut in Howth heard of his decision, one of them quipped, 'I don't think Eamonn intends to be an actor, but this will not stop him playing Hamlet if he's offered the part.'

Secretly, Eamonn wanted to be a film star. He saw the school as a first step in that direction and he was eager to learn the rudiments of acting. The money and fame attached to film stardom appealed to him, but he had first to contend with Miss Mooney: 'I soon learned that she had a fine command of blistering and colourful invective which she never hesitated to employ. I tried hard, and I enjoyed the schooling, doing plays, rehearsing speech, learning movement. But it was a slow process, and heartbreaking as well because there was little or no money in stage acting in Dublin.'

Young Philip O'Flynn was, like Eamonn, tall, thin and well spoken. One day he would become one of the Abbey Theatre's finest actors; now he was committed to learning the art with Miss Mooney. After classes, he usually sipped coffee with Eamonn Andrews. He remembers: 'My first impression was that he was quiet and sincere. When he began to talk more about broadcasting that acting I suspected his heart wasn't a hundred per cent in the School of Acting. And this was borne out when he refused to allow his name to go forward for parts in Gaiety Theatre productions. I think he didn't want anything to come between him and broadcasting.' To O'Flynn, Eamonn wasn't cut out to be an actor. 'There was nothing exceptional about him in class and I felt he wouldn't make a professional actor.'

Eamonn, meanwhile, wrote a critical radio column every Saturday for the *Irish Independent* and revealed a natural flair for writing. 'As far as I can recall, he was both fair and perceptive in his judgments,' says Micheal O hAodha.

Although Eamonn soon discovered that he wasn't destined to be an actor, he still entertained the notion of film stardom. He was consoled by stories that one hadn't to be a star stage actor to make it in films. Before long, he was able to put his new-found knowledge of speech and stage movement to good effect. At the time Dublin's biggest entertainment centre – the Theatre Royal – was proving very popular with audiences who, for their money, got a sparkling variety show, a feature film, and a new quiz, *Double or Nothing*.

It was a quiz in which members of the audience were invited on stage and asked a series of four questions each. Prize for the first correct answer was half a crown; for the second, five shillings; the next, ten shillings, and the last, one pound. After each question the compère would ask, 'Will you take the prize *now* and go away, or is it Double or Nothing?' If the contestant chose to carry on, and answered correctly, he doubled his previous prize. If he failed, he got nothing.

The fifteen-minute quiz had quickly caught on with audiences, who grew to love it. They would laugh at the stupidity of some of the answers, or if a contestant, as happened once with a woman entrant, won repeatedly and eventually had to be barred from competing; or when the compère was the butt of a joke by a contestant. To Micheal O hAodha, the quiz's popularity owed a great deal to its presenter, Eddie Byrne, a dark-haired young man with a deep resonant voice. 'Eddie handled the contestants expertly and the audience liked him for that.' When Eamonn Andrews attended the show, mostly at weekends, he agreed that it was Eddie Byrne who helped to make the quiz although he was once amused when the compère got very cross with a contestant who tried to send him up. 'Eddie was personable, fast-talking and confident,' said Eamonn. 'He was made for the show.'

Louis Elliman, the owner of the Theatre Royal, was so impressed by the success of *Double or Nothing* that he decided to put it on in the Savoy Cinema in Limerick, which he also managed. When Eamonn Andrews' name was suggested as a likely compère, he immediately agreed to give him a try in the role. By now, Eamonn was driving an old Morris car that could just about make the 100 mile road journey to Limerick – and back.

The prospect of presenting the quiz excited him. As the quiz quickly caught on he was gaining valuable experience. He compiled the questions and tried to make them as intelligent as possible, though not too difficult. But his biggest problem was making the journey back to Dublin in time for his radio work, which consisted of introducing records. It was a hectic schedule and, though he was enjoying himself immensely, he was sometimes very fortunate to make the Savoy Cinema in time for *Double or Nothing*. Once he was so breathless that he could scarcely ask the questions.

Word had already got back to Louis Elliman that Eamonn handled the quiz well in Limerick and was popular with audiences, so that when Eddie Byrne decided to try his luck in films in England, Elliman had no hesitation in offering the Theatre Royal job to Eamonn. Eamonn recalled: 'It was Eddie Byrne who recommended me to Louis and he was pleased to have me. Compared with the Savoy Cinema, the Royal was a vast place, one of the largest cinema theatres in Europe. The stage was enormous, and to get from the wings to the centre seemed to take an age. Excitement and a sort of tingling fear gripped me in the moments before I first went on. And this fear stayed with me as I introduced the first contestant in the quiz.'

After the show, he would try to relax in his big dressing-room which, he liked to tell his friends, gave him a sense of importance, as though he were a star. If his stage performance was not considered as polished as Eddie Byrne's, Eamonn nonetheless was proving a forceful and entertaining compère. When he started at the Royal, he was an unknown; now his name was spoken throughout the city. To Micheal O hAodha, Eamonn's height gave him an impressive stage presence, and his voice carried well across the footlights. 'I'm sure his natural charm appealed to audiences.'

To the variety artists at the Theatre Royal, especially Noel Purcell, Eamonn was identified more with broadcasting than with theatre. As one experienced producer summed up, 'Eddie Byrne and Eamonn Andrews were as different as chalk and cheese. Eddie was the theatre man, Eamonn, the broadcaster. It was his charm that carried him through.'

As he smoked in his dressing-room, Eamonn chatted with friends about the show. One night a young singer, Val Doonican, was introduced to him. Val was singing with dance

[38]

bands and also with a quartet, The Four Ramblers. A native of Waterford, he had worked in a factory for about a pound a week, but now he was determined to make a success of show business. He found Eamonn Andrews amiable and helpful.

'I played the guitar and simply loved singing,' remembers Val. 'I had seen Eamonn in *Double or Nothing* and was impressed by his popularity with audiences. I envied him because of the status he was acquiring. He was strong-looking on stage, the kind of person you couldn't see panicking, and every week he was getting more composed. I counted him a genuine guy who was going places.'

The Theatre Royal, which accommodated nearly 4,000 people, was opened in 1935, when John McCormack topped the bill. In subsequent years it would attract some of the biggest names in show-business, including Danny Kaye and Hollywood western star Tom Mix and his horse. Doubtless one of its biggest attractions was its own dancing troupe of twelve girls, The Royalettes, whose disciplined style and exhilarating routines proved show-stoppers. And the troupe had won great praise for dance mistresses Alice Delgarno and Babs de Monte.

Grace Bourke had joined the troupe after leaving school. Petite and very pretty, she was regarded as a natural dancer. Grace came from a theatrical background – her father was impresario Lorcan Bourke who produced plays at the Olympia Theatre in Dublin's Dame Street, and her mother Kathleen was stage manager.

Young Grace found life with The Royalettes punishing. The dancers lived an almost monastic existence. Often they arrived at the Theatre Royal at ten in the morning for rehearsals and stayed on to perform in two shows, eventually getting home before midnight. When they broke for meals, they were not allowed to bring in fish and chips. Romance was virtually out for the girls. If they happened to have steady boyfriends, they were told to go. Part of their mystique was their glamour and unattainability.

After three years at the Royal, Grace Bourke decided to quit and instead joined her uncle's firm in Dame Street where she would become an accomplished stage costume-maker. Seamus de Burce, her uncle, wrote plays in his spare time and she once appeared in one of his comedies. He encouraged her to become an actress but she had had enough of the stage at the Royal.

One evening, after an Olympia Theatre show, she accompanied her parents to the Theatre Royal where they joined some theatrical friends in the Circle Bar. When Eamonn Andrews came through the door, Lorcan Bourke, who had known him for some time, stepped forward to greet him. Eamonn shook Grace's hand and inquired how she was doing at costume-making. 'Oh, fine, Eamonn,' she replied casually. She had been introduced to him the year before but had almost forgotten.

Later that evening, he volunteered to drive her home. But on the way he said he had no money for petrol and asked if she could loan him ten shillings. It was an awkward moment, she remembered afterwards, and Eamonn blushed and was embarrassed.

But he promised to make it up to her next time.

5 Big Band Sound

THE NEWS THAT Joe Loss and his Orchestra were coming to the Theatre Royal for two weeks pleased Eamonn Andrews. Their music was familiar to him; he had played it regularly on his Radio Eireann programmes, and he liked the big, beaty sound of the orchestra.

Playing the Theatre Royal was nothing new to Joe Loss. He had first entertained audiences there in 1939, shortly before the outbreak of war, and had enjoyed himself. He was to say afterwards, 'Until you worked at the Royal, you didn't know what show business was all about.' He was particularly taken by the enthusiasm of the Sunday night crowds. As he entered the theatre, he saw long queues of people; he knew they were getting value for money because the programme consisted of a variety show, feature film and a quiz.

Earlier that year, 1949, Louis Elliman had invited him to make a return visit to the Theatre Royal. Now, when Louis came to his dressing-room, Joe commented on the great success of *Double or Nothing* and asked about the compère. 'That's Eamonn Andrews,' Louis said. 'He's very good. He took over from Eddie Byrne.'

Joe Loss came to admire Eamonn's performance. 'He had this rare quality of being able to communicate easily with audiences.' Mildred Loss was also impressed. 'My first impression of Eamonn was that this young man was sweet and charming and loved what he was doing – and the audiences adored him. Like Joe, I enjoyed the quiz. The secret of

Eamonn's success as compère was the way he handled the contestants. He wasn't arrogant, he wasn't trying to score off them, no matter how stupid were their answers, and he was adept at putting them at their ease.'

During the run of the show, Joe talked to Mildred about the quiz. 'Isn't it fantastic, love? Don't you think it would be a success in Britain?' His wife was in agreement.

Eamonn's first meeting with Joe Loss was friendly. He was thrilled when Joe and Mildred praised his performance as quiz-master, but was scarcely prepared for Joe's suggestion: 'I've got a proposition, my lad – how would you like to come over to England with the band show?'

Eamonn, who was standing in the middle of the dressing-room, laughed. He thought Joe was joking. He failed to see how *Double or Nothing* could fit into a top band like Joe's. However, he said quickly he'd love to accept the offer. The idea of working in England with a popular orchestra, appealed to him. While there he would go to Broadcasting House and see if a personal approach was successful; his scores of letters had found no response from BBC chiefs.

By now Eamonn had convinced himself that he had outgrown Radio Eireann, partly because of the frustration and disillusionment he felt every time he suggested new programmes. 'I was up against a brick wall,' he said later. 'The system was beating me.' He knew there were more opportunities in Britain, if only he could make the breakthrough. When he told his parents that he was going to London to work for a while with Joe Loss and his Orchestra, they did not see the point of it. 'Haven't you enough work in Dublin?' his mother said. 'Are you sure you're doing the right thing, Eamonn?'

He regarded the tour as an adventure, though he had to admit that £40 a week wasn't a fortune. His first engagement in England was at the Finsbury Park Empire. He felt nervous about appearing before an English audience, but as he listened to Joe Loss's enthusiastic build-up of the Irish quiz-master it

[42]

made him feel a little better. He recalled, 'I still trembled in the wings. A build-up is all very well, but the subject of it has to go out there and justify it or duck. At last Joe finished, and I went out on stage and started the quiz. It went well, and it launched me on a hectic breathless tour of one-week dates up and down the length of England, and over the border in Scotland.'

On three consecutive nights a message was conveyed to Joe Loss in his dressing-room that a young comedian wanted to see him about work. Each time he refused to see him. On the fourth night however, he agreed. The young man said his name was Spike Milligan.

'What do you do?' asked Joe.

'I play trumpet, I tell jokes. I'm a bit of an all rounder.'

'I see . . . I'll tell you what I'll do. I'm going to give you ten minutes on the show. If you don't get a laugh from the audience you still stay on, and if they just go wild for you and the applause never stops, I'll throw you the keys and you can lock up the theatre.'

In a short time, Eamonn and Spike Milligan were buddies. 'I could see that Spike liked Eamonn as a person,' recalled Joe Loss. 'He thought him a genuine fellow.'

It was accepted in the dance band business that Joe 'disliked alcohol around the theatre' and found it hard to tolerate musicians drinking. At the show's interval Eamonn and Spike usually dashed to the nearest public house for a bottle of ale. As Eamonn gulped it down, Spike would say 'Come on, Eamonn, let's get back or Joe will go crazy.'

Joe noticed that Eamonn was popular with the girls. After a show they would crowd around the stage door in the hope of meeting him or getting his autograph. If Joe Loss happened to come out first, they'd say, 'We want Eamonn Andrews.' 'Eamonn, tall and handsome, could have all the girls he wanted,' reflected Joe, 'but he never bothered. I liked him for that, because it meant he was loyal to his girl in Dublin.'

Before he left London, Eamonn went in search of

Broadcasting House, and when he eventually located it in Portland Place, he stood in the street and stared at the building thoughtfully. At that moment it represented a challenge to him. 'I tried sauntering in through the high, bronze swing doors, but at the reception desk I was always baulked.' Eventually he got an interview with Tom Chalmers, Head of Light Entertainment, and told him of his ambition to be a broadcaster; he even invited him to come to see him perform in the Joe Loss band show, but Chalmers never found the time to accept the invitation.

Travelling with the band, Eamonn forgot for a while about broadcasting. He became intrigued about the curious lives of the musicians around him, and while he enjoyed their company, he could see they were tough and hard, yet likeable. They tended to be cynical and could name every theatrical digs from Norwich to Dundee, and every nightclub they played. He had fun talking to them. The baby of the band was a quiet little chap called Bill McGuffie, who was a very good pianist and was nicknamed Jose Iturbi. They were characters in their own right, and Eamonn was able to argue with them, or go along with their practical jokes. At night, in his digs, he would sit down and write letters to Grainne Bourke in Dublin. He preferred the Irish version of Grace, which was Grainne, and she hadn't objected to his using it.

He was sorry to leave the road show, and although he ended up with less money than when he started, he returned to Dublin happy that he had learned something about show-business in Britain. He would say, 'I was richer by far on the store of experience, but I seemed no closer to becoming any sort of a name on the eastern side of the Irish Sea.'

With his fifteen pounds a week from *Double or Nothing* at the Theatre Royal, and his income from Radio Eireann, he was again able to give his parents a weekly contribution. He decided not to bombard the BBC any longer with letters; instead, he would wait for a more appropriate opportunity to approach the corporation. After a week at home, the papers

[44]

carried the news that Stewart MacPherson was leaving England. That same day Eamonn wrote to the BBC stating his experience with Irish radio, and asked to be considered for MacPherson's job as chairman of the radio programme *Ignorance Is Bliss*.

He was astonished a few days later to receive a reply. They said they were placing his name on a list of people who would be auditioned for the chairmanship of *Ignorance Is Bliss*.

Eamonn paid his own fare to London, and that brisk January Sunday morning went by taxi to Aeolian Hall, the BBC's Variety Headquarters, for the audition. He recognised few faces in the fairly crowded hall. When he was introduced to the members of the *Ignorance Is Bliss* panel, he was warmly greeted my Michael Moore and the little Cockney, Harold Berens. Both had played the Theatre Royal and remembered him as quiz-master.

He learned that there were six people in for Stewart MacPherson's job, among them Gilbert Harding. At that moment someone handed Eamonn a script, led him to a desk and said, 'Sit down there and read this.'

He sat down and read. All the questions, all the answers, and all the interjections were scripted. Almost as soon as it was started it was finished. A voice behind him suddenly said, 'That will be fine, Mr Andrews. Thank you very much.' Eamonn rose and was disappointed with himself. He didn't feel the reading had gone particularly well, and when everyone adjourned to the pub he found himself standing next to a rather stern-looking Gilbert Harding.

'I wish you well, my boy,' he heard Gilbert remark in his direction, and lifting his glass to him. Eamonn turned to face him. 'I thought you'd be the first choice for the chairmanship.'

Gilbert shook his head. 'No, no, no,' he boomed. 'I wasn't at all happy about it from the beginning. This sort of thing isn't really my line, you know. But I do hope you get it.'

For some strange reason, Eamonn felt that Gilbert was

[45]

sincere. He decided that behind the man's gruff exterior was an amiable person. Years later, Eamonn remarked, 'At that audition I was the hick, with straw in the hair, and I must say Gilbert Harding was kind and warm enough to pretend not to notice it.'

Before he left Aeolian Hall, he was approached by an individual who introduced himself as Maurice Winnick. To Eamonn, he looked a typical showman, smart and quick-witted. He explained briefly that he was the agent for the American-owned show, *Ignorance Is Bliss*, and implied that he could bring some influence to bear on the choice for MacPherson's replacement. Eamonn took a dislike to the man on the spot. His abrasive manner was a turn-off. 'I decided to promise nothing,' he recalled. 'Winnick ran an agency and wanted me to sign for him before I left the hall. I told him I'd consider it.'

Back in Dublin, his parents enquired about his audition and when he admitted that he was unhappy about his performance, their faces fell. They continued to take a deep interest in his career. When Maurice Winnick telephoned him to invite him to London to talk urgently about *Ignorance Is Bliss*, he felt for the first time that he had a chance of getting MacPherson's job. But he had been warned about the agent and decided to be cautious.

As he expected, Winnick produced a contract during their conversation at his office, but once more Eamonn stalled him. Winnick said, 'Come round this evening to my flat in Park Lane and we'll see if we can sort it out.' Eamonn agreed.

He was greeted by Winnick in a smoking jacket and was politely ushered inside the elegant interior. He felt nervous and wondered if he had done the right thing by coming. He lit a cigarette and watched Winnick puff his cigar. He decided it was going to be a cat and mouse game. As the night wore on the atmosphere became increasingly suffused with smoke, and Winnick, who had argued about the contract, asked for the last time if Eamonn was prepared to sign his name on the dotted line.

[46]

'My mind was confused by the conflicting advice I'd got,' recalled Eamonn. 'I wanted the job. I wanted to prove myself. If I missed this chance it might be the only one.'

'Look boy,' Winnick said, 'if you don't sign now....' He waved his hand dismissively, and after a brief pause snapped, 'As I say, if you don't sign you're finished. You're out. Someone else will get the job. Make up your mind, *now*!' Eamonn suspected he was bluffing but couldn't be sure. As he listened to Winnick, he looked at his watch; it was five o'clock in the morning. 'I'll sign it,' he said, with a mixture of relief and anger. Later, he observed: 'Then I went down from the flat into the deserted street, and crossed over towards the edge of Hyde Park. There, with my head against the railings, I was suddenly and violently sick.'

Eamonn was twenty-seven, and he had waited a long time for the big opportunity. When the letter arrived from the BBC confirming his appointment as successor to Stewart Mac-Pherson, he treasured it. His regard for Gilbert Harding rose when, a few mornings later, he received his letter, both friendly and warm, offering him encouragement and wishing him success as chairman of *Ignorance Is Bliss*.

The programme, which had been running since 1946, was fast-moving and amusing. It went out at seven-thirty on the Light Programme and Eamonn, who on the first night looked a little nervous, began by asking two of the show's questions.

'What flies over Buckingham Palace?'

'Pigeons,' said Harold Berens.

The second question went to Michael Moore, 'If all the women went to China, where would all the men go?'

'To Peek-in, of course.'

Although the questions were often inane, it was the way the panel behaved that guaranteed the success of the programme. The contrast in styles between funnyman Harold Berens and the more scholarly Michael Moore provided listeners with laughs, especially Berens' Cockney slang. 'Wot a geezer!' was one of his favourite lines. Gladys Hay, the only woman on the panel, had a nice line in comedy and exploited it to the full. Eamonn, in dinner jacket, settled quickly into the spirit of the programme. The radio critics regarded his performance as successful, and in Dublin, he was now being looked upon as a minor celebrity.

During the run of *Ignorance Is Bliss* he continued to fly back to Ireland to do his radio programmes. Though his father had been ill, he wasn't prepared for his death. As he recalled, 'His death came as an appalling shock to me.' He had got close to his father in the last year of his life and felt he understood him better. He was relieved that he had lived long enough to see him succeed with the BBC.

When *Ignorance Is Bliss* ended its run, Eamonn found he had nothing to turn to in London so decided to come back to Dublin. It afforded him the opportunity to be with Grainne Bourke. He was in love, and was already thinking of marriage. But first, he told himself, he had to secure his career, and that meant trying to get more work in England.

He returned to London. He stayed in a house in Bayswater Road owned by a Mrs Riddington, whose son Ken was a stage manager in a West End theatre. As Eamonn recalled, 'We had common bonds of friendship and growing poverty to sustain us when things looked bleak. He was very kind and arranged with his mother, who lived in Brighton, to have a room let to me at bargain rates. There was a phone which we shared, both of us meticulously putting our coppers in a tin box so that the bill wouldn't be traumatic when it came.'

For Eamonn, it was a particularly worrying time. His future in broadcasting seemed vague, even non-existent. The occasional parcel of food from his mother in Dublin only helped to remind him of his own plight. He found it hard to accept that no one wanted a boxing commentator who knew the sport intimately. Now and then he got promises of work, but in the end they came to nothing. The only consolation was

[48]

that eating was cheaper when shared by two people. Always he found it painful to recall the period: 'Many's the time I went out with the shopping bag for the celery, the radishes and the lettuce to supplement the cheese suppers or, on better days, when we had Irish stew, the carrots, the onions and the potatoes that would hide the scarcity of meat.

He was now with a new agent, Teddy Sommerfield, who had worked with the Maurice Winnick agency. Eamonn got on well with Teddy and believed he could help him find a broadcasting job. Before long, he was offered a reading of George A. Birmingham's novel *Spanish Gold* and this helped to pay his mounting bills.

It was his meeting, however, with a lean Scotsman, Angus McKay, that was most significant. McKay had been impressed by Eamonn's voice on *Ignorance Is Bliss* and enquired about him for his own programme, *Sports Report*. When they met he said he was prepared to give Eamonn a chance on the programme. 'Drop round on Saturday. In the meantime I want a word with your agent, Teddy Sommerfield.'

For the first time in his life, Eamonn, on that Saturday in 1950 met some of the big names in sports broadcasting. Through a glass partition he spied Raymond Glendenning, and soon he got talking to Alan Hoby. When Angus McKay told him, 'We live on our nerves here,' Eamonn believed him. *Sports Report* with its exciting format, attracted millions of listeners and he wanted to be part of it.

Although McKay could be a tough, no-nonsense Scotsman, Eamonn found him good to work with. He had taken him on the staff without a trial run, which was unprecedented in those days in the BBC. Despite the fact that he was only getting £40 a programme, Eamonn wasn't worried. As he would say, 'I'm *in* ... that's what counts.' McKay ran a tight ship and had the reputation of being 'mean' with the corporation's money.

All the time Eamonn wanted to be a boxing commentator, but on *Sports Report* he spent most of the time interviewing famous footballers. When the opportunity came to do a boxing

[49]

commentary it was for television, not radio. It was to be his first television appearance. The broadcast was coming from the Empress Hall and the producer was Peter Dimmock, who told Eamonn, 'At the end of each fight I want you to hop into the ring and do an on-the-spot interview with the winner. Nice and short, and it doesn't matter if he's puffing and blowing and surrounded by yelling fans, the atmosphere should be right.'

There was one problem. Eamonn was obliged to wear a tuxedo and at the last moment had to dash back to his digs by taxi to collect it. After the commentary, microphone in hand, he ducked under the ropes as he had done many times before, dressed in vest and trunks. Suddenly, as he bent his head there was a warning click. To his horror, the bow tie had snapped. As soon as he straightened up, he snatched the loose-hanging bow right off, and slipped it into his pocket.

Eamonn quipped, 'Imagine! on my first TV appearance I was seen tieless in a tuxedo in a boxing ring!'

6 *Eamonn or Gilbert?*

EVERYONE AT Lime Grove, the BBC's television headquarters, called him Jacko. But his full name was T. Leslie
Jackson and, unknown to Eamonn Andrews, he was destined
to play a key role in his future television career.

A slight man of medium height with a razor sharp brain, he
liked to describe himself as 'a poor Protestant Dublin boy who
left his native city in the thirties to find work in England'. His
first glimpse of Eamonn Andrews had been at the St Andrew's
Boxing Club. As he recalled, 'I was a flyweight and Eamonn
was a welterweight. I watched him spar and considered him a
good prospect. We were absolute strangers, though, and soon
I left the city.'

When he found it hard to get a job, he decided to try his luck
at professional boxing in Liverpool. 'I got a few fights and
made a few pounds, but after a year or more I drifted into
theatre in Manchester and worked there for seven years with
Irish producer Dominic Roche, doing stage direction as well
as acting. I played innumerable small parts. It was a struggle to
eke out a living, but I enjoyed the atmosphere round the
theatre and got on fine with members of the company. It was
useful experience.'

At the outbreak of war he joined the Royal Navy and
remembered a few narrow escapes from death. When he
returned to civvy street he thought of going back to theatre
again. One of his navy pals, however, who knew something
about television, suggested that he should look for training in

that medium. Jackson wasn't enthusiastic at first but was gradually persuaded to apply for a month's trial with the BBC. He adapted quickly and graduated to be a floor manager.

Live television, he discovered, was very exciting and he wondered why he had hesitated about becoming part of it. One day, Ronnie Waldman, Head of Light Entertainment, talked to him about the new panel game from America, *What's My Line?* and said they intended trying it out on British viewers.

'Who do you suggest should chair it?' Waldman asked. 'I've been thinking of Eamonn Andrews.'

Jackson expressed surprise.

'Personally I'd prefer Gilbert Harding in the chair,' he told Waldman. 'To me, Eamonn Andrews is a sports commentator – and a very good one.'

After a pause, Waldman said, 'I'll tell you what we'll do – we'll use Eamonn for the first week and Gilbert for the second and see who is best suited to the role.'

Leslie Jackson was still unhappy. But soon he realised he was wrong. 'Eamonn was terrific as chairman,' he recalled. 'And I told myself what a stupid man I'd been to think that he couldn't do it.'

When it came to Gilbert's turn, he seemed to get confused. Apparently the cards identifying the challengers in the programme got mixed. One man was a panel-beater but the card that came to Gilbert read 'Male Nurse', so that when the man started to answer questions truthfully and accurately, Gilbert became more and more impatient and almost called him a liar.

'Can your job be done equally well by a woman?' Gilbert asked him bluntly.

'Yes,' said the panel-beater.

'No!' roared Gilbert, thinking of the male nurse.

Eventually, with time running out, Gilbert announced that the challenger had beaten the panel and that he was a male nurse.

The panel-beater looked perplexed and almost in despair.

An unsuspecting Eamonn Andrews was the first subject of BBC's *This Is Your Life* in the mid-fifties.

Mrs Margaret Andrews, Eamonn's mother, was determined that her son would finish his schooling with the Christian Brothers.

Eamonn returns to Dublin in 1951 to marry the glamorous Grainne Bourke, a member of a theatrically connected family.

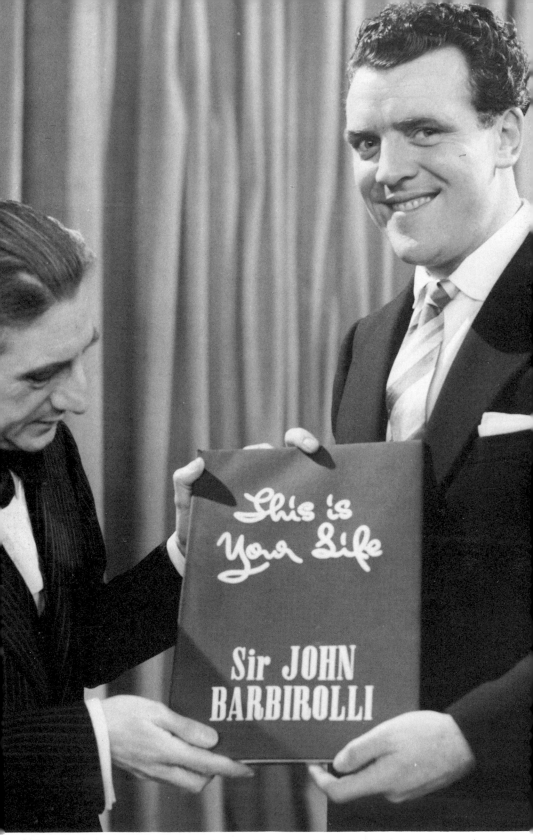

Distinguished conductor Sir John Barbirolli was fascinated by the *This Is Your Life* book on his own career.

Eamonn with actress Siobhan McKenna and Irish radio producer Michael O hAodha in Dublin in the late forties.

Relaxing over a drink at the BBC, Kenneth Adam (left), Director of Programmes, Eamonn, and Leslie T. Jackson, the first producer of *This Is Your Life*.

Eamonn in the midst of the redoubtable Behan clans for the *This Is Your Life* show on Stephen Behán, Brendan's father. Stephen is seated with his wife, Kathleen Behan.

Stanley Matthews, England's most famous footballer in the 1950s, was the subject of *This Is Your Life*, to Eamonn's obvious delight.

Bandleader Joe Loss played the Theatre Royal in Dublin in the late forties and invited Eamonn Andrews to the UK to present a quiz show with the band.

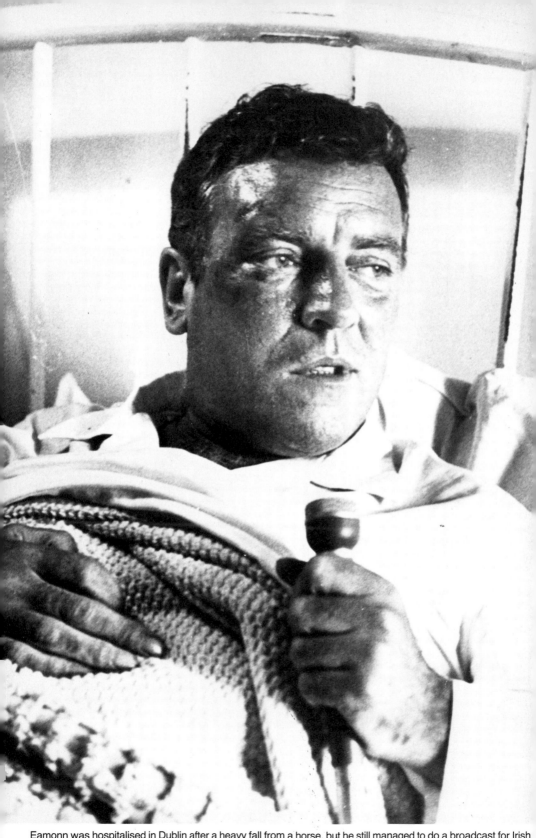

Eamonn was hospitalised in Dublin after a heavy fall from a horse, but he still managed to do a broadcast for Irish radio.

'But I'm not,' he said. 'I'm a panel-beater.'

Gilbert was enraged. 'This,' he thundered, 'is the last time I'll ever appear on television.'

To new producer Leslie Jackson, Gilbert had shown himself temperamentally unsuited to fill the chair. He now agreed with Ronnie Waldman that Eamonn Andrews should be the permanent chairman, with Gilbert a panellist. The others were Ted Kavanagh, the witty scriptwriter of ITMA fame, Canadian actress Barbara Kelly, writer Marghanita Laski and Jerry Desmonde, who described himself as 'a comic's feed'.

Although Eamonn became enthusiastic about *What's My Line?* he would say, 'Going on television was a complete mystery to me, and I excluded everything and everybody else in the effort to concentrate on what I had to do – be myself.'

Leslie Jackson found Eamonn easy to work with. 'There was no flannel about him ever. If you put something to him that he wasn't quite sure of he'd say so. Like me, Eamonn was beginning his career in television and success was important to both of us. His forte was obvious – he never got annoyed with people, and some people were very annoying. A challenger would come up determined to beat the panel by giving half-hearted answers or even wrong answers, but Eamonn always put them right without being rough with them. He wasn't nervous as chairman because his entire concentration was on the job – not on himself. As long as he got the grasp of the job he was happy.'

At the time Eamonn was living in a flat in Priory Road in Kilburn and some evenings Leslie Jackson visited him. He remembers: 'I'd tell him who the challengers for the following week were on the programme. He wanted to know everything about their trade or profession. He was a perfectionist and if we happened to have a bell ringer on the show I would have to brief him in detail about his work. Eamonn had a sense of humour but never let it interfere with his work. He was meticulous but never boringly so. I don't know why we got on

[53]

so well together. Perhaps we both loved professional boxing and that was common enough ground for a start. We were also Dubliners and could talk about our backgrounds.'

When Eamonn first met Leslie Jackson, he regarded him privately as 'a mercurial, friendly man'. Soon he came, like everyone else, to call him Jacko.

It became apparent that much of the success of *What's My Line?* hinged on the outcome of the battle of wits between Eamonn and Gilbert Harding. Viewers were intrigued. Eamonn denied that the clashes were arranged. As he tried to explain, 'I always dismissed these charges on two main counts. First, I felt that *What's My Line?* would never survive this kind of dishonesty; secondly, whatever else Gilbert may have been, he was not an actor. I don't think he would have been capable of acting out annoyance.'

To Leslie Jackson, Gilbert's irritability on the show made lively television viewing, though his rudeness on occasions did not please viewers.

The newspapers tended at the time to exaggerate the clashes between Eamonn and Gilbert, as though the two men were not even on talking terms. Eamonn would say, 'Gilbert and I had many fatuous arguments which lasted for weeks. He would then be only as civil to me as bare necessity demanded. Passing time helped him to get these contretemps into perspective. Irritations that arose over the meanings of words were silly anyway – though I must admit that I was delighted when one of the leading publishers sent me the present of a dictionary and said, "Here you are, now you will know what the real meaning of the word is." More often than not Gilbert was right.'

Gilbert did not try to give the impression that he was Eamonn's sworn enemy. As he said himself, 'It is very useful I suppose to the newspapers to pretend that we don't get on together, but the truth is that Eamonn and I have had never a cross word and he is one of the very few friends I have of whom

[54]

I can say that'.

Sometimes, after the show, they enjoyed a drink together in a nearby public house. Eamonn felt the big man was misunderstood. He gave the impression of being an intellectual, but he was not. In reality, Gilbert felt insecure. He was restless. He thought he was wasting his talents. Contrary to general opinion, Gilbert in his estimation was not a proud man. 'He never believed he was as great as his public thought he was, and he had a sense of guilt about the money that he received. I think he felt he should be achieving greater things. Some of his friends chided him about misusing his abilities on such a simple game as *What's My Line?*'

As a panellist, the schoolmaster in Gilbert often shone through. 'The urge to correct was with him innate,' a critic remarked. He was, as Fanny Cradock rather wickedly pointed out 'physically fat and temperamentally thin'. But everyone agreed that his television performance could be dazzling. The trouble was that people either liked him or hated him. Eamonn Andrews once observed, 'I wouldn't want to try to portray Gilbert Harding in depth. All his friends, and whatever enemies he had, had a different slant on him'.

With a reasonably-sized bank account to his name, and his future in television seemingly assured, Eamonn popped over to Dublin and talked to Grainne Bourke about marriage. As they sat one warm August evening in his car within earshot of the sea at Dollymount strand, he asked her, 'Will you marry me?'

It was a simple approach to romance in the Dublin of the time and no one made any surprise of such little rituals. Grainne was in love and instantly said 'Yes'. Later, Eamonn drove her back to her own house to break the news to Lorcan and Kathleen Bourke. Mrs Bourke was thrilled, but Lorcan wasn't home so Eamonn decided to wait until he arrived.

When he did eventually arrive, about three in the morning, he was somewhat surprised to be met by Eamonn who asked to see him privately. Lorcan, being a theatre man, did not make a fuss.

Grainne was a little nervous, and admitted later, 'I don't think Daddy was a bit pleased. I mean he was happy about Eamonn but he was the sort of man who didn't want his daughters to get married.' When Eamonn emerged, smiling, from the adjacent room, followed by her father, she felt relieved. She knew that all had gone well between them. Lorcan liked the idea of having a show business celebrity in the family, but he was genuinely fond of Eamonn.

Next day Eamonn and Grainne went into town where he bought the engagement ring and placed it on her finger. It was a five-stone one which was exactly the kind she wanted. Grainne thought it was the most beautiful thing she had ever seen in her life. That weekend they fixed the wedding date for November the seventh. The year 1951 was proving a remarkably lucky one for Eamonn. Almost immediately, Grainne set about making her wedding dress. Lorcan Bourke, with his flair for the theatrical, was intent on making his daughter's wedding reception one of his most 'colourful productions'.

Eamonn didn't arrive in Dublin until the day before the wedding. On the wedding morning, Grainne was disappointed to find none of her neighbours outside the house as she came out; it was raining, making the November morning look bleak. Her father Lorcan accompanied her to her seat in the Corpus Christi Church and by the time she took her place beside Eamonn at the altar, she felt almost numb.

She was relieved when the ceremony was over. Walking hand in hand with Eamonn down the main aisle of the Church afterwards, she felt herself once more – but it was only when she stepped outside the Church that she realised why her neighbours hadn't turned up that morning to wish her well. Now, they all seemed to be ready to greet her. Masses of people surged forward and tried to shake her hand.

For the first time in his life, Eamonn realised he was a

celebrity. Photographers clicked their cameras and asked for more photographs of himself and Grainne. Reporters took down the names of the guests in their notebooks. It was proving one of Dublin's biggest show-business weddings for some time. Grainne looked radiant with happiness.

In keeping with his love of the theatrical, Lorcan Bourke chose a ballroom – the Four Provinces – for the reception and wedding breakfast. He had supervised the seating arrangements, ensuring the lighting was right, and that the general setting was to his satisfaction. On the way to the ballroom, Eamonn, seated beside Grainne in the back seat of the taxi, said, 'I'd love a cigarette.' The driver stopped the car and Eamonn got out and went into a nearby public house for a packet of cigarettes. The publican, in an unexpected gesture of generosity, came out and handed the newly-married couple a large glass of whiskey each. As Grainne cautiously sipped hers, Eamonn threw back his and lit a cigarette.

It was late afternoon before the festivities ended and Eamonn and Grainne were off on their honeymoon. They would spend a week in Parknasilla in County Kerry, then return to Dublin. When it came to the time for Grainne to go to London with Eamonn, she was crestfallen. It was her first time away from Dublin for a long period and she knew it would take her time to adapt to life in London.

Eamonn, with his busy radio and television schedule, had hardly time to think of his new married status. Yet he admitted he found it 'very exciting'. The more serious, indeed responsible, side of his character emerged later when he wrote: 'It was frigthening, though, suddenly to realise that I was totally responsible for one other human being as well as myself. And I still wasn't in the most secure business in the world'.

Among the first visitors to their flat in Priory Road was Leslie Jackson. He found Eamonn a very caring husband, yet he felt for Grainne because he realised that Eamonn's was a hectic lifestyle, and she might experience some lonely hours.

[57]

'They are very much in love,' he told himself as he dined one evening with them.

It was here that Grainne was introduced to Gilbert Harding and, to her surprise, found him pleasant company. Eamonn invited his mother to stay for a short while and brought her along to the studios to see *What's My Line?* Gilbert's own mother had not been long dead and as he discussed her with Mrs Andrews, Eamonn saw the tears roll down his face. 'There was something very pathetic about him that night,' he remembered.

Exactly eighteen months after their wedding Grainne developed a pain in her knees which made her limp. She holidayed in Ireland but found movement of the knees painful and dancing almost out of the question. On her return to London her doctor sent her for X-rays to the Orthopaedic Hospital in Great Portland Street. That week, Professor Herbert Seddon, a slight, studious man, asked to see Eamonn. He broke the news gently: 'Your wife has a tubercular infection of the hip, Mr Andrews. I don't know what we can accomplish, but we shall do our best. You will have to be patient'.

The news shattered Eamonn. It was the last thing he had expected. By now Grainne's limp was noticeable, and Professor Seddon said to her, 'I'll try to cure it. But it will be a long job.'

Grainne found it hard to accept that she was ill. She was sent to Stanmore to the Orthopaedic Hospital, and found she was in a ward with nineteen other women. 'It is very hard to be brave,' she told herself.

Being a devout Catholic, Eamonn prayed more than ever before that Grainne would get well. To forget his worst fears he worked hard. 'It was a terrible time for Eamonn,' recalls Leslie Jackson. 'Grainne's illness bothered him greatly, but no matter how busy he was he seemed to find time to visit her in hospital. 'Because I worked closely with him, I knew of the sacrifices he had to make to be with her. Sometimes he worked through the night so that he could take time off the following day to go to Stanmore.'

During the subsequent months, Eamonn had much faith in Professor Seddon, who never built up false hopes about his wife; in a quiet voice he'd tell Eamonn, 'The treatment is going well, Mr Andrews. But we cannot say anything for certain until the bandages are off and your wife starts working her hip again.'

For Eamonn, the nine months Grainne spent in the hospital seemed endless. She had plenty of visitors, among them her parents from Dublin. The treatment consisted of rest and traction; inevitably she put on weight. She was now, however, more contented. She started to knit, and after that she sewed and weaved and read as voraciously as ever. Gradually she responded to the treatment. She knew she was fortunate that the infection hadn't got into the bone in her hip.

The hospital staff reckoned that Grainne's singular determination to get well had worked wonders. In April 1954, she was released on crutches and driven back to Eamonn at the flat. He told her, 'We're going on a long holiday abroad so that you can recuperate, darling.' Later, he wrote: 'My heart was full, and I was excited and right up on an emotional peak'. He bought a new car with an open hood so that Grainne could take the sunshine.

Although she was 'weak and fat', Grainne experienced an incredible feeling of joy that she was at last out of hospital. She wanted to do so many things, but she knew she would have to be patient until she was able to walk again. Now she could not wait to be alone with Eamonn in Cap Ferrat. In the warm evenings they sipped coffee and cognac and talked hopefully about the future. Professor Seddon had been cautious. 'Mrs Andrews is not cured yet,' he had said. 'She will have to have more tests.' But in the sunshine and tranquillity they tried to forget the painful experience.

Joe Loss and his wife Mildred were holidaying in the South

of France at this time and spent hours talking to the Andrews. Mildred was impressed by the kindness of Eamonn towards his wife. 'He was so caring and they appeared so happy together. Grainne was recuperating from her serious illness and tried to be cheerful. At this time she was using a walking stick but had some difficulty trying to move, but all the time Eamonn would help her along. As he held her hand, he looked so much in love.'

On their return to London Grainne took some time to settle into a routine. She still visited Professor Seddon who, as always, advised her to be patient. Then, one evening, he seemed less cautious than before, and told her that she was cured. To Eamonn, it was a miracle. Grainne wanted to diet and to shed the stones of weight she had put on.

'Eamonn seemed a new man,' remembers Leslie Jackson, who called on them shortly after their return from France. He smiled again, his humour returned.' While Eamonn was on vacation the chairmanship of *What's My Line?* had been taken over by Australian actor, Ron Randell. He had surprised producer Leslie Jackson by throwing kisses to the girls in the audience.

Afterwards, Leslie felt Randell was more showman than chairman and tended to react to the audience rather than to the panellists. 'The newspapers had noted Randell's flamboyant performance and expressed mixed views about it. But there was no denying he had made an impact. One Fleet Street columnist hailed the actor as 'a sensation'.

The reaction worried Eamonn Andrews and secretly he wondered if his role of chairman of the programme was safe. But he needn't have worried. As he was to recall, 'It was reassuring to know that despite Mr Randall's explosively successful start on *What's My Line?* the BBC still wanted me.'

PART TWO

'This Is Your Life'

After my first viewing of *This Is Your Life*, I said to myself, 'This *is* Television.'

Eamonn Andrews

7 *Air of Secrecy*

ONE MORNING IN April, 1955 Ronnie Waldman telephoned
Leslie Jackson, inviting him to a small studio in Lime Grove to
watch an American TV show called, *This Is Your Life*.

'I think you should see it, Jacko,' enthused Waldman,
'because I'm thinking of you as producer of the English
version, and Eamonn Andrews as its presenter.'

Jackson, who had faith in the judgment of the BBC's Head
of Light Entertainment, quickly replied, 'I'd be delighted to
see it, Ronnie.'

That afternoon, they both sat through a showing of the *Life*,
which featured the actor Victor McLaglen, whose tough guy
film image was already legendary. But, as they watched in
silence, they saw him reduced to tears as paraded before him
were his seven towering brothers from all parts of the world,
and the rest of his family. Although it came across as
sentimental and laden with emotion, there was, Leslie Jackson
reckoned, something riveting about the programme and
obviously it would generate huge popular appeal. It opened up
also fascinating possibilities; already he visualised in the
British version war heroes, show-business stars, and not a few
compelling unknowns.

'Well, Jacko,' said Waldman, as the film stopped rolling,
'what d'you think?'

The producer could not disguise his unbounded enthusiasm.

'What a programme!'

'You'd produce it, then?'

[63]

'I'd love to.'

Waldman rose and prepared to leave the studio.

'It won't be easy. It's going out live.'

Jackson was adamant. 'I still want to do it.'

As they sauntered along the corridor, Ronnie Waldman turned to him and asked, 'And Eamonn Andrews – what d'you think of him as presenter?'

'He's my unanimous choice.'

'And mine.'

Leslie Jackson said, 'Eamonn's already a big name. His friendly style is so right for a programme like *Life*.'

Next day they discussed the show. 'Eamonn was enthusiastic,' Jackson recalls, 'but not over-enthusiastic. But then that was always a characteristic of his – he tended to be over-cautious until he learned more about a programme. He quizzed me about possible changes for the British version and I assured him that we'd strive for a better balance than the Americans had managed to achieve. Before we parted, I knew he wanted to present the programme. It was *his* kind of show. He was good with people; it was the reason for his success on *What's My Line?* which was enjoying top ratings.'

Earlier that year, Eamonn had been to America to view television generally and pick up new ideas. *This Is Your Life* was one of the shows he saw and it made an immediate impression on him. He thought: 'This *is* Television'. It was fast-moving, told an absorbing story, and he could see it having strong appeal for the average viewer in Britain. But some restraint was needed, otherwise viewers might find it heart-stopping.

Nonetheless, he subscribed to the view that the British people liked a bit of sentiment in their lives, indeed were not above expressing emotion. As he liked to explain, 'At heart, an Englishman just as badly wants to tell his wife how much he loves her as any American or Frenchman. The trouble is that he has been the victim of centuries of sustained conspiratorial brain-washing. He's been made to believe that not only has he got a stiff upper lip but that not having it would be shameful. A massive, subliminal campaign that helped build empires, increase trade, and reduce the birthrate.'

On his return from America, Eamonn had discussed *This Is Your Life* with Ronnie Waldman, whose opinion he valued. They agreed that it wasn't exactly a BBC type programme but that was no reason why the Corporation should not screen its own version. Waldman expressed his confidence in getting the idea through, despite resistance by some of the top brass. Eamonn said he was prepared to present it. As always, he never discussed money; he left that question for his agent, Teddy Sommerfield. All he was worried about now was getting *Life* off the ground in Britain.

In subsequent weeks, after BBC chiefs had given the go-ahead for the programme, Eamonn, Leslie Jackson and Ronnie Waldman regularly conferred. It was decided to screen the show on a monthly basis. Numerous names were suggested as possible subjects and, in this respect, Eamonn put his own views forward strongly. 'Even then, he wanted to have a say in who the subjects should be,' says Leslie Jackson.

The first programme, scheduled for Friday, July 29, 1955, would be put on by the original American production team Ralph Edwards, as presenter, and Axel Gruenberg, producer. They were very experienced in radio and television and between them had presented hundreds of *Life* programmes.

Eamonn was particularly impressed, though also amused, by the loquacious Gruenberg, a big man who wore thick glasses. He talked endlessly about the *Life* subjects they had surprised in America, detailing the precise circumstances and the immediate reaction of each subject. Eamonn concluded that the American was 'a delightful sentimentalist,' though Leslie Jackson was more sceptical than that.

The Americans were shown a short list of likely subjects for the first *This Is Your Life*. After a comparatively brief discussion, it was agreed that the honour should be conferred on the country's greatest footballer, Stanley Matthews. To

Leslie Jackson, the programme was taking on an air of secrecy and mystery. The team's greatest fear now was that the secret of the first subject would be leaked.

News of the new series on BBC was attracting wide interest. The American version was discussed by journalists who had seen it in America and viewers in Britain were warned to have 'their handkerchiefs ready'. At least one critic believed it would have a short life in Britain. Nonetheless a script was prepared of Stanley Matthews' career in football and everything seemed to be running smoothly until Fleet Street got hold of the story.

To the consternation of the *Life* team the *Daily Sketch* headlined Stanley Matthews and predicted he would be the first subject. Copies of the paper were delivered to Ralph Edwards' hotel room and, in turn, Alex Gruenberg, Leslie Jackson and Eamonn Andrews read the details. It was an agonising moment. 'We were astounded,' recalls Leslie Jackson. 'We had no idea how the secret could have been leaked.'

'I felt numb,' Eamonn would say later. But neither of the Americans showed astonishment; it had happened once previously in their case. However, Ralph Edwards tried to retrieve the situation.

'Where is Stanley Matthews?' he asked.

'He's away fishing,' Leslie Jackson said.

'Well, can't we get a ring around him to stop newspapers getting to him?' suggested Edwards.

Eamonn told the presenter that this might be done in the United States where papers were local rather than national, but it would never work in Britain. In all probability, the famous footballer had been told the news by now.

For a moment they sipped their coffees in silence; then it was agreed to drop the idea of Stanley Matthews. Momentarily, when Eamonn Andrews left the room, Leslie Jackson looked at the others and said, almost furtively, 'Why not Eamonn...? He'd make a good subject.'

The thought hadn't struck the others; now they were unanimous that he would make an ideal subject. To Leslie Jackson, there was logic in the choice. With limited time at their disposal to compile a script, Eamonn's life story, though eventful, could be written at speed. Nor was there any question of inviting guests from across the globe; mostly, they would come from Ireland and England.

Later, Eamonn was told of the team's choice, which he was led to believe was his friend, boxer Freddie Mills. As far as he was concerned, it couldn't be better. Mills was popular and had fought some great fighters. It would be an exciting *Life* and undoubtedly get the show off to a great start.

Arrangements were made to put on a special sports programme on which Mills would be a panel member, with Eamonn acting as chairman. This was designed to keep the boxer busy.

Inevitably, Grainne Andrews was drawn into the plot. Being a practical person, she found the mystery surrounding the show rather funny at first, but gradually entered into the spirit of the programme. On the evening of the show they would entertain Freddie Mills to dinner in their flat and afterwards Eamonn and Freddie would drive to Lime Grove for *This Is Your Life*. Keeping the secret from Eamonn was, she soon discovered, not easy. Earlier that day she told him she was going to see her doctor, but in reality she was off to the Television Theatre to meet the guests, including Eamonn's mother, and receive a briefing. When she returned to the flat he instantly asked her where she had been, having already checked on the phone with the doctor's receptionist and been told that Mrs Andrews hadn't called.

Grainne casually made the excuse that she had gone shopping after the doctor's and had forgotten to mention it to him. For the first time she started to feel insecure about the plot, fearing that in some bizarre way she might let the cat out of the bag. She was relieved when Eamonn said no more about it. That evening, however, during dinner with Eamonn and Freddie, she felt the strain but tried to act as normally as possible. She was glad to see that Eamonn hadn't suspected a thing.

After dinner, her real problem arose. She had to ensure that she got to the theatre before her husband and, of course, without him knowing it. When he and Freddie Mills had driven away, she quickly changed clothes with the assistance of her housekeeper, Alice, and dashed off in a waiting taxi to the Television Theatre.

In the crowded foyer there was a perilous moment for Leslie Jackson and the *Life* team when Freddie Mills spotted heavyweight Don Cockell and, at that moment, wondered if after all he was going to be the subject of the programme. But he made no remark and agreed to Jackson's suggestion that he sit beside Eamonn among the studio audience. Around them were seated stage and screen stars Boris Karloff, Bebe Daniels and Ben Lyon.

At 7.45 the red studio light flicked on and millions of viewers were about to get their first glimpse of the BBC's version of *This Is Your Life*. Presenter Ralph Edwards moved smoothly among the audience and welcomed some well-known personalities; heads turned sharply when he came to Boris Karloff, star of numerous horror films. 'Maybe it's your life tonight, Boris?' hinted Edwards without conviction. 'Not likely,' he said softly.

Eamonn sat smugly in his seat as Edwards moved up beside him. He looked at the American presenter and grinned confidently. The preliminaries were exciting, he thought, and Edwards expertly conveyed the suspense.

'Now, who have I here?' Edwards said, looking in the direction of Eamonn and Freddie Mills. 'I guess it's Eamonn Andrews! And I see he has brought along with him a guest everyone knows – Freddie Mills!' His words were followed by loud applause from the audience, who by now were finding the tense build-up absorbing. At that moment, Edwards handed the red volume, inscribed in gold letters with the title *This Is Your Life*, to Eamonn and said, 'Here, you read it.'

Eamonn took the book eagerly. Before he even had the wrapper off that hid the name, he was reading aloud: 'This Is Your Life – Oh blimey!' There, beneath the title, was the name *Eamonn Andrews*.

The grin disappeared from his face. For a moment he blushed and hardly knew what to do. He heard Ralph Edwards say, 'Tonight we have turned the tables on you, Eamonn.' There was more enthusiastic applause.

Edwards led his victim to the stage where, paraded for the next thirty minutes, were members of his family and some show-business stars. Eamonn smiled and still looked in a daze. Leslie Jackson thought the most moving moment of the evening was Eamonn's embrace of his mother. 'Eamonn doesn't cry easily,' he would say later, 'but that night the tears rolled down his face.' Unfortunately, it was also the kind of scene that provided ammunition for the critics who accused the BBC of trivialising the channel with 'cheap emotion'.

At the party afterwards, Eamonn was able to relax. Secretly, he had one regret – that his father was not alive to be part of the unique occasion. He felt proud to be the first subject chosen for *Life*, and even though this was by default, he knew it was an important boost to his television career.

He was now thirty-two. He had made it. Already he had achieved more than he could ever have hoped for in his relatively short time in Britain. The presence of Don Cockell at the party was a vivid reminder of his first broadcast of a World Heavyweight title fight from America – something he had always wanted to do. And though Don had been defeated by the powerful American, Rocky Marciano, millions of listeners had stayed up until 3 a.m. in Britain and Ireland to hear his commentary. 'That commentary was one of the proudest moments of my life,' he would declare later.

Next morning, the newspapers concentrated on the emotional

impact of *This Is Your Life*, and a few carried photographs of Eamonn embracing his mother. It was said that some viewers wept during the show. Leslie Jackson said the success of the show vindicated the BBC's courage in putting it on. 'I think before very long,' he predicted, 'it will be screened once a fortnight.'

Eamonn was emphatic: 'I believe in *This Is Your Life*. In the business of television, if you don't believe in a thing, it's no good carrying on with it.' Repeatedly he was asked his own feelings at the moment he was surprised by Ralph Edwards; 'My reaction was that of getting a shock. I felt myself tremble. It is so unbelievable that you are going to be thrown into the spotlight. You don't know what is going to come, and when it begins, the memories keep flooding back. It's like a dream, it goes so fast. I don't think you enjoy it or not enjoy it, while it is happening. I know I was in a daze, and it was all great fun and wonderful, but I enjoyed it even more in retrospect.'

Mrs Margaret Andrews had always remarked on her son's innate shyness, and after his *Life* performance, she was still not sure whether Eamonn had entirely cast it off. 'I felt for him as he stood on the stage not knowing who next was going to greet him,' she said, 'But I was very proud of him.'

Eamonn looked forward to his role as presenter. Watching Ralph Edwards, he recognised the risk of being carried away on a tide of emotion. It was something he would have to avoid, though he saw the programme itself as essentially moving. It also highlighted heroic lives that might otherwise go unnoticed by people. He agreed with the Americans that the surprise was everything. After his own experience, he was utterly convinced.

8 *Surprise for Sue*

EARLY IN 1956, Eamonn jotted down in his notebook the name Sue Ryder as a potential *This Is Your Life* subject. The papers were describing her as the 'Sister of Mercy' and three years before the Sue Ryder Foundation had been formed for the purpose of helping the sick and the homeless. Ostensibly, her story was one of human courage, the type that appealed to viewers. Asked once if heroic stories made the best *Life* programmes, Eamonn replied: 'I think they are essential to the whole pattern of the programme, but I am equally convinced that no matter what viewers think the show would pall having them every week.'

Sue Ryder's story seemed of exceptional merit. A frail and slender woman of 33 years with intense blue eyes and gold-coloured hair, she was from the landed gentry with estates in Yorkshire and Suffolk. Her parents, especially her mother, had a strong influence on her childhood. Mrs Ryder was a woman who took on the problems of others and often invited them into her own house for attention. Sue was sent to Benenden School, which in the thirties was offering free places to the children of families fleeing from Nazi Germany. In 1938, when she was fifteen, she wrote to her mother: 'I wonder how much longer we will enjoy peace and poetry? Probably only a short time now – shorter than many realise or want to hear.'

A few years later she served with SOE (Special Operations Executive) mainly in the Polish section, and when the war ended she was in Europe. Around her she saw despair in the faces of hundreds of thousands of sick and displaced persons. She was determined to bring them hope and assistance. Men and women at the very limits of human despair had for her, she said, beauty. 'I think they're beautiful. I can't think of any other word. The real love that comes from the heart is what I feel for them.'

Back in England, she begun to work for various welfare organisations and when they were withdrawn she carried on working on her own. Driving herself relentlessly, working literally a twenty-four hour schedule, existing largely on tea and biscuits, she rattled endlessly the length and breadth of Germany in her battered car, travelling hundreds of miles to help the displaced persons. Never, since 1941, had Sue spent a Christmas with her mother in the quiet Suffolk countryside.

With the forming of the Sue Ryder Foundation, her work began to be noticed, yet there were still millions of people in Britain who had never heard of her. It was this and other aspects of her story that interested Eamonn Andrews. To promote her work, she needed money. Already he had read that more than £1,000 of her personal savings had been used up by her welfare activities. By now she was dedicating her life to helping over 1,000 of the 220,000 Displaced Persons still in European camps whose world was dark and without a future.

When producer Leslie Jackson and the *This Is Your Life* team checked out Sue's mother as the key contact for the programme, they found she was prepared to assist them, though she felt that her daughter was rather shy of publicity. The team did not see this as the real problem. A woman who travelled so extensively was hard to pin down in one place long enough for Eamonn to present her with the red book.

By now, Eamonn was intrigued by the work of this unselfish woman they called 'a modern day Florence Nightingale'. To thousands of the sick, crippled, jobless, displaced persons of Europe she was a link with hope and sanity. She was 'Mamma' to many youngsters whose childhood was spent in the

[72]

nightmare stench of Nazi concentration camps, whose parents died in the gas chamber. She was 'Sister Sue' to thousands of men and women whose bodies and minds were shattered in the hells of Buchenwald, Belsen and Auschwitz.

As the *Life* researchers pieced together other aspects of Sue Ryder's extraordinary life, they learned that she would be in London for a few days that November. But what they or Eamonn hadn't known, or could not be expected to know, was Sue Ryder's total ignorance of *This Is Your Life*. So busy was she with her work, that she had not heard of the show, despite the fact that the series had now run for over a year and was attracting millions of viewers. Unsurprisingly, when Eamonn handed her the red book that evening in the King's Theatre in Hammersmith, she looked absolutely bewildered. As she was greeted by her mother, friends and fellow workers she hardly knew what to say. She stood there, a small, unassuming woman, her face pale, her eyes deep-set and tense.

Today, Sue – or Lady Ryder of Warsaw as she prefers to be known – remembers the occasion. From the Foundation's headquarters in the picturesque Suffolk village of Cavendish, she said she was at first a little baffled by the *Life* programme. 'When Eamonn Andrews handed me the red book I couldn't comprehend what was happening to me. I had never before seen the show, so it was new to me. I couldn't understand the nature of the programme, but I know now I felt happy. Seeing my mother so happy, and my smiling friends around me, made me feel proud and secure. I didn't find it an emotional experience.'

What was to please her greatly in the subsequent weeks were the many congratulatory messages, as well as postal orders and cash, that poured into the Foundation's headquarters. To Eamonn, the programme had served its purpose. In addition, in his view, to being good television, viewers had met a remarkable woman with a stirring story. As he had pointed out, there was a place in the series for the heroic story. It showed that *Life* could be meaningful despite what some of his

[73]

detractors liked to think.

Lady Ryder of Warsaw was to be guest on two further *Life* programmes when she was able to study Eamonn's role as presenter more closely. She was, as she says, enormously impressed. 'I thought it was amazing how he handled the programme. His personal approach, his anxiety to put people at ease – these things, as well as his obvious sincerity and dedication, ensured the success of the show. I admired also the way he coped with different people.'

As time passed she was delighted to find that Eamonn continued to take interest in her work for the Foundation. 'He used to send me these little notes asking me if he could help in any way. I knew he was under a lot of pressure and for that reason I didn't want to bother him. As far as I could see, he never spared himself. He always worked so very hard.'

She and Group Captain Leonard Cheshire married in 1959 when both the Cheshire Homes and the Sue Ryder Foundation were firmly established. Before doing so they wrote to their colleagues: 'We assure you that our sole aim is still the good of the work.'

Although Eamonn never cared to take the credit, it was generally believed that certain *This Is Your Life* programmes, especially in the early post-war years, helped to further good causes. In the case of the Sue Ryder homes this is probably true; there are now twenty-two in Britain and twenty-eight in Poland.

A few years later Group Captain Leonard Cheshire would be the subject of *This Is Your Life*. Leslie Jackson counts the show as among the most exciting he has produced. 'For one thing,' he recalls, 'I think that Eamonn wasn't at all sure that he would accept the book.'

Today Leonard Cheshire confirms this. As he says, 'When I found Eamonn looming over me, with a broad smile on his face and a camera somewhere behind him, I agreed to go on the programme, but at that moment he seemed to think that I would not, for he enquired rather anxiously whether I really meant what I said, and continued to appear slightly ill at ease in the car as we drove to his home. We sat there for an hour or so, before going on to the studio.'

For a number of years he had no intention of going on the *Life* show if approached by Eamonn. His wife, Sue Ryder had complained of pressure on her family when her own story was being done, and despite her affection for Eamonn Andrews she advised against going on the show. 'As a result,' recalls Leonard Cheshire, 'I told my mother and father this, and asked them to have nothing to do with it, should they ever be approached. However, a week or two before my *Life* story, Sue casually said to me, "If Eamonn Andrews ever does ask you, though I doubt he will, perhaps it would be better to accept, for the sake of the work."'

At the time they had approximately twelve Cheshire Homes in England, six in India, one in Singapore, Tangier, Bethlehem and Sierra Leone. In addition, there was their first joint project, Ryder-Cheshire at 'Raphael', Northern India. As in the case of the Sue Ryder Foundation, Eamonn was interested in the work of the Cheshire Homes and was anxious to help in any way possible. He planned to surprise Leonard Cheshire in Vincent Square, London, where he had an appointment to see Duncan Guthrie in his offices.

'Duncan was then in charge of a major charity for the handicapped and I had high hopes that he would give me some money for a special project that I had in India,' remembered Group Captain Cheshire. 'My wife came with me and, not long after we had sat down, began to make signs, greatly to my surprise, that it was time to go. I objected quite strenuously, saying that we had not yet got down to the business on hand, but Duncan also indicated that it was time to stop; and, two or three minutes later, he stood up and said that he must go. Outside in the street, Eamonn was waiting.'

Now, as he sat with Eamonn in his home he found him very caring and anxious to put him at ease. He had met him once before, in 1950, when he came to open the first garden fete he ever held at his first Cheshire Home, Le Court. Their paths would cross from time to time later on, and they exchanged cards at Christmas.

He was to find his own *Life* programme a memorable experience.

'How could it be otherwise, with so many different people coming out of the wings to bring back personal memories of days gone by? I was greeted by Mick Martin, of Dambuster fame, and others from my RAF days as well as from the Homes. One particular memory is of somebody from Limoges. We, the Dambusters, were given as our target the Gnome-Rhone areo-engine factory on the outskirts of the city on which to demonstrate our newly-developed, high-level, precision-bombing technique, using 10,000-pound bombs dropped from 16,000 feet. But we had instructions from the War Cabinet not to destroy surrounding property, nor to cause any civilian casualities. There was a night-shift of 500 at the time we attacked but, by doing three very low-level runs over the factory, and then waiting five minutes, we warned them to get out, so that not one bomb dropped outside the factory, and there were no casualties. This, I believe, is still remembered in Limoges today, and a representative came over at Eamonn's invitation, really just to say thank you on the show. It was probably for me the most moving moment of all that evening – and the most unexpected.'

In retrospect, he was glad that he had agreed to accept the large book from Eamonn, although he reckoned his parents were a little puzzled by his change of mind. He was to participate in another unforgettable *Life* programme when the subjects were Father Michael and Father Kevin Doheny. As he recalls, 'Father Kevin is our representative for Africa, and Father Michael was a frequent visitor to the office; in fact, when in London they usually "dossed down" on camp beds in the office. For us, this posed considerable problems, as they were there for several days prior to the programme, with each

[76]

of them coming up to us and saying, "Whatever happens, don't tell Kevin (or Mick), but he is about to be on *This Is Your Life*, little knowing what was going to happen. Eamonn was at his best that night and, once again, the caring side of his nature came out. As the truth, that he himself (and not just his brother) was going to be the subject of the programme, began to dawn on Father Kevin, he looked in such a state that Eamonn interrupted his questioning and leaned forward to ask rather anxiously, "Are you alright?"'

It struck Group Captain Cheshire that Eamonn was interested, where possible, to project the good side of life on his programmes, in particular worthy causes. In this respect, he thought that *This Is Your Life* could be very meaningful. He was happy also to make the friendship of Eamonn Andrews.

By now, *This Is Your Life* owed much of its undoubted popularity to the contrasting personalities it continued to bring to the screen. When Eamonn was asked for his definition of the ideal *Life* subject, he said thoughtfully, 'The basic requirement is a good story, a varied story, and if you can add to that a pleasant, bubbling personality then you have something else going.'

Coping with such a variety of subjects could have posed a problem or two for a lesser professional than Eamonn. But it was acknowledged that as presenter he was able to sum up quickly the kind of approach needed for certain subjects. As one veteran researcher put it, 'If Eamonn sensed it was advisable to adopt a light-hearted approach, he did so; if he thought a more direct approach was necessary that's the way he did it. Sometimes it could be tricky, but Eamonn's long experience as presenter was a great asset to him. His instincts were rarely wrong, and he was able to cope easily with most *Life* subjects.'

He could not have looked for a more bubbling subject than comedian Jimmy Edwards. Regarded as a larger-than-life individual, and a healthy mocker of false emotions, he posed

[77]

an undoubted challenge to Eamonn. Would the presenter try to match his ebullience? Or would he be content to stick to his script and let the irrepressible Edwards poke his wicked fun without provoking him?

The comedian had been born in Barnes in 1920 and served as a pilot in the war with the RAF and was awarded the DGFC. It was a gamble whether he would become a school teacher or go on the stage. Deciding on the stage, in 1946 he made his debut at London's Windmill Theatre, the famous training ground for most of the country's comics. However, it was in the radio series *Take It From Here* that he eventually made his name. Eamonn made no secret of the fact that he was a fan of the programme.

It was now 1958. Jimmy Edwards was being described as 'a gruff bachelor, whose prowess on the hunting, shooting and polo fields were as well known as the shape of his moustache.' When not working, he liked to retire to his 400-acre farm in Sussex and keep an eye on the dairy herd and horses.

The fun began as Eamonn led the comic, protesting loudly, to the stage of Shepherd's Bush Theatre. As his friends in the business were paraded before him, Edwards ran his fingers lightly through his moustache and poked fun at all and sundry Eamonn kept resolutely to his prepared script and refused to be drawn into verbal combat. It seemed the only course he could take, otherwise his words would be lost in the welter of audience laughter.

Meanwhile, the real drama was taking place behind the scenes.

The *Life* team had been experiencing considerable trouble in locating Jimmy Edwards' sister in Australia, but eventually contacted her. When they explained to her the reason for the call, she said enthusiastically, 'I'd love to be a guest in the show. I know Jimmy would love it also. But how do I get over at such short notice?'

'We'll fly you over,' the *Life* researcher told her. It meant some hectic, last-minute flight arrangements, and when she eventually arrived it was only hours before the show, or just enough time for flowers to be delivered to her hotel room in Lancaster Gate. When Eamonn introduced her at the climax of the show there was spontaneous applause from the audience. Even Jimmy, a compulsive talker, was almost lost for words.

At the outset, he said he had anticipated a programme of such sentimental impact that there wouldn't be a dry eye between Land's End and Val Parnell. He was wrong. As one critic observed, 'There were no dry eyes last night. They were wet with laughter.' And he added, 'Edwards made wicked fun of Andrews. Andrews, playing himself, saw his programme ripped to shreds.' Leslie Jackson disagreed. He felt that Eamonn, as presenter of the show, coped admirably with the comedian's non-stop wise-cracking. 'It was a fun programme and Eamonn helped to make it so by refusing to take on Jimmy.'

Off-stage, Eamonn and Jimmy were friends. Eamonn, a radio man to his finger tips, admired the comedian's technique and how he disguised it so cleverly behind his large moustache. To radio listeners he came across, as one critic put it, 'with the subtlety of a battering ram, flattening resistance and sweeping the audience on wave after wave of hilarity,' but to Eamonn, Jimmy knew how to make an audience laugh and sound extremely funny on radio.

Later, when both men met in America, Eamonn was amused by Jimmy's impact on the Americans. He observed: 'A moustache like the Edwards glory had never before, I'm sure, been seen in Miami. When Jimmy's commanding voice and very English accent were added, there resulted (for Americans) a triple attraction to vie with any three-ring circus. He may not have been aware of it, but Jimmy's moustache had the patrons and hotel staff entranced. From where I was sitting I could see the waiters whispering among themselves, nudging each other, pointing in our direction, and then coming back time

[79]

after time ostensibly to check our orders, but really to take another look-and-listen to this transatlantic phenomenon.'

Eamonn was there to do a commentary for the BBC on the World Title fight between Patterson and Johannson. Jimmy Edwards had flown in that day to see the fight. When he discovered that he had a wretched view, he appealed to Eamonn to try to do something, but nothing could be done. After the fight, they talked to Schnozzle Durante. He made Jimmy very welcome. Eamonn was taken by the comic's 'enormous nose and his reddish face'.

They were in Durante's dressing-room with three other people, among them Floyd Patterson's manager. The outspoken Edwards, who hadn't bothered to get names, began to criticise Patterson's 'low blows' until Eamonn reminded him that it was Patterson's manager he was talking to. Jimmy kept talking, as though he was a boxing authority, while at the same time the manager stared at his moustache, fascinated by its size and shape. Eamonn thought a lesser man than Jimmy would have fled the scene. But he stayed and bluffed it out.

Eamonn felt he understood Jimmy Edwards, in the same way that he was at home with the more eccentric Gilbert Harding. Jimmy had been a panellist on *What's My Line?* and he found him both quick-witted and entertaining. He subscribed to the view that both radio and television needed characters, the funnier the better. Jimmy, he knew, revelled in the limelight and liked to hit his audience where it hurt. But there was more than a modicum of truth in the PR handout that 'his personality attracts fans from six to ninety-six'.

9 *Frankie's Friend*

IN THE MID-FIFTIES, Frankie Vaughan was playing the Theatre Royal in Dublin for a week, along with comedian Harry Worth, when he was introduced to salmon fishing in the River Boyne, near Drogheda.

'I fished every day – it was wonderful,' he recalls, 'and before the week was out I caught this magnificent twenty-five pound salmon which I decided to bring back with me to England.'

Eamonn Andrews had heard about Frankie's success as an angler and invited him as a guest celebrity on *What's My Line?* After the panel had guessed his name and occupation, Eamonn said, 'I gather you caught a fish in the River Boyne the other day and it weighs twenty-five pounds and is fourteen inches long?'

Frankie: 'No, no, it's much longer than that.'

Eamonn: 'That's impossible.'

With that, Frankie opened a large box and brought out the salmon and proudly showed it to Eamonn. 'It was a good gag,' he remembers, 'and Eamonn thought it very funny.'

Frankie Vaughan regarded Eamonn as his friend. He had come to admire his boxing commentaries and sometimes they discussed the sport. 'I found him very knowledgeable about boxing,' he says. 'Around this time I had been introduced by Bessie Braddock in my native Liverpool to a young black fighter, Hogan Kid Bassey. Bessie convinced me he was going to be great. I mentioned his name to Eamonn and he showed a

[81]

lot of interest in him. He was also interested in my work for boys' clubs and once told me he had belonged to a boxing club in Dublin and placed real value on well-run clubs for boys.'

As he got to know Eamonn better, he grew to enjoy his company. 'Eamonn had a nice, charming manner that got through to you. One didn't feel afraid of talking to him, and one trusted him. He was accepted in show-business as one of us. Often you find that media people and show-business people are afraid of one another, but one never felt this with Eamonn. He was the ultimate all-rounder in my eyes – writer, radio broadcaster, and television presenter.'

Like Eamonn, Frankie Vaughan had made it during the fifties. His big break came when he auditioned for impresario Val Parnell and was booked for a tour of the famed Moss Empire theatre circuit – the same circuit that Eamonn Andrews had toured with Joe Loss and his Orchestra. In 1953, Frankie made his movie début when he landed a small part in the comedy *Ramsbottom Rides Again*. Soon afterwards he began a highly successful cinema association with Anna Neagle and Herbert Wilcox. Soon he became the first British singer to top the bill at Las Vegas. But today he likes to recall one of the truly outstanding moments of his career, when he became the subject of the American version of *This Is Your Life*, and presenter Ralph Edwards handed him the red book.

Later, he would mention the experience to Eamonn Andrews. 'Like me, Eamonn found the advertising that punctuated the hour-long show ridiculous. But it was for me a very moving experience, and in showbiz terms, a very important programme. It was, if you like, an American version of a Royal Command Performance and was counted one of the top programmes in the States.' They flew in from England his relatives, friends and show-business friends, but Frankie disliked the show for one reason only – he cried like a baby for much of it. After the show he said to himself, 'That's it. I'll never have to bother about the programme again.'

Watching *This Is Your Life* presented by Eamonn Andrews

prompted him now to draw comparisons. While he agreed that Ralph Edwards was the more professional, there was no doubt in his mind that Eamonn added an extra dimension. He had his own way of getting people to talk; he avoided hogging the limelight – and the 'mike' – and managed to make the show his own. To Frankie Vaughan, the show was identified solely with Eamonn, and in his view he was a great success. It didn't worry him that *This Is Your Life* could be over-emotional or sentimental. As far as he was concerned it was refreshing television and brought to the screen the lives of a wide variety of people, sometimes people with extraordinary stories to tell.

Eamonn's thoughts were divided between *Life* and *What's My Line?* He was relieved that BBC chiefs had granted a reprieve to *Line*, for he had been sure it was to be taken off. He hadn't agreed with the decision and had argued with Ronnie Waldman that there was plenty of life left in the programme. Recalling his feelings at the time, he wrote: 'I felt as if I'd had one of those agonising experiences where the train whistles, the doors slam, you kiss your loved one, babble your sad farewells and messages; and then stare at each other as the train decides it was only joking and doesn't leave for another ten minutes.'

The reprieve was vindicated, for when the show resumed it quickly got into the top ratings. Eamonn felt he had established a fine rapport with his panellists, even the often rude Gilbert Harding. Yet, he told himself, life indeed would be strange without their battle of words.

By now, they had acquired a new panellist in Isobel Barnett, a doctor by profession, who sometimes found it difficult to cope with the rumbustious Gilbert Harding. 'Gilbert's passport to fame was his rudeness,' she would comment later. 'He allowed his impatience to show instead of masking it with a false bonhomie. He lost his temper with volcanic suddenness instead of controlling it. He could be deliberately rude, but deliberately unkind – never.' To the observant Lady Barnett, Gilbert was at the same time an intelligent and deeply

[83]

sentimental man with a streak of brilliance. He lacked however the desperate single-mindedness of purpose and hard work needed to train for and pursue an academic career. She believed he was a sick man.

Producer Leslie Jackson thought that one of the best things about *What's My Line?* was that it introduced viewers to people with all kinds of odd jobs. 'What I mean is, that viewers learned how other people lived up and down the country. In this way the programme was fascinating.'

To Barbara Kelly, Eamonn's role was punishing, even nerve-racking, for it was up to him to keep the panellists in check and the questions flying between the panel and contestants. Once, Leslie Jackson asked the almost impossible of Eamonn when he suggested that he'd be the guest celebrity. As Eamonn good-humouredly recalled, 'It was impossible to get anyone else to the studio at such short notice. So as soon as the panel members had put their masks on somebody else "signed in" for me, walked with heavy footsteps towards the vacant seat by my side, and then sneaked quietly away to leave me to adopt a dual personality. Hopping from one chair to another, I asked myself questions and answered them in a high falsetto voice that almost choked me. I argued with me, whispered to myself, and nearly died laughing. And I beat the panel!'

Funny thing is, Eamonn would probably not have missed *What's My Line?* as much as he reckoned, because he was extremely busy with other television and radio programmes. On *Crackerjack*, the BBC's ambitious children's show, he showed how adept he could be with young people. As producer Johnny Downes recalled, 'Eamonn had the happy knack of putting them at their ease and, at the same time, getting the best out of them.'

When the Andrews moved to a more spacious and ornate flat in Lancaster Gate, Leslie Jackson joked, 'Eamonn's climbing up in the world.' It was true. His was by now one of the best-known faces in television. He betrayed no shyness when he welcomed Queen Elizabeth on *Crackerjack*. And when he was introduced to the Duke of Edinburgh both men talked for a while about their own roles in life. Eamonn's natural courteousness made him a favourite with the Royal Family.

On Saturdays he continued to present *Sports Report*, a programme that still attracted millions of listeners, while he was also presenting *Pied Piper*, a late night radio chat show. With this heavy workload it came as a surprise when his agent, Teddy Sommerfield, accepted a new television show for him. Producer of the show, Ernest Maxim, had been eager for some time to have Eamonn sing and dance and he reckoned the time was right for such a daring venture. He knew that Eamonn was anxious to extend his scope.

Maxim had said, 'We'll call it the *Eamonn Andrews Show*. It's bound to be a fabulous success.'

When Eamonn asked what he was expected to do on the show, the producer explained, 'Everything! The lot! You'll sing, dance, take part in funny sketches, meet guests.'

'I can't sing,' protested Eamonn. 'I'll make a fool out of myself.'

Maxim was adamant: 'You'll be taught how to sing. I know you can do it. It's a new opportunity for you.'

It was a moment when Eamonn's agent should have stepped in and said 'No' to the show. He didn't; nor did Eamonn have any serious second thoughts; instead he went along with the BBC's plan for six shows. Eric Robinson was the musical director, Dick Hill and Syd Green the scriptwriters, and guest artists would be people like Frankie Vaughan, Jill Day, Yana, and the Vernon Girls. Despite his qualms, Eamonn mustered up enough enthusiasm to make the rehearsals look promising. Ernest Maxim was impressed as his 'new star' rehearsed the song, *You May Not Be An Angel* with Yana and Jill Day. The voice, though ordinary, sounded good in the song, but in the middle of the dress rehearsal Eamonn began to sing out of tune. The trio repeated the song and this time everything seemed to go right. It was pointed out to Eamonn that there was a key-change in the middle of the number and he was asked to watch for it.

Since the show would be going out live, he began to feel nervous. However, as the trio sang *You May Not Be An Angel* Eamonn looked across at the pianist, who was accompanying him and misinterpreted what he was trying to convey by a wave of his arm. The pianist was humming the tune, but Eamonn, for some inexplicable reason, thought he himself was singing off key and suddenly his voice began to wobble and he lost it.

At that moment his face reddened, he felt terrible. But his big solo number, *How Deep Is The Night?* was still to come. There was no way he could wriggle out of it. 'It was a nightmarish experience,' he admitted later. 'I could feel millions of viewers glaring at me from the cameras, daring me to sing again.'

That evening, the BBC received numerous calls about the show from irate viewers, some of whom asked if the Corporation was going to take it off altogether. Next morning, the newspapers called it 'a shambles' and begged Eamonn to confine his singing in future to the bathroom.

Eamonn was to describe it as 'a ghastly business'. But the BBC decided to continue with the series; however, more emphasis would be placed on comedy sketches in the future. When Frankie Vaughan was a guest, Eamonn intimated that he'd like to sing with him. But as they rehearsed *Give Me The Moonlight*, Frankie noticed that Eamonn was having difficulty managing the hat and cane routine.

'He got into a bit of a mess,' he recalls. 'I remember he blushed in his lovely Irish way. He looked at me and said, "You take it from here, Frankie". I think Eamonn knew he was no Frank Sinatra.'

Although Eamonn labelled the affair, 'a tremendous crisis' in his career, he was exaggerating. Obviously he was too established a name now to be ruined by one poor television series. In future however he would have to learn when to say no to programmes that were obviously unsuited to his talents. It wasn't a question of money; he was by now one of the biggest money earners in the business and there was no reason for him to take silly risks.

Coming from a shrewd show business family, Grainne Andrews was quick to see the folly of her husband's decision. She told him, 'If you ever again try to sing on television – I'll leave the country. I'll emigrate.'

Incredibly, Eamonn found time to pursue his business interests in Ireland. He was a director of a recording studio that produced sponsored programmes for Radio Eireann. Fred O'Donovan, a freelance producer and the owner of a small recording studio in Dublin, felt that Eamonn's company wasn't cashing in on his name. Both men arranged to meet and discuss a merger.

'I agreed on condition that Eamonn lent his name to the new company. I pointed out to him the obvious possibilities and he agreed to let the company be known as the Eamonn Andrews Studios. He was a celebrity and I felt we could plan together major interviews and documentaries.'

To O'Donovan, Eamonn was not only an outstanding broadcaster but also a keen businessman. 'Before long I was impressed by his enthusiasm. He would fly over from London to attend our monthly meetings. It was my job to run the company on a day to day basis. We had a good working relationship, though Eamonn was not a person who was easy to get to know. He had a quiet sense of humour and a certain reserve.'

In a short time, the company built up a large business. Based in a top floor apartment in Henry Street, it catered for the needs of radio, television and cabaret. Soon it would expand further to involve itself in hotels; another company would be set up to lease the city's best-known theatre – the Gaiety.

Dubliners, who tended to regard Eamonn as a showman-cum-businessman, were not surprised by his involvement. Friends felt that he wanted to maintain his links with the city. It was a fact also that since he regarded fame as ephemeral he thought it wise to seek security by promoting profit-making companies.

To his television colleagues in London, Eamonn was rich and famous. They wondered why he bothered to dissipate his spare time by pursuing business interests in Ireland. To some of them it was illogical and they argued he was taking on too much. Producer Leslie Jackson would say, 'Presenting a nerve-racking programme like *This Is Your Life* was a week's work in itself. I don't know how Eamonn found the time for business.' Occasionally on Sundays, when Jackson was invited to the Andrews' flat for a Sunday drink, he noticed that Eamonn had gathered around him television colleagues and the conversation tended to be 'shop' talk. He wondered if he was able to relax.

In a year or two the Irish Republic would have its own television service and already Eamonn's name was being linked with it. It was expected that the Irish Government would make an approach to him to act as adviser, or even become its first director. To Fred O'Donovan, the new service opened up new possibilities and he hoped that Eamonn would be involved.

10 *Mildred's Secret*

MILDRED LOSS WASN'T surprised when she was approached by the *This Is Your Life* team for her cooperation. Knowing Eamonn Andrews' affection for her husband, she knew it was only a matter of time before the name Joe Loss would figure in the famous red book.

But she was scarcely prepared for subsequent events. 'They told me that Joe would be surprised by Eamonn at Hammersmith Palais, where he was doing a season,' she recalled. 'Every night as he left the house at 7.30 he'd remark, "I'll see you later, love." His departure was the cue for a BBC researcher to visit me to work out details of the programme. I found the plotting at first rather funny, but after a while I wondered what some of my neighbours must be thinking. I began to feel the strain in case any of them might take Joe aside and ask him if he knew what was going on.'

In fact, the only time he did suspect anything was when he thought his secretary was acting 'strange' and he asked Mildred, 'What's wrong with that woman. Is she looking for another job?'

Eventually she was moved by the programme. 'I think that Joe really felt honoured to be handed the red book by Eamonn. In my own case, I felt a little guilty keeping my big secret from him. We never kept secrets from one another.'

Eamonn had pencilled in another of his friends, Noel Purcell, to be the next recipient of the red book. Fred O'Donovan had convinced him that the tall, white-bearded actor would make a popular subject for *This Is Your Life*. However, when Fred and Eamonn's sister, Kathleen, called on Noel's wife, Eileen, they found she wasn't keen on the idea.

'Take a little time to make up your mind,' they suggested to her. 'We'll call by later.'

Eileen Purcell, who wasn't a television fan, did not want to put her husband to any trouble and, for her own part, wasn't keen on all the fuss involved. A week later she relented. As Fred O'Donovan recalled, 'It was very amusing really. If Noel happened to be in the house, I'd wait with Kathleen in a car nearby and pop in when he was gone so as to brief Mrs Purcell about the programme. I think she found all the secrecy off-putting at first but soon appreciated it was necessary.'

As in the case of Mildred Loss, the *Life* show was to prove an agreeable surprise for Eileen Purcell. Eamonn had tricked Noel Purcell into believing that the actor Barry Fitzgerald – a leprechaun of a man – was to be the subject, when in fact Noel, described by Eamonn as 'the biggest leprechaun in Ireland,' was told: 'Noel, tonight this is your life!'

The towering actor looked bewildered. He hadn't suspected a thing. Eamonn agreed with Fred O'Donovan later that it was one of his most interesting *Life* programmes.

By now the programme was being screened on a weekly basis. For producer Leslie Jackson, it meant extra strain. 'When Ronnie Waldman told me the programme was going weekly I remember saying to myself, "Can my nerves stand the strain?" There was always the possibility that someone would say no to Eamonn and walk away.' But he continued to find it exciting. In his own view *Life* had given Eamonn a new dimension. 'I could see his confidence grow every week. He was totally in command of the show. He was the star.'

Working as a researcher or scriptwriter with Eamonn wasn't easy. As one young researcher explained, 'He demanded a script that was simple and straightforward in its narrative; everything had to be written down, even the asides.'

The web of secrecy surrounding the show intrigued

newcomers to the *Life* team. 'Any of us involved were so guarded in our talk that we dared not tell our wives what we were doing,' remarked one producer. Eamonn Andrews had absolute integrity; he expected those concerned with the programme to dine together if necessary. At all times total secrecy was urged. The pressures in other ways on the team could be intense. The friends and relatives of the subject concerned were almost sworn to secrecy. In television circles the *This Is Your Life* team was soon to be described as 'a secret army, with the secrecy only ending when Eamonn Andrews stepped in front of the cameras to speak the words, "This Is Your Life".'

Despite the demands of the weekly programme, Eamonn and the team found no difficulty in finding suitable *Life* subjects. When they finally caught up with Stanley Matthews, it was agreed that sportsmen didn't always make the most exciting subjects. One of the programmes that Eamonn liked to remember involved the veteran actor A.E. Matthews. It stretched his nerves to breaking point. Even now, some years after *Life* was first introduced to British viewers, Eamonn was nervous at the pick-up moment and was often seen to perspire freely. He knew he faced in Matthews a warm-hearted but unpredictable 'rebel'.

'I had a tough assignment on my hands once the decision was made to present his life,' he said later. 'On transmission he did just about every solitary thing calculated to wreck the show's intricate timing and drive me up the drapes.'

Viewers at one point watched in amazement as Matthews contradicted, interrupted and laughed aloud. He was seen to stretch out on the couch and told all and sundry he was going to have a snooze. But there was a happy ending when he told the audience with tears in his eyes, 'Ladies and gentlemen, I would just like to say, that it has been the greatest experience in my whole life. . . .'

He wanted to go on, but his voice broke. Then after a slight pause, he muttered, 'Thank you, God Bless You.' For

Eamonn, it was a memorable moment. The old actor was nearly ninety years of age and had all the fame theatre can offer, yet that night he had tasted an altogether new experience, or as Eamonn put it: 'Two minutes before Matty had been full of mischief and fun. Now, near the end of his life, he was saying that he had to wait until this night for his greatest experience. There was nothing I could say.'

Eamonn was pleased for another reason. Occasionally the newspaper critics sniped at him – and at the programme. They accused him of 'intruding in people's private lives' and of 'inflicting a kind of torture'. He dismissed these accusations out of hand. He saw *Life* as a celebration. As he liked to say, 'We do not shock, nor do we pry. We try to make the show a joy. It brings people together.'

The ratings for *This Is Your Life* got a remarkable 89, and the average index for the series since it began was in the seventies – and over. The weekly audience averaged twelve million, which underlined the wide popularity of the programme. If some producers tended to ignore ratings, Eamonn was the direct opposite. 'Like it or not,' he once argued, 'the ratings decide whether or not a series shall carry on. Only a fool ignores them.'

There were certain people the *Life* team avoided as potential subjects, among them was Brendan Behan. Although producer Leslie Jackson would say that Eamonn was at one stage keen to hand the red book to the Dublin-born playwright, he changed his mind after considering the implications. 'I think he was afraid of Brendan's unpredictability and concluded he wouldn't be worth the trouble.'

The ratings for *What's My Line?* meanwhile afforded Eamonn much satisfaction. He experienced a buzz of excitement when Princess Margaret was presented to the panel and the contestants after one particular show. He found she possessed a fine gift for putting people at their ease, and he was pleased to hear from the Princess that she enjoyed *Line*.

'I almost always watch it,' she said, 'but the time seems to go too quickly, and the programme is over before you know it.'

Panellist Barbara Kelly was unhappy with the paltry money paid by the BBC. 'I kept quitting the programme,' she recalled, 'but I also kept coming back to it. At heart, I really loved the programme, despite the fact that at times I would have liked to argue with Eamonn, but he always remained calm. That infuriated me.'

It was now 1960, and Eamonn and the panellists were increasingly worried about the state of Gilbert Harding's health. To Lady Barnett, Gilbert looked ill and had lost a lot of his fire on the programme. Eamonn said, 'He wasn't really strong enough for the old, great gales of irritability. Now and then a storm would blow up – but a small storm, and he would let it pass. He didn't feel like sustaining an onslaught – but the image he had built was always there.'

It was common knowledge that Gilbert liked a drink or two before *What's My Line?* but now Eamonn discovered that he didn't drink as much any more. 'In the old days I could see a storm brewing way ahead of time. Gilbert would come straight from a dinner party or a session with some of his friends, heave himself into the seat, feel the heat of the lamps, and I could *see* the annoyance and the edginess rise in him. He would scan the faces of the challengers looking for a target, not caring very much what the target was so long as it gave him a chance of firing off some of his accumulated, if not completely understood annoyance.'

That autumn Gilbert collapsed and died on the steps of Broadcasting House. Lady Barnett would say, 'Gilbert knew that he was going to die: so did his friends; and when his death came we were shocked and deeply sad, but still surprised. Surprised because he had surmounted so many illnesses with such a superb physical courage that we imagined he could surmount even death itself.'

Eamonn was in Dublin when he heard the news of Gilbert's death. 'It was a terrible shock to me. Suddenly I felt very

[93]

lonely.' Later, he would recall, 'Gilbert was kind. He was religious. He lived in a beautiful home in Brighton and liked to sit and hold court and call the male members of his staff "Brother". He was attached to his mother, and frequently told me how she scolded him for being rude to me.'

With Gilbert's death, the future of the programme was said to be in the balance. It was argued that he had become an integral part of *Line* and was irreplaceable. As one observer put it, 'Mr Harding was to *What's My Line?* what Eamonn Andrews is to *This Is Your Life*. I can't see the programme ever being as entertaining again without the rumbustious Gilbert Harding.' It seemed only a matter of time until the BBC would decide to end the series.

Eamonn Andrews was among the 2,000 mourners in Westminster Cathedral for the Requiem Mass. He had once asked Gilbert, 'What qualities in life – which experience tells you are essential to happiness – are the ones you feel you most lack?'

Gilbert replied, 'Companionship, security and a sense of purpose.'

He had died a lonely man.

For Eamonn, it had been an eventful year. He had found the time to pop over to Ireland to accept the Chairmanship of the new Advisory Committee set up in connection with the establishment of Irish Television. He felt an honour had been conferred on him, though soon afterwards a political row erupted when it was claimed that his appointment would cause a conflict of interests. He was still a director of Eamonn Andrews Studios which made programmes for Radio Eireann. But the Minister for Posts and Telegraphs assured his colleagues that Eamonn Andrews would resign if he found he was compromising his position as Chairman of the Advisory Committee.

Later in the year, Eamonn was appointed Chairman of the new Radio Telefis Authority, while at the same time he decided to silence critics by not appearing professionally on Irish radio or television as long as he continued to act as Chairman of the Authority. He would remark, 'I had a hard time explaining that I wasn't going to make any profit out of it anyway.'

Friends in Ireland knew that he had accepted the part-time appointment in the first place out of a sense of loyalty. He was anxious to make a worthwhile contribution to the setting up of the new television service. Irish people expected him to accept the first offer of chairmanship of the Advisory Committee, and he could hardly say no. Eamonn was aware of this when he commented, 'It was the most exciting and the most challenging question I had ever been asked.'

But he had one reservation: 'I told the Minister that if I accepted the offer some people were bound to say that I had a commercial and selfish interest in the inauguration of the new service. He assured me that the government knew enough about me to know that I would not take advantage of the situation, and besides that, they knew no one who knew as much about television and also, as much about Ireland as I did.'

He worried a little about finding the time to attend meetings in Dublin. Coping with tight schedules in London was already a problem and this new appointment would eat up his spare time. Furthermore, it could mean having to say no to lucrative broadcasting offers in England. But the more Eamonn argued with himself, the more he realised he had no choice really. As he said, 'It wasn't as dramatic as the soldier going to war, but somehow it had the same undertones of duty. I believed strongly that Ireland must have its own television service. I decided to accept the offer.'

It was the kind of loyalty that his BBC colleagues would appreciate. If some of them remained puzzled why he should devote time to business interests in Dublin, they thought it rather noble of him to involve himself in the launch of Radio Telefis Eireann.

*

It was while Eamonn was in Dublin that his co-director in the Eamonn Andrews Studios, Fred O'Donovan, suggested a filmed interview with Brendan Behan.

'I had met Brendan one day at Dublin airport,' O'Donovan remembers, 'and since we were old friends I asked him if he was interested in being interviewed by Eamonn. I knew that he was fond of him. Brendan agreed and Eamonn promised to find the spare time.'

It was decided to do the interview at Ardmore Film Studios near Bray. To ensure that Brendan Behan would be there Fred O'Donovan booked him into the Royal Hotel in the Main Street. Eamonn, Lorcan Bourke and himself would also stay there. On the way to Bray, they decided to pick up Brendan at his home in Anglesea Road, near the Royal Dublin Society headquarters. Eamonn was startled to find Brendan had produced a half-bottle of whiskey and two champagne glasses. He handed these to Fred and Lorcan Bourke and poured whiskey into them. Then he turned and said to Eamonn: 'Fame is a great thing, but you know all that – on the television.'

Eamonn asked, 'What do you mean, Brendan?'

'Well, I came home today in a taxi, and when I got here the taxi-driver wouldn't take the fare. He recognised who I was. Marvellous.'

As the car headed for Bray, Eamonn wondered what he had let himself in for, though Fred O'Donovan had assured him that Brendan was 'off the gargle' and promised to behave impeccably.

It was late when they booked into the hotel. 'We stayed with Brendan until two in the morning,' says O'Donovan, 'to ensure he didn't go to the bar. I then saw him to his bedroom. He was in amiable mood and very sober when I told him I'd see him in the morning.'

O'Donovan did not sleep well. He found the room cold and uncomfortable and woke at 3.30. Suddenly he heard loud singing from somewhere downstairs. 'I decided to investigate,' he recalls, 'because I feared the worst. I trotted downstairs in my dressing-gown and there, before me in the bar, was Brendan leading a sing-song. I decided to stay in the bar until dawn, then went to my room and got dressed.'

Brendan Behan had sobered quickly and seemed all right to Eamonn and the others as they drove to the studios. The filmed interview, which was scheduled to take two days to complete, was finished at ten minutes to ten. Fred O'Donovan was astonished by the professionalism of Brendan. Eamonn remembered: 'During the interview there was a jug of Guinness hidden out of shot, and when we had to reload cameras we reloaded Brendan too. In fact, he was a perfect, sober, entertaining and philosophical interviewee.'

O'Donovan decided to pay Brendan on the spot. 'When I asked him to sign the contract, he looked at me and complained, "Do yous not trust me?" I told him it wasn't a question of trusting him, but rather that he'd forget I ever paid him.'

Three days later Brendan came into his office in Henry Street seeking to be paid for the interview!

Although Eamonn had coped confidently with Brendan in the filmed interview, he still was reluctant to have him as the subject on *This Is Your Life*. Apart from his unpredictability, he feared he would steal the limelight from everyone else on the programme and that was something he had tried to avoid, even in his own role as presenter.

Eventually, when it was decided to hand the large *Life* book to Brendan's father, Stephen, Eamonn said to producer Leslie Jackson, 'We mustn't allow Brendan to upset the show. Can we keep him in check?' Jackson, a seasoned producer, knew it wasn't going to be easy. Brendan could be boisterous if he had too much to drink. When Eamonn met him before the show, however, Brendan promised, 'I won't let you down at all. I give you me word.'

It was decided to pre-record the show at the RTE Studios in

Dublin, thereby ruling out a 'live' performance by Brendan Behan, for the programme would not be screened until two weeks later. Eamonn recalled, 'When I got to where Stephen Behan was sitting among the audience, I could see him staring up at the monitor screen above his head. In the picture he could see himself, with me standing close by. I said, "What's your name?" We had never met. Without turning to me, still trying to fathom the mystery of seeing himself in a picture, he just said, "Behan".' The audience looked in Eamonn's direction as he asked the genial old man, 'Are you anything to Brendan and Dominic Behan?'

The audience laughed as Stephen remarked, 'I'm married to their mother.'

Eamonn: 'When Brendan comes home, who does all the talking?'

After a puzzled pause, Stephen said, 'Their mother.'

The audience was enjoying the fun. Just then Eamonn sprang the surprise, but Stephen did not appear to comprehend fully what was going on. When Brendan was announced as the first guest he seemed to ignore Eamonn and, instead, began to talk about Tony O'Reilly. 'D'you know him, Eamonn? I played soccer with that fella once.'

Eamonn did his best to try to steer him back to the programme.

'It's your father's life you know, Brendan. Tell us about him.'

Brendan shrugged his shoulders. 'Oh, I'll tell ye about him.'

Leslie Jackson was on tenterhooks in the wings, wondering what Brendan was going to say and if, afterwards, they would be able to get him off to allow the other guests on. Brendan was acting as though he was in a Dublin 'local' and chatted affably with Stephen, oblivious of Eamonn. The audience by now had entered fully into the spirit of the show.

To Eamonn's relief, Stephen was holding his own and refused to allow Brendan to steal the limelight. Eventually, Brendan shuffled off, muttering to himself. It was the cue for

[98]

the entry of Stephen's wife, Kathleen Behan, and she quickly endeared herself to the audience, with her witty stories about her husband and sons. There was a spontaneous laugh when she announced she would 'love a bottle of stout.'

Eamonn admitted later that he enjoyed the programme despite the obvious Behanesque hazards he had to contend with. He liked to recall one particular incident which he was to find almost moving: 'I was actually a helpless witness to it. It concerned Stephen Behan's pipe. Stephen and the pipe were inseparable. It was part of his character. But when I helped him out of his overcoat in the audience, the pipe was left behind in the top pocket. When this was realised, Peter Moore, the writer, slipped down, recovered the pipe and the little brown paper bag of baccy that nestled with it in the pocket. Thus, when one of the later guests in the show came on, the pipe and paper bag were handed over again to Stephen. Unfortunately the wrong bag was handed to him. I knew it as soon as I saw his forlorn face. All the way through I could only stand and watch as poor old Stephen tried to get his pipe going on sugar and tea!'

At the party after the show in a nearby hotel the Behans and their friends had one big celebration. As Leslie Jackson would joke later, 'I was glad I wasn't picking up the bill!'

The show again demonstrated that Eamonn was able to cope with the unexpected. Yet he was not able to say, as he left the hotel, that he was prepared to hand the *Life* book to Brendan Behan, as much as he would have loved to.

11   *Danny's 'No Regrets'*

DANNY BLANCHFLOWER sat alone in a couch in the ornate foyer of a Dublin hotel. At the age of 62, he looked fit enough to play a game of football, except that on his own admission arthritis had set in in his right knee. The fair-haired celebrity had arrived that January afternoon in Dublin to receive a Hall of Fame Award to mark his outstanding contribution to football.

It was nearly 27 years since he had walked out on the *This Is Your Life* programme and greatly embarrassed his fellow Irishman, Eamonn Andrews.

Monday evening, 6 February 1961, was a date, Danny said, he could not easily forget. 'I'm sometimes reminded of it, and I can recall every moment of the episode because it was so personal to me. I suppose I'll never forget it.'

He spoke calmly and without any hint of rancour in his voice. Although his performance at the time created a sensation, it did not leave Eamonn with any bitter memories. As he explained, 'Danny Blanchflower was completely within his rights in refusing to go on with the programme and owed no explanation to anyone.' Television viewers, who imagined that both men had fallen out over the episode, were wrong. 'I met Eamonn afterwards and there were no hard feelings between us,' Danny says. 'Once, he laughed as he said to me, "Maybe you'll oblige us the next time".'

He said that his reasons for not accepting the famous red

book from Eamonn were, in his own view, perfectly valid. 'First of all, I never cared for the *This Is Your Life* programme and felt that if anyone wanted to say no he was entitled to do so. I suppose I resented the air of secrecy around it, the way I had been lured to the studio under false pretences and taken through a back door to meet certain people. I wasn't dressed for the occasion and felt I was being imposed upon. Anyway, I wasn't interested in seeing my life reconstructed in these circumstances, and there were, I realised at that moment, one or two people I didn't want to meet. Not that I had anything to hide. I had nothing whatsoever to hide from anybody. I would do exactly the same thing again if I was approached by a *This Is Your Life* presenter. I've no regrets.'

To Eamonn Andrews, Danny was a natural choice for a *Life* show. He was Captain of Tottenham Hotspur, the renowned London club. Among his fellow professionals, he was regarded as a brilliant half-back, at once stylish and disciplined. He had won most of the top honours in the game. As a Belfast-born footballer, he was colourful and an international player of distinction. A long time before Eamonn had pencilled his name into his notebook as a potential *Life* subject, and when the team checked with his relatives in Belfast there seemed to be no particular obstacle in the way of an exciting sporting *Life*.

Eamonn came to know Danny when he interviewed him on the BBC's *Sports Report*. He considered him very articulate, intelligent and blessed with a typical Belfast sense of humour. Furthermore, he was a fluent conversationalist and could analyse a football game as a professor would a new thesis. They got on well together and it was one of the reasons why he wasn't unduly worried about the forthcoming *This Is Your Life*.

'I knew Danny, not only as the star footballer he was,' Eamonn remembered, 'but as a radio and television performer. He had written about himself, and by no stretch of the imagination could I imagine him as being adverse to publicity. So I relaxed as we prepared to spring our surprise on him.'

To Danny, Eamonn was a thorough professional – and a nice, friendly Irishman. 'I found no difficulty working with him. His radio interviews with me were sharp and to the point. He was a man who enjoyed what he was doing. We didn't mix socially or sportingly, but I admired him as an outstanding broadcaster and boxing commentator.'

Eamonn's plan to surprise the footballer was a simple one. Danny would be invited by Angus McKay, the BBC's Sports Editor, to discuss players' wages with Matt Busby, manager of Manchester United, and Denis Law, a famous United player. This was scheduled to take place in a news studio opposite Broadcasting House, and here Eamonn was waiting to do the pick-up.

As Eamonn recalled, 'It was intended to tape the opening sequence. We had meanwhile a fast car standing by to get him to the theatre where we'd show the opening all over again to the audience and the viewing millions and then carry on with the programme and the surprises we had in store for him.'

Now, as the camera started operating, Eamonn pretended to be reading a newspaper. The *Life* book was hidden under a table. When Danny sauntered into the studio, Eamonn said, 'Do you see that camera?' Danny casually replied, 'Yes, that's an automatic camera. It's not controlled from here; it's controlled from upstairs. I've seen it work before.'

Eamonn's face showed surprise, his smile faded. 'Yes,' he said to the footballer, 'but the red light means it's on.'

Danny nodded, looking at the picture on the monitor. He still suspected nothing unusual. Eamonn said, 'It's not just on in the studio. It's on in the real sense. We're now being photographed for a special reason.'

Danny at that moment was standing beside him. Eamonn bent down to pick up the large book, saying as he did so, 'The reason is, because tonight Danny Blanchflower, this is your –'

Before he could utter another word, Eamonn watched in

dismay as Danny, showing the speed of a footballer, headed for the door. It was the last thing Eamonn expected to happen. For a moment, he looked bewildered, hardly knowing what to do next.

Angus McKay tried to stop Danny by hastily reaching out to grab his coat but in his haste nearly tumbled down the stone steps. Danny was heard to exclaim, 'Let me out of here!' By now, Eamonn, looking perplexed, caught up with the star footballer and appealed to him, 'Come on, Danny, be a sport will you?' He pointed out to him that there was a theatre full of people waiting to greet him. But Danny turned to him and snapped, 'It's not my concern. I didn't invite these people, did I?'

Among the guests at the theatre was the whole Spurs team, including goalkeeper Bill Brown who had let his wife into the secret so that she was now sitting at home with neighbours and friends expecting to see her husband greet Danny Blanchflower on the show.

'There was still fifteen minutes to go. In desperation, Eamonn went across to the BBC Club and telephoned his producer Leslie Jackson at the theatre to tell him of his dilemma. He warned him of the stark possibility of no programme because of the unprecedented behaviour of Danny Blanchflower. Jackson, a cool customer in a crisis, was stunned by the news. 'I couldn't think of any good reason why Danny should walk out on us,' he says today. 'The production team were confident that Eamonn would experience no trouble picking him up. I begged Eamonn to go back to Danny and make a final appeal to him.'

Eamonn was shattered. He found it hard to accept that one of the country's greatest footballers would say no to publicity. He hated to think also that so much preparation had gone by the board. Later, when he was asked about the *cause célèbre*, he said philosophically. 'I feel uncomfortable when people ask me didn't I think Danny Blanchflower was a bad sport not to have gone on the show. Whatever my opinion may be, it doesn't matter. When we throw the book at someone on *This Is Your Life*, we do so in the knowledge that this person has the right to come back with "Do you mind if I don't?" or any words he cares to choose to that effect.'

The audience at Shepherd's Bush Theatre was naturally disappointed that the show was cancelled. Among them was Danny Blanchflower's wife, Betty, who appeared cross that her husband had refused to go on the show. The frustration of the Spurs team was reflected by their rather glum faces, and Bill Brown knew that his wife would be furious at Danny's decision. But it was decided to carry on with the after-show party. The millions of viewers had not seen the 'walk-off' by Danny at the BBC's news studio. Another programme had been put on in place of *This Is Your Life*.

Next morning the newspapers headlined the history-making *Life* incident. Some of them felt that Danny Blanchflower should have been sport enough to accept the red book; others tried to speculate on the footballer's real reasons for his refusal, which weren't at all clear. Eamonn admitted that he had been disappointed by Danny's 'unexpected performance' and hoped it would not be repeated by others in the future.

Danny meanwhile was unrepentant. In the subsequent days and weeks he received numerous letters from ordinary people as well as footballers and football fans, most of whom seemed to agree that he was entitled to take the action he did, although some people regretted the hurt it obviously caused to Eamonn. As Danny recalls, 'I realised that my decision was a controversial one. Everyone I suppose expected me as Captain of Spurs to go on the show, but I had my own reasons for not doing so. I talked to my team-mates and they agreed with my decision, even my friend Bill Brown who had to face his wife and friends after the no-show. The team had after all given up their evening to be at the theatre. I appreciated their frustration and was sorry for them.'

The top brass at the BBC appeared even more concerned than Eamonn Andrews. They considered Danny Blanchflower's action as a direct slight on the Corporation. They insisted that henceforth every *This Is Your Life* show must be pre-recorded. Their decision, taken rather hastily, upset Eamonn. The live aspect of the programme appealed to him because it generated excitement; now, he worried about the future. Leslie Jackson agreed that the show would not have the same powerful impact as before and he discussed with Eamonn how they might surmount the problem.

'We decided to record the show a week before transmission,' he recalls, 'then a day before, then an hour before.' He was cross with Danny Blanchflower for walking off because he felt it gave BBC chiefs a reason for pre-recording the show. Even today, Leslie Jackson can find no good reason for the footballer's decision and prefers to attribute it to the 'stubbornness inherent in Irishmen'.

Eamonn's ambition, which he never tried to disguise, as well as his eagerness to think ahead, gave him little time to dwell on past disappointments. From time to time he was asked if he would care to try his luck in television in America. Presumably his mid-Atlantic accent would be an advantage. He was known to respect the professionalism of the Americans, as well as the way they devised their shows. Two of these shows, *What's My Line?* and *This Is Your Life*, when expertly fashioned to the tastes of British viewers, were to serve him exceedingly well. But uprooting himself at this stage of his successful career was something he would have to consider seriously.

Nonetheless, he accepted with alacrity the opportunity to be a guest panellist on the American version of *What's My Line?* Once more he was, on his own admission, impressed by what he described as 'the meticulous professionalism with which these people treated their work'. He wasn't allowed on the screen until such time as he was thoroughly briefed as to how the show was run over there, the kind of questions that should

[105]

be asked, the different terms used, and the differences between State laws and Federal laws.

John Daly was the programme's chairman and the panel comprised a New York columnist, a publisher, and an actress. Eamonn was surprised how nervous he himself felt by the time the transmission came, and during the show he found the team strangely aloof in their attitude towards him. However, he was pleased with his own performance, despite the fact that he failed to recognise the celebrity guest.

To his surprise, the other panellists, and the celebrity guest, seemed to disappear into thin air after the show. In England, he had become accustomed at the after-show party to mix with the participants. It made him feel good, however, to receive a number of invitations to guest again on the show.

It was an important show, as it received coast-to-coast transmission and Eamonn was often stopped subsequently by people who asked, 'Oh, you're the guy who was in *What's My Line?*' He liked America. Las Vegas left him breathless. Hollywood, with its glamour and big names, appealed to the showman in him and also for another reason. Secretly, he wanted to 'surprise' some of the legendary movie stars, such as John Wayne, Cary Grant, Bob Hope, Charlie Chaplin and Mae West for *This Is Your Life*. He proposed one day to persuade the BBC to give him his head.

Although it had thrilled him to broadcast big fights from America he still wasn't sure if it was the country for him. Soon he would have to think again. One day in New York, he lunched with the promoters of *What's My Line?*, Mark Goodson and Bill Todman and listened carefully as they offered him $250,000 to chair the show. It seemed too good to be true. They pointed out that it was possible for him to earn twice that amount in a single year if he took on an extra new show.

Compared with the kind of income he was earning at the BBC, he told himself that the money offered in America seemed like 'pure gold'. He had to admit it was very tempting.

As he would remark later, 'Five years of this kind of success and I could retire with Grainne to Florida and never work again.'

On his return to England, he pondered the offer. He discussed it with his friends. Leslie Jackson was one of the people in whom Eamonn liked to confide and on this occasion the producer encouraged him to consider the offer seriously. 'I told Eamonn it may never come his way again.' Presenting the show, Eamonn could commute between London and New York. The more he thought about it, the more tempting it became. But his mind was made up. As he said, 'I had gone to London intending to stay no longer than five years. When I reckoned the same thing might happen in New York I decided against it. It was tempting but only for a brief moment.'

At the time it seemed a poor excuse. He had, after all, made a tangible impression on the American promoters of *What's My Line?* and they had expressed confidence in him. Perhaps he was thinking of his age? At thirty-nine, Eamonn might have felt it was too late to be starting a fresh career in an unpredictable scene like America where fame could be more fleeting than in England, however attractive the financial rewards. By nature, he was cautious and he was inclined to count the risks involved in any such move, for he felt that if he accepted the offer he would have to move to America.

He saw no particular reason why he should take the risk. Now among the top television earners at the BBC, his business interests were beginning to boom in Ireland. The truth was he didn't need the money. That he wasn't prepared to take the gamble disappointed a few of his friends who believed he could have created a niche for himself in the States.

Eamonn wasn't a man to be influenced by friends in this way. Happiness meant being with Grainne in London, also not too far away from his relatives and friends in Ireland. He was happy, though, to accept periodic work in America.

12 *The Big Deal*

BRIAN TESLER POSSESSES the self-confidence and urbanity that can be counted among the hallmarks of the successful television executive. His shrewd professional judgment is another useful asset. He occupies a bright and spacious office on the thirteenth floor of the towering block that houses London Weekend Television, which is located within a stone's throw of Waterloo Station. Quietly spoken and alert, he prefers thin cigars to fat ones.

Tesler is in his fifties, lean and sallow-skinned, a man who clearly thrives on the television challenge, particularly in the creative sphere of new programming. He became a friend of Eamonn Andrews after they worked together in the mid-fifties on a number of *What's My Line?* programmes. As a young producer, he was impressed by Eamonn's professionalism as well as his infectious enthusiasm.

'I thought he was a nice guy with an attractive personality,' he says today. 'I know one can become terribly irritated with nice guys who bumble on screen, but a competent nice guy is an asset. Off-screen, I found Eamonn sincere and honest.'

Late in 1956 Tesler met Eamonn's agent Teddy Sommerfield. 'Do you want to leave the BBC?' the agent asked. 'I can get you more money in Independent Television.' Tesler explained that he was under contract and only worked with the BBC. 'Anyway, it looks very frightening out there,' he added, with a note of caution. However, when his contract expired, and he applied for an increase of £100 a year, he got a flat refusal.

His mind was made up. He approached Teddy Sommerfield and by January, 1957, he was on his way to join ABC
Television. He was so impressed by the increase in money
negotiated by Sommerfield that he decided to make him his
business manager. Sommerfield began to see more of Eamonn
Andrews socially.

Eamonn meanwhile was enjoying his work enormously at
the BBC, and he still found time to pop over to Dublin to
attend monthly meetings with his business partners. In
November of that year, 1960, he was named for the second
time television personality of the year in Britain. He was given
his award by the Guild of Television Producers. Earlier in the
year he had been awarded the Television Society's silver
medal for the most outstanding television personality. With
their marriage as secure as ever, he and Grainne now talked
about buying their own house and eventually counted
themselves fortunate to find the ideal one in Chiswick. It had
two storeys and was very quaint, ideally situated in its own
attractive grounds. It was secluded enough to meet Eamonn's
requirements for privacy. They decided to name their new
home Parknasilla, after the picturesque resort in Count Kerry
where they had honeymooned nearly ten years before.

Soon Eamonn and Grainne were inviting people around at
midday on Sundays for drinks. Leslie Jackson sometimes
wondered if Eamonn could truly relax in such company,
for most of the guests were television people and the conversation was often 'shop' talk. To Brian Tesler, these
lunchtime get-togethers were very enjoyable. As he liked to
recall, 'Eamonn chatted casually with everybody. We talked
gossipy things, interesting things. If you can show me a "pro"
who doesn't come up with things about the business when
relaxing, then you'll show me someone who isn't happy with
the business.'

However, he discovered another side to Eamonn. 'I think I
can say that he was a private man, and that is no exaggeration.
There was one little door that he kept locked for Grainne and

himself, and he kept the key.'

Since Parknasilla was a spacious house, it seemed strangely empty when Leslie Jackson occasionally went there to talk to Eamonn about *What's My Line?* and *This Is Your Life*. After their work they chatted for a while over drinks. It was on such occasions that the producer felt he got to know Eamonn more than most people.

'By now we had worked together for a long time,' he recalled. 'I knew that Eamonn missed children very much. It was obviously a void in his life. One evening he confided that they were thinking of adopting a child. I told him it was a marvellous idea. Since his own career was very busy I knew that he could probably manage without children, but I sensed that he was taking the step as much for Grainne's sake as his own. I could see they were very much in love.'

They were by now ten years married. 'Eamonn was pressing me to adopt,' remembered Grainne. 'He was very gentle. He knew that, even after I agreed, I could change my mind at any moment. I was frightened about the prospect of bringing home a baby to the house for the very first time. But I realised that Eamonn, as well as myself, would never feel a family without children. We had everything else.'

They had both wanted children. However, as the years wore on it became obvious that their chances of having the children they longed for were receding. 'It was nothing to do with my old TB illness,' Grainne said, 'though people seemed to assume this was the reason. I had the usual tests for infertility, and Eamonn had all the normal, humiliating tests too. There was no reason why we shouldn't have had children, but it didn't happen.'

Adoption was, they painfully discovered, a slow and rather elaborate process. It was three months before the papers were signed and they were able to take the baby girl back to Parknasilla. A special nursery was built upstairs. Eamonn and Grainne were both overjoyed with the new arrival. They decided to name the baby Emma Margaret Mary.

[110]

Being of an unselfish nature, Eamonn wanted to share his world with little Emma. 'When I saw her first, I felt she was enchanting,' he recalled. 'The whole thing was too exciting for words. It was new responsibility. A new world. A new awareness. A tremendous joy at being able to share our happiness with someone else. I knew that Grainne had been terrified about adopting a baby, but now she would say, "I needn't have been terrified at all, because the moment I saw her I knew I loved her. I knew I'd been looking just for her".'

Dinner party guests were amused when they saw the big man with the tiny baby in his arms. He laughed when someone called him 'Papa Andrews.' Instead of making stage costumes, as she had done before she married, Grainne now made clothes for Emma and some of them were admired by visitors to Parknasilla. Eamonn never liked to hear children being labelled 'kids' and he always referred to their baby as Emma or the baby. What pleased him most of all was that at last they were a family. Even now, he was already thinking of adopting another baby.

The adoption was one of the best kept show-business secrets of the year. Although friends in Ireland and England were aware of the adoption, nobody in Fleet Street seemed to have heard a whisper. Eventually, when the news leaked out, Eamonn said, 'My wife and I tried to keep the adoption secret. The baby has brought tremendous happiness to us both. We have had her with us now for three months. We took her to the Church of Our Lady of Grace in Chiswick last week to have her blessed.'

Eamonn stressed that the new baby had made Grainne exceedingly happy. 'She was seriously ill for two years and the doctors were doubtful if she would be able to have children. We have never given up hope entirely, but we decided to adopt. When we saw Emma we both fell for her. She's a beauty.'

Grainne soon found herself the focus of magazine and newspaper attention, but with her theatrical background she

[111]

took it all in her stride. Photographs of her and Emma showed her smiling and relaxed and she was amused to read, 'Friends say that Emma looks like Grainne as a child.'

Just at a time when Eamonn's married life had taken on a new dimension, his agent Teddy Sommerfield was showing concern about his career at the BBC. As he explained. 'We are not dissatisfied with the BBC but we have to look for really first-class programmes. We hope they will come from the BBC, but Eamonn has been with them a long time and must find new things. When it comes to ITV we are biased towards ABC, because we have the greatest admiration for its Programme Controller, Brian Tesler. I regard him as a most creative brain.'

As the newspapers speculated about his future, Eamonn decided to continue with the BBC. His new two-year contract was said to be worth £30,000 a year, giving him a total of £60,000 over the two years. It made him one of the highest paid artists under contract to the BBC. It was the first time that he had signed an exclusive contract, although he had always confined his appearances to BBC television. In the past he had merely undertaken to do so many programmes a year, which included *This Is Your Life*, *What's My Line?* and *Crackerjack*. He could always have appeared in Independent Television if he wished, although his many programmes for the BBC left him little time for other work.

Teddy Sommerfield hastened to emphasise that 'it was not the money that had made Eamonn Andrews decide to stay with the BBC, but the promise that he would be given the right programmes to do'.

Sommerfield had been concerned for some time that if and when the BBC decided to drop the *Line* and *Life* series they would have alternative programmes ready for Eamonn. It was now eight years since the Corporation had launched *This Is Your Life*. Producer Leslie Jackson felt that it had run its course. He asked to see Tom Sloan, Head of Light Entertainment.

'We've got to stop doing this programme at the end of the present series,' he said.

'Why?' asked Sloan.

'For we're now doing lives we'd never have touched. I know the show's in the top ratings, but some of the subjects are not good enough.'

'What are you suggesting we do?'

'I'm suggesting you drop it.'

Sloan looked surprised. After a short pause, he looked across at the producer. 'I do think it's better that we give it another year, Leslie. After that, we'll consider it.'

Leslie Jackson was disappointed. They were now doing the lives of pop stars who had been so widely publicised by the papers that they could hold little appeal for viewers. However, he was aware that *This Is Your Life* meant a great deal to Eamonn and for that reason alone he was determined to see the series through.

Eventually, when the BBC decided to drop *What's My Line?*, Eamonn and his agent, Teddy Sommerfield, were taken by surprise, although Sommerfield had always felt that with the death of Gilbert Harding the programme had lost its impact. However, the BBC's decision was a serious blow to Eamonn and he soon became restless. What also hurt was the BBC's cancellation of the series without consultation with him.

Inevitably, Brian Tesler heard about Eamonn's unrest. At this time he was worried about the poor ratings for their sports programme on Saturdays. 'We were being beaten hands down by the BBC and I was asked to come up with some new ideas. I went away and devised *World of Sport* and, at the same time, told myself that I needed a star front man to ensure its success. It would be a live show so it needed someone who could think on his feet, someone who'd sound knowledgeable and be knowledgeable. The programme would run throughout the afternoon.'

It took him less than ten seconds to think of the man he

wanted – Eamonn Andrews. He was experienced on sport and would be a popular choice. He decided to approach Eamonn's agent, Teddy Sommerfield. He agreed that he could talk to Eamonn. They both lived in Chiswick and one afternoon he put the proposition to him.

'Are you interested in taking over *World of Sport*?' he asked Eamonn. As always, Eamonn was cautious.

'I'll consider it. I like boxing. I like football but I don't know much about racing or rugby football.'

Tesler felt Eamonn was showing real interest.

'But I couldn't leave the BBC just for a sports programme,' Eamonn suddenly said. 'I'd have to have something else. I'd like to do a children's programme.'

'I can't give you a children's programme but I will make you available to the other networks.'

Donald Baverstock, the Assistant Controller of BBC Television, felt that *This Is Your Life* had by now lost a lot of its spontaneity and excitement. Even Eamonn, whom he admired as presenter, was in his view finding it hard to inject life into the programme. As he would say, 'There is a repetition about them I don't like. Nor are some of the subjects world beaters.'

It was no surprise when Baverstock made the decision to end the series after nine years. To Leslie Jackson, its producer since the outset, it was inevitable. Eamonn took the news badly. He was convinced that *This Is Your Life* had still plenty of zest in it and he regarded Baverstock's action as premature. His biggest worry now was whether the Corporation wanted him. When he met Baverstock shortly afterwards, he tackled him about new programmes. The BBC chief replied, 'We'll think of something for you.' The reply wasn't good enough for Eamonn. When he was assured he would get more money, he retorted, 'I've enough money; it's programmes I want.'

Brian Tesler meanwhile had been watching Eamonn's progress. He decided the time was opportune for him to make another approach. Some time previously he had been in

America and had enjoyed the Jack Paar Show. It was very popular, worked well, and as a chat show attracted some of the biggest show-business names in the States. There was, he knew, no equivalent in Britain and on his return to ABC Television made up his mind that Eamonn Andrews would be ideal as the presenter.

In addition, it would provide him with a new challenge. It would be live and transmitted as a late-night show. He called Teddy Sommerfield and explained the position. Was he prepared to negotiate on Eamonn's behalf? Sommerfield instantly agreed but insisted that any negotiations must be conducted in the strictest secrecy. Brian Tesler knew that his business manager had always had a nice sense of the dramatic and was fond of spy movies. 'Teddy would pass for a spy without any trouble.'

The rendezvous was to be 'a central square' in London. On the afternoon that Tesler arrived by taxi it was like a scene out of a Pinewood thriller. A black Mercedes was parked discreetly in a corner of the square and when he walked in its direction he saw it had tinted windows. On reaching it, the chauffeur got out of the front seat, opened the back door where Teddy Sommerfield was seated. Tesler's arrival was the cue for the chauffeur to take a walk until negotiations were completed.

After an hour, the deal was clinched and Eamonn was on his way to Independent Television. Tesler recalled, 'When I talked to Eamonn next day, he was both delighted and relieved that we had reached a decision. He saw the new programme as a challenge. It was never a question of money with him. Eamonn was always more interested in the nature of the programmes. The idea of fronting Britain's first chat show was enormously appealing to him.'

That January, 1964, the news made headlines in all the papers. Brian Tesler wasn't surprised. 'As far as ABC was concerned, we had achieved a major coup. Signing Eamonn Andrews was the equivalent of a football club signing the biggest star in the business.'

It was clear that Eamonn, at the age of forty-one, had made his biggest decision since joining the BBC in the early 1950s. His three year contract was reputed to be worth £40,000 a year, which made him the country's highest-paid TV commentator. It was again emphasised that he was changing channels because the BBC could not find him programmes suitable for his talents. He was quoted as saying, 'I was very happy with the BBC. I expect I shall be happier with ABC.'

What irked him was the paradoxical attitude of the BBC chiefs. As he would say, 'In the same breath that they killed off my programmes they offered me a huge amount of money to stay on. But they wouldn't say what programme they wanted me to do. I suspected they didn't know themselves. And that for me was very important. I must always know what vehicles I have.'

In Leslie Jackson's view, the BBC simply had nothing for Eamonn. 'He had reached a cross-roads in his career. He could be forgiven for feeling at a low ebb. In retrospect, I think he had made his contribution to the BBC. It was a very significant one and in the process he had become a household name. Offers were coming in for him from Independent Television and I don't believe he could have said no.'

In Brian Tesler's opinion, it was a question of Eamonn's unhappiness. 'Programmes meant everything to him. I could see how excited he was, for instance, when I tossed around new ideas for new programmes.'

Eamonn Andrews as the popular quiz-master in *What's My Line?*, one of his own favourite TV programmes.

Eamonn with *What's My Line?* participants Ernie Wise (left) and George Gale. The seated panellists are Jilly Cooper (left), Simon Williams and Barbara Kelly.

Group Captain Leonard Cheshire with his wife Sue Ryder and their daughter Gigi. They became friendly with Eamonn Andrews through *This Is Your Life*.

Spike Milligan first met Eamonn when they toured the Moss Empire circuit with Joe Loss and his band. Spike was later surprised by Eamonn on *This Is Your Life*.

The morning after boxing champion Henry Cooper was beaten by Cassius Clay. Cooper admired Eamonn's talent as a fight commentator.

Eamonn with Lord Louis Mountbatten and Commander Alfred Hughes, Mountbatten's first shipmate on HMS *New Zealand*, in a special edition of *This Is Your Life*.

Football star Danny Blanchflower walked off the *Life* show despite desperate pleas by Eamonn.

Eamonn popped into Broadcasting House to surprise Terry Wogan for *This Is Your Life*. Terry admitted he never suspected a thing.

Val Doonican admired the judicious way Eamonn Andrews managed his television career.

Despite his illness, Eamonn enjoyed a round of golf at Portmarnock with actor Patrick Mower.

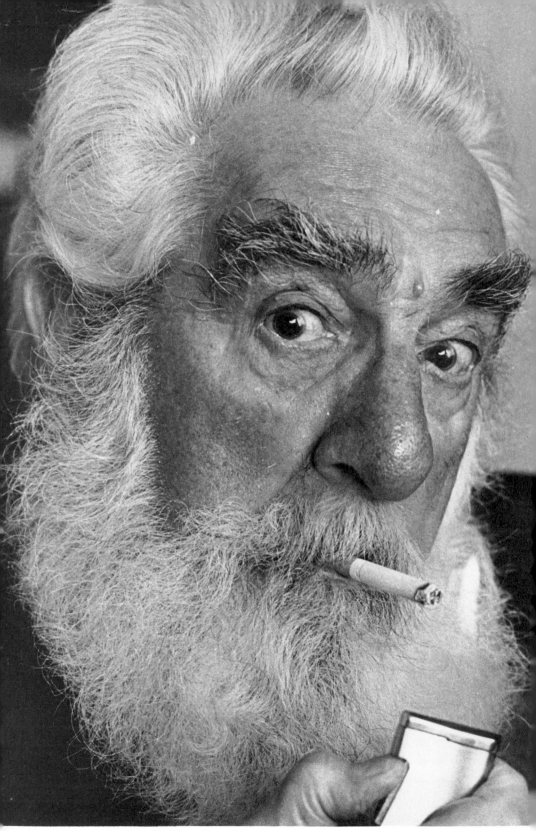

Film-goers came to admire Noel Purcell's magnificent beard, so did viewers of *This Is Your Life* when Eamonn Andrews handed his old friend the big red book.

PART THREE

Chat Show Host

We got nearly any guest we wanted for the show.

Eamonn Andrews

13 *In The Hot Seat*

THE CHAT SHOW has come to be reviled as disposable, even trivial. In modern television terms, chat is cheap – as little as £13,000 for 30 minutes compared with £150,000 for half an hour of drama. Although it has been labelled complacent – 'creating a chummy conspiracy between host, guest and studio audience which helps disguise the emptiness of the programme's contents', there is no doubt that it enjoys huge popularity among viewers, as shown by the ratings of the Terry Wogan show.

In 1964, the chat show was virtually unknown, which made the task facing Eamonn Andrews all the harder. As its first host he would be bringing to the screen on Sunday nights the famous, the funny, the frank, the frivolous and those known as the 'fab' people – all off their guard. The man chosen to produce the show, which was scheduled to start at 11 o'clock, was Eamonn's friend, Malcolm Morris. They had first met in the fifties when Morris, a young photographer, took pictures of celebrities in *What's My Line?* and *This Is Your Life*; he was by now a talented producer.

To Morris, Eamonn was an obvious choice to host *The Eamonn Andrews Show*. He was unflappable and an experienced interviewer – and he liked people. Immediately he sensed that Eamonn was enthusiastic. 'He saw the show as an exciting new challenge, and like everything else he approached he was painstaking,' he recalls. 'I suppose both of us were nervous as we were exploring completely new territory.'

[119]

Eamonn had decided not to meet the guests before the show; instead, he would stay in his dressing-room. Even then, it did not appear a wise decision. Guests could hardly be expected to know how outspoken they could be. As a voice announced, 'Live from London ... The Eamonn Andrews Show', Eamonn was a bundle of nerves.

Although the studio audience, which earlier had had a warm-up, were eager to join in the fun, Eamonn looked taut and nervous, as though over-eager to get the show off to a successful start. At times, he was so wary of letting the show get out of hand that he kept too tight a rein on it. It seemed a mistake also to have all the guests from show-business.

Later, the show received mixed reaction. Observed one critic: 'Eamonn says himself that nobody has ever been given more freedom than he has, with this new show, and obviously no expense was spared with the trimmings, or the guest list. The trouble was that nobody except perhaps the singers seemed to know what to do or even what to talk about. It seems Eamonn must now decide whether to project himself as a personality in his new show or whether to use his talents to project his guests.'

Maurice Wiggin, the experienced critic of the *Sunday Times* thought that the first show would have encouraged few to wait avidly for 11.05 p.m. on Sunday nights, and he added: 'It was a throw back to the emptiest sort of jolly-jolly pre-Coronation TV – when it was believed to be enough just to have people appear. Mr Andrews trying desperately to get a topic going – "Does the studio audience like men with moustaches?" – that was a sad sight. The paid guests kept giggling loyally, but at what, I never discovered. In sum, we learned that Terry-Thomas owns several waistcoats, Honor Blackman is afraid of spiders, William Rushton can imitate a squeaking door. There was a teenage beat group and a teenage pop singer who all made very unpleasant noises, which everyone present, being either with-it or scared of not being with-it, politely applauded. I've been at livelier wakes.'

Some other English and Irish critics were less caustic. Their verdicts ranged from 'a lively show' to 'very entertaining' and 'Eamonn Andrews at his best'. The majority were prepared to give Eamonn and the show 'time to find their feet'. Eamonn knew that it would be some weeks, if not months, before he mastered the subtle chat show technique, but at the same time he was determined to be himself – imperturbable, polite and reasonable.

Soon all three virtues – if you like to call them such in the unpredictable chat show world – would be put to the severest test. Some guests began to play up and be down-right rude; a few indulged in bawdy stories. When complaints continued to be received by ABC about the show the Independent Television Authority ordered guests who appeared in the show not to be too outspoken in future. The order arose from complaints from viewers after the previous Sunday's show.

Jimmy Edwards, Diana Dors and Freddie Trueman had taken part in the programme. At one stage Jimmy Edwards jokingly referred to his moustache as a kind of sex indicator. Some viewers felt that the remark went too far, even though it was made in a late-night show. The ITA called for a special showing of the programme and afterwards condemned the conversation as too outspoken.

The ITA was emphatic: 'We and the Company both feel that last Sunday's conversation in the programme, even though transmitted very late and of course *live* was more outspoken than we would have wished. We have consulted ABC, the company which produced the show, with a view to avoiding such conversational excesses in future programmes. Before future programmes guests will be asked not to go too far. The producer will not ban any subjects but will advise guests not to let the conversation get out of hand.'

'It is a programme which is feeling its way,' a spokesman for ABC pointed out. 'We share ITA's view that perhaps things went a little too far on Sunday. The broadcast is live. It is unscripted and unrehearsed.'

[121]

In the previous week's programme there had also been complaints from viewers after some remarks made by the Earl of Arran. One of the guests, Laurence Harvey, was heard to comment that he did not know that British television was so broadminded.

Diana Dors considered that certain people were taking too prudish a view of *The Eamonn Andrews Show*. 'I was not offended by Jimmy Edwards' moustache joke,' she said. 'I thought it amusing. Nobody is asking anybody to look at the show. If it offends certain people the answer is to switch off. To succeed, a show like this which is based on conversation must create all kinds of excitement. I think ITA's decision is a shame.'

Brian Tesler thought that Eamonn, from time to time, was genuinely embarrassed by some of his guests. 'It was a question of some people showing off. Since Eamonn was an inherently decent chap, he would not say to them, "Shut Up! You're a bore. You're misbehaving." If he had been that sort of person the show wouldn't have been the success it was, nor would we have been able to engage suitable guest celebrities. Just because a few people took advantage of Eamonn's niceness didn't mean that he failed as host of the show. On the contrary, he put his own unique stamp on the show.'

Producer Malcolm Morris argued that Eamonn's forte was the way he pretended to be hurt by what some outrageous guests said, when in reality he was acting the straight man. 'I think that viewers didn't always understand his approach. It worked very well when Woody Allen or Dick Gregory told funny, though somewhat risqué, stories with a New York setting.'

'Eamonn enjoyed hosting the show enormously,' recalls Morris. 'He absolutely loved it. Only a few guests were offensive or tried to send him up. Eamonn also admitted that failing to meet the guests before the show had been a mistake, so he began to talk to them before 11 o'clock.'

Although he was supplied with ample background material

[122]

on his guests, and a number of key questions, it couldn't in reality be a scripted show. Sometimes he had to ad lib for all he was worth. Malcolm Morris felt that Eamonn was an extremely fast thinking ad libber and was at his best when confronted by ad lib situations. Later Eamonn would say, 'I was over-produced at the time and given the wrong kind of research but I was worried about using all the research I got. Now I know that you don't use it all. You just have it or you don't have a question line in your head before you sit down. It's too rigid. I know my work suffered from that, but we got nearly anyone we wanted for the show.'

He always had a hand in the selection of the guests and showed a particular interest in those from America. Some tended to be less inhibited than their British counterparts. As the show continued to cause controversy, Howard Thomas, ABC Managing Director decided to take action to preserve the programme's good features and to safeguard as far as possible against a lapse in taste. Eamonn was asked to exert stricter control over his guests and to 'come down hard on any attempt to introduce comment which would be offensive.'

Thomas acted after 'incidents' in a programme involving Jimmy Edwards and Kenneth More, although no complaints had come from viewers. ITA called for a transcript and a private screening of the film. Lord Hill, chairman of ITA, and Sir Robert Fraser, Director General both expressed disapproval of certain remarks introduced during the programme.

Were some viewers too sensitive in regard to the show? The question hadn't worried Maurice Wiggin when he wrote in the *Sunday Times*: 'Instead of fussing and clucking like an old hen about a few regrettable and rather juvenile bawdy quips in *The Eamonn Andrews Show,* or non-show, the ITA ought to be concerned with all the other things that are wrong with it. Not for the first time, all the uproar and furore divert attention from more important matters. The publicity chaps promised that Mr Andrews would be meeting fabulously interesting people with interesting things to say. What we actually get is a procession of very well-known show-business people who accept the publicity and pay for it with a little desultory chit-chat, hardly worth staying up for, even when Laurence Harvey sends the whole thing roof-high.'

Wiggin, who was tending to ignore the light entertainment value of such a show, warned his readers that since the censors were at work those who intended staying up for something spicy would be disappointed. 'The whips are out and without its fortuitous touches of titillation the show is desperately dull. I wonder what Mr Andrews, pre-eminently the family favourite in his BBC days, really thinks of his new show's notoriety? It's like seeing Barbirolli compèring *Top of the Pops*.'

Curiously, Eamonn refused to be drawn on the 'notorious' aspects of the show. He preferred to dwell on the entertainment value and the ratings, yet he admitted he was aware of the risk factor: that certain celebrities could not easily be controlled. He must have thought now that dealing with his old adversary Gilbert Harding was kindergarten stuff compared with Laurence Harvey & Co. The main trouble of course arose because Eamonn was by now regarded as among the 'nice guys' of television and for him to accept smut and crudities with a smile was at variance with the viewers' image of their popular host.

But the fun continued, despite Eamonn's tight holding of the rein. For instance, a furious row broke out between Zsa Zsa Gabor and satirist Peter Cook – a few hours before the actress was scheduled to leave England. Eamonn unwittingly fuelled the fire when he invited Cook, a regular guest on the show, to give his opinion of the forty-five-year-old Hungarian-American actress. The languid Cook puffed on his cigarette and said crisply that she was vain, had no talent, and altogether 'a non-event'.

Eamonn looked embarrassed as Zsa Zsa retorted, 'Why do

you say these things? You are the rudest young man I have met for many years.'

Cook: 'I was asked to speak the truth.'

Zsa Zsa: 'How dare you say I have no talent? I get 150,000 dollars a picture.'

Cook: (to a loud round of studio applause) 'That is not necessarily talent.'

At this point a perplexed Zsa Zsa Gabor appealed to Eamonn: 'I don't even know what he does. I don't know his name, and I don't want to know his name.'

She patted her fluffy white cat which she balanced on her lap and affectionately called Madame Pompadour. 'I want to let this man know that I'm very fond of animals,' she said, looking directly across at Peter Cook.

Cook: 'If you really cared about animals you would not bring that cat under these hot television lights.'

Eamonn grinned and seemed relieved that time was up. Later, at the after-show party at the Royal Lancaster Hotel, Bayswater, the controversy continued between Cook and the actress. Said Cook: 'I hope you are not going to throw your cat at me, Zsa Zsa.'

It was plain by now that viewers could not remain indifferent to the show; they either loved it or hated it. Frivolity was the keynote. It was fun without profundity. Its daring and irreverence suited the Swinging Sixties. If, in the previous year *That Was The Week That Was* had been a television landmark, then *The Eamonn Andrews Show*, with its occasional sprinkling of four-letter words, was preparing the way for the more liberal seventies and eighties. Eamonn could be forgiven for thinking he had been unfairly given the role of catalyst.

Occasionally the show sparkled, depending on the merit of the guests. At other times it was consistently dull, leaving Eamonn with the hard task of keeping the fun alive. He looked embarrassed when fashion photographer David Bailey acted up. The sound technicians were not quick enough to cut out one four-letter word from the tele-recording. And Bailey's remarks were heard in full half an hour earlier by ITV viewers in East Anglia, South Wales and North Scotland, where the show went out live. When the recording of the ABC programme was put on by Associated Television in London, Bailey – the man who discovered Jean Shrimpton – was twice seen mouthing words on a silent screen within minutes of joining Eamonn on stage.

Eamonn looked uneasy and his face reddened. The first three-second cut came after he referred to Bailey's leggy pictures of Miss Shrimpton, and the photographer replied, 'I just like girls with lots of legs.' Eamonn said he had only ever seen girls with two legs, and Bailey countered, 'Haven't you ever been to...'.

The rest was cut. Eamonn looked flustered as he said, 'That's a good question. I am afraid I haven't got a good answer.'

A few seconds later Bailey again appeared to be miming as engineers made an even longer cut in something he was saying – but not before viewers heard him explain, 'That's a lot of–'.

Eamonn commented, 'That was a good old English phrase.'

The photographer, dressed casually in sweater, jeans and suede jacket, three times referred to sex maniacs. Once, talking about his girl pictures, he remarked 'I'm a sexual maniac.'

Eamonn looked unhappy, as though not knowing where next to steer the conversation. Viewers who had come to admire him in *What's My Line?* and *This Is Your Life* must have asked themselves how he ever got himself involved in such trivia. Where was the spontaneous and effortless wit? What viewers were seeing was not even satirical nonsense but rather tiring superficiality.

While some of the critics continued to snipe at Eamonn – and the show – a number of guests talked afterwards of the success of its host. Val Doonican found it enjoyable and made no secret of the fact that he stayed up to watch the show. Eamonn was, in his view, 'a polished and likeable host who handled his guests with skill.'

'Eamonn invited me on the show after my big success at the London Palladium,' he recalls. 'He said to me, "It has taken you a long time to crack the show-business scene, Val, but you did it in style." I told him that I had been trying for seventeen years to make it and then it happened overnight with my appearance at the Palladium. I could see he was a star. I was remembering the days when I first got to know him at the Theatre Royal in Dublin. Although he was a raw entertainer, I had predicted he would scale the ladder. Now, he was a big, smooth star who didn't panic easily; he was confident and had learned how to cope with situations. He was himself and that, of course, was the secret of his success. Only a few of his guests on the show were ever rude to Eamonn; most of the times the late night show was entertaining.'

Brian Tesler thought that after a few weeks Eamonn had come to terms with the chat show technique; his timing had improved and he was more at home with guests. Some of his American guests were more outspoken than their British counterparts, but Eamonn was not upset by them.

Perceptive commentators had no doubt that his politeness and charm were sometimes liabilities in his role as chat show host. They argued that more aggression was needed to cope with some ego-tripping guests, or guests who regarded vulgarity as an easy way to win laughs. As one commentator put it, 'Some of Eamonn's guests have no outstanding ability in the field of entertainment. They do a disservice to Eamonn.'

The private Eamonn Andrews looked to his home in Chiswick for the peace and quiet he sought away from the turmoil of the television studio. He found time to watch Emma grow, smile, cry. Friends from Ireland who called at the house were surprised to find how adaptable Eamonn had become in his new role as father. 'I think he revelled in it,' recalls Leslie Jackson. 'Both he and Grainne were intensely happy to have Emma.' But their Sunday pattern had not changed. People like Brian Tesler and Malcolm Morris joined Eamonn's friends for drinks at midday and had fun talking 'shop'.

Autumn had come to Parknasilla and this was reflected in the garden and lawn, which still managed to look attractive. Occasionally newspaper and magazine people came to Chiswick to talk to either Eamonn or Grainne, especially now that Emma was in their lives. The visit by the writer Ursula Bloom was treated as rather special and Eamonn took a little time off to show her around.

Miss Bloom concluded: 'Eamonn Andrews lives in one of the loveliest houses in Chiswick. There's a high wall round the house – and it's almost as if that wall shut in the personality of the man. Open a yellow door and you enter a garden of vivid flowers (his wife Grainne paints flowers) and meticulous paving. The facade of the house has yellow shutters buttoned back against white walls. Fragile curtaining. The wrought-iron front door has glass behind it and shows a wide hall. You enter the double sitting-room on the right. Here is a wonderful backcloth for the man himself. Grainne planned it; she chose the white walls that are only lightly patterned, the soft blue carpet everywhere, and rosy red armchairs. The vista of the dining-room is in the same colouring.'

Together she and Eamonn strolled in the garden. It was spacious but not vast. The lawn was well manicured. Half across it swept the lowest limb of a tree some 300 years old. Eamonn said it was a Cedar of Lebanon. 'A fantastic piece of engineering,' he mused. 'This tree limb which does nothing save to be there, is in my view breathtaking.' Beyond the lawn and shrubs, beyond the fruit trees and behind the wall, ran the Thames. To Ursula Bloom, on this October day, it was tranquil, its mood matching the setting of the house, and also the feeling you got of the occupants.

As they talked, she deduced that Eamonn had been frustrated in his earlier attempts to get into Fleet Street. He had found it almost a locked door. She observed: 'This was his testing hour. He had the courage to force a foothold on his disappointment. He went on. The scars of time are still in his heart. You cannot erase them. But they teach. He knows that now.'

To Miss Bloom, determination and inspiration were the two keen friends who set Eamonn on the road to fame. 'He has the shrewd outlook. He has raw, cold commonsense. He loves people. I think, if you are interested in a person, a person is interested in what you're asking him. He saw television ahead of him as the career with great chances.'

As they sat in the sitting-room she decided that his warm personality was the heritage of the shamrock. 'Most sympathetic, he is always understanding. Yet able to draw a curtain over his real self. As he chats, you see him as a man veiled. It is difficult to know the real Eamonn Andrews. The owner of the lovely home, the devoted husband of Grainne, and the adoring father of Emma.'

In May, 1966, there was some surprise caused in Ireland with the unexpected resignation of Eamonn as Chairman of the Radio Telefis Eireann Authority. He made it clear that he thought the service was on its feet and it was not a case of opting out at the half-way stage. As he stated: 'After less than four and a half years on the air, it has brought television within range of over ninety-five per cent of the population, is staffed by competent and imaginative people, is a profitable concern, and is technically well equipped.'

He warned that it could not continue like this unless it maintained communication with and enjoyed the confidence of the majority of its viewers. His main bone of contention was that in the projection of the Irish language programming they were in danger of moving too far ahead of their audience's capacity to maintain communication with them.

'As the people of Ireland themselves implement revival of the language, so too do I believe the service should keep pace and even be slightly ahead – but only slightly.'

He expressed a second fear that they might have been going

too far too fast in seeking self-sufficiency. As he stressed, 'I felt that we in the television service would have less danger of slowing down our development if we continued for some time in the future to be courageous in finding skilled people to help us from other countries.'

There was some criticism of the course he had taken, but generally it was accepted that with the great pressure on his time his resignation was inevitable. Later, Eamonn reiterated that he had real fears about the future of the new Irish television service, in particular because of the 'narrow-minded' attitudes of some of his colleagues on the Authority. 'I found,' he said, 'I held different views on important questions of communications and expertise. I felt in conscience I could no longer lend myself to policies with which I could not agree and which I believed to be a danger to the service.'

In Ireland, it was felt he had made a valuable contribution towards the development of the new television service. He probably felt it was time to leave it to others.

14   *A Colourful 'Life'*

FOR EAMONN, THE year 1969 promised to be crucial. The changing of his late-night chat show from Sunday to Monday night wasn't a success. It was apparent that the glitter had faded. When it was later switched to Thursday night the result was unfortunately the same – a marked drop in the ratings. 'We both agreed it wasn't working,' recalls Brian Tesler, who was by now Head of Light Entertainment at Thames. 'Viewers had become accustomed to chat on Sunday and wouldn't accept it on other nights.'

Eamonn took the dropping of the show philosophically. 'I saw it coming,' he said later. 'Anyway, I did get five good years out of the show and learned a thing or two about chat show techniques.' However, he did not disguise the fact that he was hurt on occasions by the excesses in the newspaper criticism. 'I think they overplayed it a little. They decided I was a shockable person, which I'm not really. The guests probably thought that if they could shock me they might make the headlines next morning. And I suppose some people used to watch the show to be shocked. My only concern was to send the viewers to bed happy. I agree that early on it was nerve-racking, but the more experienced I became the better I was able to handle the guests. Some savage things were written about me; that's one of the sad things about this kind of journalism: they decide on your image and then go on repeating themselves.'

But Eamonn was resilient. Ideas for possible new

programmes were jotted down religiously in a notebook. Occasionally he discussed them with Brian Tesler. Programmes meant everything to him. Money by now wasn't his prime concern. Although he had been identified with *This Is Your Life* for nearly a decade, the programme was long forgotten in television circles. However, Eamonn had other ideas. He had never lost faith in *Life*, even if everybody else regarded it as old hat.

One afternoon Brian Tesler was at his desk when Eamonn came into the office holding in his hand a piece of paper. Before he could utter a word, Eamonn said, 'I think this is what we should do, Brian.'

Puzzled, Tesler took the piece of paper and began to read. The note simply said, 'This Is Your Colourful Life'.

'You don't mean we should call it *that*?' remarked Tesler.

Eamonn said, 'No, no, no. I mean that the programme for the first time will be screened in colour, I think this could be an added attraction for viewers.'

After a slight pause, Tesler shook his head as he reflected, 'Don't you remember that the BBC dropped it and then tried it with Cliff Michelmore? I'm sorry, but I honestly don't think we should revive it. I feel the critics will murder it, and can you really see audiences liking it?'

Eamonn was by no means put off. He continued enthusiastically, 'I think it will work. I believe the BBC killed it off too soon. In my view it had years of life left in it. Didn't it have always high ratings?'

To Brian Tesler, the more he listened the more he was inclined to agree that Eamonn sounded very convincing. As he would say later, 'I had a healthy respect for Eamonn's judgment. True, it wasn't always functioning a hundred per cent, but it wasn't too often wrong. I took into account that there was a new generation of viewers who might find it exciting television. Before he left the room I told him I'd probably try it.'

Malcolm Morris, who was named producer of the new

series, expressed the view that he was amazed in the first place that the BBC dropped *This Is Your Life* in the sixties.

'I think they thought the programme was played out and decided rather hastily to end it. They would admit later their decision was a big mistake. There were plenty of potential *Life* subjects around and it was up to Thames to inject new life into the programme. I had great faith in Eamonn; he had matured greatly from the early days of *Life* in the fifties.'

To Morris, who remained a close friend of Eamonn's, the programme was based on a simple idea and the simplest ideas in his experience were the most effective and tended to last the longest. He saw *Life* as a party in which the subject and the guests enjoyed themselves.

When Leslie Jackson heard the news that Thames intended reviving *Life*, he could scarcely believe it. Yet, because he knew of Eamonn's obsessional interest in the programme, he reckoned it could be a success, provided Malcolm Morris and his team could get the right guests. 'By now it was agreed that war heroes were thin on the ground,' he recalls, 'and that a new *Life* programme would have to search around for other exciting subjects.'

The first programme in the new *Life* series was screened on the evening of 19 November, 1969. The subject was to be the popular comedian Des O'Connor, who was surprised by Eamonn on the stage of the London Palladium. The show was not due to start until eight o'clock, but the audience and the cameras were in by seven, apparently under the pretense that tests were being made for the new colour outside broadcast units.

Des O'Connor was so utterly staggered by Eamonn's interruption to his 'act' that he seemed, as one critic would say later, able only to speak in capital letters: 'I AM JUST SPEECHLESS AT ALL THIS'. As the ghosts of his past sauntered on stage, the comedian was heard to exclaim, 'Are there really enough of them to make a programme?'

[133]

Next morning, the Fleet Street critics gave a mixed reception to the programme. Although most of them paid tribute to Eamonn's 'infectious enthusiasm' as presenter, the experienced critic, James Thomas summed up: 'Back to TV comes the old hoary epic, full of emotions which sometimes smack of the phoney, still a mine of manufactured enthusiasm as the people turn up from the past – *This Is Your Life*. And back comes Eamonn Andrews, his sweat now glistening in colour, transferring the BBC's success to the commercial channel. Is it really so good that they could not think of something else? But I could not help wondering just how surprised was Mr O'Connor when Mr Andrews burst in upon him at the Palladium.'

Brian Tesler was relieved: 'The critics didn't actually savage us. The audience loved the show and from day one I had no misgivings about the programme once it got on the air. Eamonn's judgment had been absolutely right. As the series climbed the ratings I could see he was getting better every week. He was a success as presenter because he was passionately interested in people and here was an opportunity every week for him to get into his subject. He was getting an enormous kick out of the programme and his enthusiasm was communicated to his audience.'

Tesler found that Eamonn could on occasions be self-critical about his own performance. 'When he came into my office I might remark, "Well done last night". But he would shrug and say, "It wasn't so hot. I didn't get that point across well."' To Malcolm Morris, the programme was turning into a celebration. 'Eamonn stayed a little in the background and let the guests join in the fun. It was a very personal moment in their lives.'

Eamonn continued to have an important say in the selection of the subjects. There were a number of potential subjects he vetoed because he disliked them as people. Names he noted for future programmes included Joe Loss, Ronnie Corbett, Spike Milligan, Dudley Moore and Rolf Harris. As time passed

[134]

there were some subjects who were checked out and research work begun on their backgrounds, but who for reasons only known to the team never came to the screen. Usually, though, the reason was that a wife or relative advised against the programme.

Since his *Life* had already been screened in America, Frankie Vaughan felt that he was secure in England and that Eamonn would not consider him as a subject. He was wrong. It was Eamonn's own idea to surprise him, and when he did so in London's Caesar's Palace night spot, Frankie's astonished response was: 'Nonsense! My *Life* has already been done, Eamonn.'

Frankie had been in the recording studios for most of the day and when he went home for a short break he was surprised to find the children back from school. When he enquired, his wife Stella told him that they were going to a party. After that, he didn't take any more notice. In the afternoon he returned to the studios to complete the album. That evening when he arrived at Caesar's Palace for his cabaret show, he saw television cameras around the place. 'I was told they were doing a promotion for the night club,' he recalls. 'I knew that Eamonn Andrews had some connection with the club and was expected to pop in for a while to ensure that everything went right.'

That night, when he was on stage with his band, the V-Men, and was finishing his big number, *Give Me The Moonlight*, Eamonn jumped onto the stage. Frankie was amazed. He snapped, 'Cut it out, Eamonn, I'm not finished yet.'

Eamonn interjected, 'Can I just stop you here, Frankie?'

'No, you can't, I'm not finished yet.'

Frankie was still arguing with him when Eamonn suddenly said, 'This Is Your Life, Frankie Vaughan!'

A look of disbelief swept over the singer's face. At that moment, Eamonn whispered to him, 'Don't worry, Frankie, it's going to be a happy affair.' Now, as Stella held her husband's hand, he felt it was a very happy event. Paraded

[135]

before him were his sisters, his children, show-business friends, including his close friend, Jimmy Tarbuck. Frankie would say later, 'This programme was a much happier one for me than my American *Life*, because Eamonn was my friend.'

Eamonn still found the pick-up moment nerve-racking. He never knew when a potential subject would say no and walk away. The Danny Blanchflower affair was still fresh in his memory. Yet, subsequently, when Richard Gordon, best-selling creator of the famous 'Doctor' books and television series, refused to appear on *This Is Your Life*, Eamonn admitted that he experienced the same kind of agony as when Danny Blanchflower walked off. 'I really don't know why he refused. Perhaps he just didn't want to face the cameras.'

More than twenty million saw the author walk off the set at Thames Television, with Eamonn following him close behind in a desperate bid to persuade him to stay. After a few moments' confusion, the screen went blank. Then a recorded version of a standby programme, featuring the actor Sam Kydd, was shown.

Richard Gordon had been brought on as a mock 'Doctor' sketch was being played by members of the *Doctor In The House* cast from London Weekend Television. Eamonn held up the large *Life* book and told him, 'You won't need a script tonight because, Richard Gordon Ostlere this is your life!' It was at that moment that he decided to snub Eamonn. He later returned to the studio however and explained to the audience of 200 that he was 'pathologically shy'. He then went ahead with a recording of the programme.

After the incident Thames Television was inundated with telephone calls from viewers wanting to know what had happened. A spokesman for Thames explained that sometimes the show was recorded and sometimes put on live. 'As luck would have it tonight's show was live. But live or recorded, it is always a surprise to the subject. Tonight was a surprise to us. We hope to show the Richard Gordon *Life* at a future date.'

At the point of the author's refusal to cooperate, Eamonn

[136]

had looked shaken and pale. It was obvious that some programmes were proving more nerve-racking than even he cared to admit. But he was prepared to endure the pain for the sake, as he would say, of the thrill of a live programme.

If 1969 had proved another milestone in Eamonn's remarkably successful career, 1970 opened as though it held out for him even greater promise. He was listed in the New Year's Honours List and named OBE, but because of his Irish citizenship it was considered only an honorary award and would be conferred on him by Foreign Secretary, Michael Stewart, and not at Buckingham Palace by Queen Elizabeth.

Eamonn was intensely proud of the award, despite some snide suggestions in Ireland that he should refuse to accept it. He saw it as a glowing recognition of his television achievements during his twenty years in Britain; a kind of royal accolade. The Irish government made no official objection to his accepting the award.

By now he was at the peak of his career. Driving his Mercedes coupé to work, he smoked cigars and made no secret of the fact that he was pleased with the way his career was shaping. He was reckoned to be earning more than £50,000 a year from television alone. Just as important to him was that his marriage was as secure as ever. A journalist visiting Parknasilla described how she found 'a home full of happiness'.

The Andrews now had three adopted children, Emma, who was eight, Fergal, five, and a little girl they called Niamh. On the street in Chiswick where they lived, Eamonn was like any other father. He did his stint of ferrying his and the other local children to school, and carted them off to films once in a while. He also cooked dinner occasionally and, as Grainne remarked, he even baked bread.

It was a busy time for her. She made most of her own clothes and all the children's. When she was asked what she thought about the man she had lived with for eighteen years, she said with a wry smile, 'Talking about our private life is like going to confession, only worse, because you know everybody's going to read about it. If you really want the truth, he's the nicest person I ever met in my life. I find him very hard to live up to. But he can be a bit maddening on occasions like all men. He doesn't see all the things that go on around him. I think he's an escapist.'

In the quiet of Parknasilla Eamonn and Grainne began to discuss seriously the future of their children and where they wanted them educated. Grainne was in favour of an Irish education and felt that it was time perhaps they moved back to Ireland. If that was what his wife wanted, Eamonn was prepared to go along with the arrangement. It was a vital decision, he knew, to distance himself from his work, and he hoped it worked out. It meant that in future he would have to commute regularly between Dublin and London. He decided to invest in a flat in Chiswick which he would also use as an office. When Parknasilla was sold it made a considerable profit.

The Andrews' decision to sell their home came as a real surprise to their friends. It would mean the end of the little Sunday drinks ritual, that convivial get-together which delighted Eamonn. His colleagues were also surprised that he had decided to distance himself from his television commitments, thus putting an extra burden on himself. A few of them at Thames wondered if, after all, it was a logical or even wise decision. Knowing how terribly hard he worked, they feared that in time the extra burden might tell on his health.

Everyone agreed, though, that the Andrews had made the 'painful decision' solely for the sake of the children's education, otherwise they would not have considered uprooting themselves from their idyllic home in Chiswick. In another sense their decision to move made sense. Grainne had many relatives and friends in Dublin, while Eamonn's Irish business interests were becoming increasingly profitable. He was particularly proud that his company had made a success of running Dublin's Gaiety Theatre. It was a beautiful theatre, he said, and very important to the life of the city.

They proposed to move back to a bungalow near the sea at Portmarnock. Eamonn had asked his friend, architect Sam Stephenson, to design an extension to make it as roomy as their house in Chiswick. Meanwhile he had joined the board of Butlin's Holiday Camp empire and in future would take charge of all entertainments throughout the organisation.

Eamonn went to great pains to point out that there was no question of his quitting television. Talking about his new job, he said, 'Tastes in entertainment are constantly changing and these very real changes in requirements open new fields. I think there may be a new demand for more intimate forms of entertainment, such as late-night cabaret, and so on.' When questioned about his earnings from this latest source, he said he would receive a share of the directors' emolument.

Eamonn's colleagues at Thames wondered how he would find the time for his new business commitments. In Ireland, he was by now regarded more as business tycoon than showman, which was rather confusing. While the English tended to envy him his business flair, they preferred nonetheless to see him solely as a star television presenter. Everyone agreed that he had never lost sight of himself.

Eamonn was showing his undoubted versatility in another sphere. He was link-man in the new Thames magazine programme, *Today*. Designed to be at once topical and informative, it was screened five nights a week. At six o'clock each evening without a hint of panic, he coped expertly with the stories of the day and some of the personalities behind them. Brian Tesler thought that the programme showed another side of Eamonn – his flair for assimilating news. He revelled in bringing topical events to the screen and his enthusiasm never once waned. As he would say, 'TV is vital to me now. I like going in and being involved. I feel I'm seeing life and taking part in it. At the end of the week I've been in touch with every major story that's been written. I could never sit on the sidelines now.'

He admitted that to stay in the centre was a grind physically and mentally. To keep himself in shape, he went to a gymnasium two mornings a week. 'With five shows a week I didn't think I'd last the season. You've got to be fit to do a job like mine.'

Controversy was sometimes unavoidable. When Richard Harris arrived in London from New York with his new book of poetry, he was invited on *Today*. 'My book was a bestseller in America,' he recalls, 'and I wanted to talk seriously about it on the programme. But I got the impression that Eamonn Andrews was trying to ridicule the book. I love confrontation and welcomed the opportunity to meet him head on. I don't think Eamonn had ever a particular regard for me, but I hadn't a particular regard for him, either. I thought my poetry was worth considering in a serious vein. Americans had treated it as such.'

Later, Eamonn had a run-in with disc jockey Jimmy Savile also, on *Today*. Jimmy had made a bet that Eamonn would not dare call him a bastard on the air. On the programme he was in a typical wise-cracking mood as he tried to talk about his new book, *As It Happens*. Finally Eamonn looked his 'tormentor' in the eye and said with a grin, 'You bastard'.

The interview had been pre-recorded. Executive producer Andy Allan said, 'From all our audience in the South-East there were only two complaints. And these were just a couple of people puzzled over why Eamonn should cast doubts on Jimmy's parentage. 'Jimmy didn't mind paying up – for the money went to one of the disc jockey's favourite charities.'

People around his sometimes found it difficult to get to know the real Eamonn Andrews. A programme associate at Thames commented, 'I've been working with him for six months and I barely know him.' Another colleague described him as 'a cool, shrewd guy'. Liz Cowley, who produced the *Today* show, felt that Eamonn kept away from the females as much as possible. 'I don't know him off-screen at all. Apart from the odd joke I don't think we've had one personal conversation. He is old-fashioned about women. He liked them to be glamorous and feminine, not strike leaders or political pundits. He found it very hard to come to terms with a woman producer. We've got used to each other because I think he has forgotten I'm a woman. If I were to squirt perfume at him he'd be embarrassed. Let's say for Eamonn I'd wear deodorant not perfume.'

Amazingly, he found time occasionally to present a private showing of *This Is Your Life*. The first took place in a London hotel where the 'subject' was Stephen J. Conway, retiring chairman of the National Cash Register Company. It proved a moving experience for Mr Conway and, for his trouble, Eamonn collected a fee of £1,500.

Later on Eamonn would figure in another private *Life*, when newspaper proprietor Sir Max Aitken planned a celebration for the seventy-eighth birthday of Lord Thomson at the Dorchester Hotel with hundreds of guests. Sir Max had the idea of putting on a film called *Lord Thomson – This Is Your Life*. When Lord Thomson's son and heir, Kenneth Thomson heard about the plan, he phoned Sir Max to complain that the film was 'not dignified'.

Despite the cancellation Eamonn collected £2,300. Because of increasing TV and business pressure, he decided in future against all private *Life* shows, though he would say that invitations to present them continued to arrive on his desk.

Eamonn was to join comedian Ted Ray and football manager Sir Matt Busby as being among the elite few who were surprised twice on *This Is Your Life*. Eamonn had first been the 'victim' in 1955; it was now May 1974 when Thames decided to hand him a second red book. He was lured to the studio under the impression that he was to make a guest appearance on a David Nixon show.

'It was the most fantastic security operation,' Eamonn

would say later. 'When David Nixon threw the book at me I thought for several minutes it was a gag. Then my wife Grainne walked through the doors and I realised it was for real.'

But he was a willing 'victim' after he had recovered from the initial shock. 'When the realisation dawned on me everything was fine,' he said. 'I was quite knocked out by it all.'

In the case of the most famous football manager in Britain, Sir Matt Busby, his appearance on *This Is Your Life* coincided with his impending retirement as Manchester United boss. Eamonn had first surprised him in 1958. Four weeks later the manager would have a miraculous escape from death in the Munich crash that saw star members of the United team perish.

It was decided on this occasion to surprise Sir Matt at a match between Manchester United and Manchester City at the latter's ground. To avoid being spotted Eamonn sat head downwards in the back of the car on his way to the ground. It was an emotional moment for everyone – Eamonn, Sir Matt and the 50,000 fans, – when Eamonn, standing in the middle of the pitch, presented the red book to a smiling Sir Matt. As he recalled, 'Out there on the pitch the atmosphere was electric. I'll never forget the look on Matt's face when I opened the second box and told him, "For the first time, for the second time This Is Your Life!"'

Eamonn was to say that he got an even bigger kick surprising subjects for a second time. It was true in the case of Ted Ray. He had first presented him with the red book in the fifties, but only just, for the comedian had been delayed for six minutes getting to the theatre, which meant that Eamonn had to keep the audience in chat. 'I was never more happy in my life to see anybody than when Ted finally walked into the theatre.'

On the second occasion there was no such agonising wait. Ted was appearing in a television programme in Birmingham when his wife called him to come to London the next day to 'meet someone important'. The VIP turned out to be Eamonn. Ted's reaction was swift: 'Not again, Eamonn!'

It was inevitable that Eamonn should put Joe Loss's name forward at the Thames *Life* conference to receive the famous red book for a second time. They had always remained the best of friends. Once again Joe's wife, Mildred, was the link. She again found it very hard to keep the secret from her husband. 'I found it a bit trying really,' she recalls. 'We always talked openly and I found that I had to be on my guard in case I let anything drop.'

It had never entered Joe Loss's mind that Eamonn and the *Life* team would try to surprise him for a second time. When it happened, he found the experience even more profound than the first time. 'I was shattered. I deemed it a great honour of course to be chosen as the recipient of a second red book.'

15   'His Voice Painted Pictures'

IT WAS EAMONN'S voice that captivated Henry Cooper.

'Eamonn had a great voice. I used to love listening to him on radio. In his commentaries he was able to paint pictures, making you feel that you were at the ringside alongside him. He managed to catch the bigtime boxing atmosphere and you knew he wanted you to be part of the occasion.'

Today, the former British heavyweight champion, who is best remembered for his exciting fights with Muhammad Ali, lives with his Italian-born wife Albina in a spacious semi-detached house in Hendon. Although he is director of a number of business companies, he still finds time to attend fights and do radio work. Off the hallway of his house can be seen a large glass showcase of trophies which he won over nearly twenty years of boxing.

He first met Eamonn in the fifties when he was a guest on the BBC's *Sports Report*. They soon became friends. To Henry Cooper, Eamonn was a big, friendly man. 'I think you could say he was a handsome man and he always had this grand smile when he met you. There was no affectation about him. For a big man he was gentle, never aggressive, and I never imagined him as a boxer. I like to reminisce, and so did Eamonn. He used to tell me about the boxing club he attended when he was growing up in Dublin. Boxing was his first love and he had always a genuine interest in the sport. He used to say that he got into broadcasting through boxing. He was very proud of his connection with the sport.'

In his view the secret of Eamonn's success was that anything he attempted, he did it well. 'Eamonn was a thorough professional and talking to him on a radio or TV programme you realised he had done his homework. I remember in the early sixties he was delighted when I told him that *Sports Report* was proving a good omen for me. Like most boxers I'm a bit superstitious – I mean the way I put on my boots or what I wear – and soon it struck me that every time I went on *Sports Report* I won my fight. It became so common that I began to invite myself on the programme.'

Socially they were to meet at charity dinners and at boxing receptions. He found that Eamonn liked to recall the great fighters of the past and had their names at his fingertips. 'He once asked me who I considered were the five greatest boxers of their eras. I think I told him Jack Johnson, Jack Dempsey, Joe Louis, Rocky Marciano and Muhammad Ali. We agreed that Ali was probably the fastest heavyweight the world has seen. Eamonn admired Ali's skill and craftsmanship and, as a person, found him good company.'

Although Eamonn tended to be selective in his choice of sportsmen as potential *This Is Your Life* subjects, because some of them were unable to articulate on screen, he had no objection when Henry Cooper's name was suggested at the *Life* conference. The boxer had a good story to tell, was respected by the public and the boxing profession, and was a fluent talker.

Henry has happy memories of the programme: 'I was invited to the television studios for a boxing discussion but when I arrived by taxi I was confronted by Eamonn. At first I was naturally taken aback but after a short time I got this marvellous feeling of satisfaction when Eamonn handed me the red book. I counted it an honour as well as recognition of my achievements in boxing.' He was amused when he recalled the phone calls he had been receiving during the previous weeks. A voice would say 'wrong number' when he lifted the receiver. Although he considered it odd he hadn't suspected a thing. The most moving moment in the *Life* programme, he would say later, was when Eamonn introduced the man who had started him off in boxing.

'I had been brought up in South London during the war years. This man was in the fire service and gave us young chaps a love of boxing. Now he was in his eighties. I recognised him straight away. It was wonderful to shake his hand again.'

Paraded before him were boxers like Billy Walker and Joe Erskine, men he had fought in the ring. There was a film clip of Muhammad Ali, who was unable to be in the London studio. It was a satellite link-up from America and Ali was in characteristically buoyant mood. 'I remember he good-humouredly shaped up to me on screen,' recalls Henry Cooper. 'Outside the ring I found him a nice guy. He never tried to belittle me. His sense of humour was very original.'

Later on when Eamonn achieved one of his *Life* ambitions – to surprise Ali – he agreed that the show was one of the most memorable he had ever presented. It was a longer show than usual and was screened at Christmas time. 'It was very, very exciting for me,' he recalled. 'I had to think fast to keep up with him. Ali wasn't called the Louisville lip for nothing. In some ways I considered him a genius.'

What millions of viewers did not know then was that it was no surprise to Ali to be given the red book. He and his 'camp' had to be informed about the programme weeks in advance, otherwise he would have refused to participate. But it in no way spoiled the fun. Ali gave one of his most scintillating performances, a combination of Hope and Milligan.

To Henry Cooper, it was an unforgettable *This Is Your Life* event, the greatest boxing programme of them all. 'I think this was because of the star names paraded before viewers, all of them paying tribute to Ali. There was obviously tremendous organisation put into the programme. When I came on briefly Ali shaped up to me as Eamonn reminded him of my big punch that once floored him. Ali admitted it was a good one, but for me of course it came too late in the round, for the bell saved him. He was undoubtedly the greatest fighter of his era.'

Today Muhammad Ali, who lives with his fourth wife on a farm in Michigan, is a victim of Parkinson's Disease. At forty-six, he is only a shadow of the man he was. Doctor Stanley Fahn, a leading New York neurologist, was the one who diagnosed the disease. The specialist is adamant, however, that the former world champion is not suffering from punch drunkenness as he is far too mentally sharp. Yet he does concede he should have quit the ring long before he did so. Ali says, 'If I had to do it over again I would have packed up after losing to Leon Spinks in 1978.'

Henry Cooper argues that because of his phenomenal speed in the ring Ali was able to avoid heavy punches to the head and brain. 'I don't think boxing had anything to do with his present condition.'

When Eamonn was told that Ali had contracted Parkinson's Disease in 1984, he was saddened. He had greatly admired him from the beginning of his boxing career. 'My own impression of him is of a highly intelligent individual with a brain like lightning,' he would say. 'Watching him box was an experience.' Like the majority of Ali's admirers he found it hard to accept that the former champion's speech was now slurred and his voice barely audible.

In subsequent years Henry Cooper would be invited on *This Is Your Life* more than a dozen times to pay tribute to boxers and other subjects. Sometimes when Eamonn rang him he would tell him, 'Eamonn, you don't want me again, do you? I don't know the individual all *that* well, you know; he's only an acquaintance. But Eamonn would insist. I used to joke with him and say viewers will get tired of seeing Henry Cooper on the programme.'

Henry's wife, Albina, invariably found the programme touching. 'I think really it is more of a woman's show than a man's because one can get very sentimental about it. But it is nice to know what other people do for a living, or how they won their VC; in that way it can be very fascinating. When I was on Henry's *Life* programme I remember I was tense. I didn't relax for the whole show because the focus was on the family. Watching Eamonn presenting the programme, you immediately appreciated all the hard work that had gone into it. He made everyone feel as if they were at a party. I enjoyed that part of it.'

She admitted that she found it terribly hard to keep the secret from Henry. 'I think I would have let it slip if I had to wait for another week.'

Henry Cooper is convinced that Eamonn got his biggest kick out of watching the expression on the faces of the 'victims'. The bigger the surprise the more he liked it. 'Eamonn told me once that everything hinged on the surprise. I knew he meant it. I came to regard *This Is Your Life* as *his* programme; I couldn't see anyone else do it.'

Sincerity was, in his view, one of Eamonn's virtues. 'Eamonn always gave me the impression that he was pleased to see me. If I was in a room full of people he'd come across to me and shake my hand and ask how I was. When my eldest boy was getting married I invited Eamonn and Grainne to the wedding and they stayed all day. He liked being in the company of friends and boxers. He never let fame go to his head.'

Eamonn made no secret of his admiration for the boxing skills of John Conteh, who was crowned World Light Heavyweight champion in the seventies. 'Pound for pound,' he would say, 'John's as good as any fighter I've seen.'

For that reason, he was eager to present him with the large red book. To do so, he called on the assistance of Paul and Linda McCartney, who were both fans and friends of the boxer. He also asked Henry Cooper to join the guests on the programme. On this occasion Henry did not hesitate to say yes. He never missed a chance to be among his boxing friends.

More than once, Eamonn had spoken about the traumas surrounding *This Is Your Life*, his favourite television programme. Some people felt he overstated the point, but to keep the secret required, he said, tremendous security and no little integrity.. He never failed to be bitterly disappointed when the secret was leaked. Therefore when he learned that packages containing special *Life* research papers had been lost he was almost in despair. He immediately feared that the John Conteh show would have to be cancelled. It happened when a despatch rider's vehicle skidded on the wet road and the papers were scattered about. Although slightly hurt, the rider gathered up the papers but left behind him a vital envelope. On returning to the spot it was nowhere to be seen. Next day a frantic search was undertaken with Eamonn being kept informed of progress almost every hour.

Imagine his relief then when the missing envelope eventually turned up. 'I was more relieved when I heard that the envelope had been found unopened,' he said. It had been sent to Robert Reed, one of the programme directors. Eamonn admitted it was 'a panic moment'. It tended to make him more nervous than usual about surprising John Conteh.

Paul McCartney had arranged to meet the boxer at a recording studios. A few minutes before John Conteh's arrival Eamonn was smuggled inside and hid behind a screen. After a nervous wait he was able to deliver the surprise punch to the boxing champion, who had been taken completely off his guard. It was a happy programme, with the boxer's nine brothers and sisters joining in the tribute. Henry Cooper and the eight British boxing champions found it hard, as Henry said later, to compete with the Conteh family.

Malcolm Morris, the experienced Thames *Life* producer, does not like to say that one programme is better than another. 'I find it hard to measure one against the other,' he says. 'In their own way they are almost all totally different because the subjects are themselves different. What I do remember are the exciting moments – like landing by helicopter on a ship for Eamonn's "pick-up", or when the River Thames traffic was stopped for twenty minutes to surprise a subject. These are the moments that make the programme such an exciting experience.' Eamonn, on the same subject, would say, 'I never compare one programme with another. I think this would be fatal. To me the moment of the hour is the most stimulating.'

On reflection, though, Malcolm Morris felt one of the programmes he liked to remember best concerned the English doctor, Michael Wood. He flew to Kenya with Eamonn and planned to surprise Dr Wood as he flew into a village on one of his mercy missions, then drive him back to Nairobi, and that evening fly him to London where he would be met by the *Life* guests.

Both producer Morris and Eamonn considered Dr Wood's story one of the most fascinating they had encountered for some time. A big, burly man, with receding grey hair, he had been troubled in his youth by an asthmatic condition, but when he was sent to school in Switzerland his health improved greatly. On his return to England he qualified as a surgeon. Later, he decided to follow in the footsteps of the legendary Albert Schweitzer and devote his life to the welfare of Africans. In the course of his mission work he flew thousands of miles across Kenya, Tanzania and Uganda.

'The idea of surprising Dr Wood in the African bush intrigued Eamonn,' recalls Morris. It would become his most unusual pick-up. On arriving in Nairobi he and Eamonn joined members of the *Life* team in their hotel. As they studied the map, it looked more like a military operation than a *This Is Your Life* story. Eamonn was to notice a pressure among the team, mainly because of the elaborate arrangements to be made to fly Dr Wood back to London. They encountered the usual red tape but eventually smoothed out the arrangements, so that everything now depended on Eamonn to make a successful 'pick up'. But where? It took some time before the precise area in the bush was pinpointed. It was a weary

Eamonn who finally retired to bed, more hopeful than confident that the mission would succeed.

As he would say, he experienced a restless night's sleep. Next morning with Malcolm Morris and the *Life* team, he set out on safari. 'It was the oddest safari ever,' he would say later. 'A convoy of Mercedes limousines rough-riding through the bush. I felt somewhat embarrassed under the collar of a safari suit – hired from Moss Bros. But I knew the kit was not just for show as we headed further and further away from Nairobi and into the heart of the bush. When we pulled up at Wilson Airport the natives were being summoned to the village by drumbeat. Some arrived pushing old ladies in wheelbarrows; others had obviously walked miles, ready to welcome the doctor when he arrived to set up his mobile clinic.'

It was the first time that Eamonn had travelled 4,000 miles to surprise a subject. To Malcolm Morris, it was a very exciting moment as he watched Eamonn prepare for the pick-up. But Eamonn was nervous. He was in unknown territory. How would the busy doctor react? He began to worry. All kinds of disturbing questions ran through his mind: 'Would Dr Wood have any idea at all what we were about? Would he have any memory of the programme from his time in England? Would he look at me with a blank expression, thinking that one of the more dangerous cases had escaped and that it was his medical duty to chloroform me quickly and then to do a more detailed examination?'

Suddenly, it began to pour with rain, and in the distance came the sound of thunder. The *Life* crew were drenched. A few moments later a small plane descended out of the sky and slowly taxied to a halt on the ground. It was the cue for Eamonn to move forward and present the red book to Dr Wood. Eamonn recalled, 'When he saw it we were all relieved and flattered that he recognised it. But I still had to do some fast talking to convince him that we were actually serious about taking him back to London with us.'

As if there was not enough excitement for one day, Malcolm

Morris eventually found there was no seat for him in the plane back to London. However, he was able to grab a seat on a plane that would take him via Entebbe to Rome and on to London. Even Eamonn was amazed to find his producer the next day at his desk at Thames.

It was a *Life* programme that afforded Eamonn immense satisfaction. Not only did it manage to grip the viewers, but the whole operation had gone without a hitch. To Malcolm Morris, it was a story of courage and hope and adventure. It was the kind of *Life* programme that brought the very best out of Eamonn, for he happened to admire people like Dr Michael Wood, The Flying Doctor.

He also happened to like Welsh folk hero Max Boyce, who in the late seventies had helped him to surprise renowned Welsh rugby forward, Mervyn Davies.

The player had been carried off the pitch at Cardiff Arms Park in a coma and close to death. Later, his fight for life had been, as Eamonn would say, more inspiring than many of his sporting achievements. That evening in Swansea, he was handed the red book before 1,000 fellow Welshmen. Recalled Eamonn, 'It was Max Boyce who scored this match-winner by inviting the rugby star on stage to join him and then make way for me to say, "Mervyn Davies ... this is your life!"'

Evidently, Max had made a good impression on Eamonn, for shortly afterwards he put the folksinger's name forward at the Thames production conference as a potential *Life* subject. It was planned to spring the surprise after an inter-club game in his village ground at Glynneath. Just as Max was being interviewed for local television about the international rugby match next day between Wales and Scotland in Cardiff, Eamonn stepped forward and sprang the surprise.

'It was a total surprise to me,' Max recalls. 'I remember, though, saying to myself a split second before, "What is Eamonn Andrews doing around here?" It was early in my

[152]

career and I didn't think Eamonn would hand me the red book.'

Lined up in the street outside the rugby ground were about half a dozen big, black limousines which would whisk the local *Life* guests to Swansea for the recording of the programme. An old man was heard to ask, 'What are these limousines for then?' Someone else replied, 'I think they're for Max Boyce.' The old man shook his head and mumbled, 'Jesus, I didn't know he was dead.'

Eamonn liked to tell the story to his friends. Max Boyce believes he enjoyed coming to Wales, in particular doing his own *Life* story. As he explained. 'He met ordinary people, warm-hearted people. Since Eamonn was a genuine person, he was able to relax with them and enjoy their conversation. He got to know my mother Elizabeth quite well and because my father, who was a miner, had been killed in the ground, Eamonn showed great interest in her story. Every year for ten years he sent her a Christmas card with the greetings written in green ink. The gesture was typical of him. He could so easily have forgotten all about her.'

Max noticed that his mother afterwards liked to take down from the shelf the red *Life* book and proudly leaf through the pages. She had, he knew, enjoyed the show, just as all the family had. Yet, in his own view, it was in television terms an old programme and depended on its continued success on the freshness of its subjects. But he attributed its real success to the fairytale element, as well as Eamonn's own personality.

Sometimes he was disappointed by the preponderance of show-business stars on the show. 'I think that ordinary people have often more to say. This was true about my own *Life*.'

16 *Eamonn, The Commuter*

SHOWING NO OUTWARD signs of strain, Eamonn appeared to his TV colleagues to be only too happy to play the taxing role of commuter. By the mid-seventies he was a familiar figure in airport lounges as he strode towards customs carrying nothing more than a worn briefcase. He liked to travel lightly. To his friends, his return to Dublin was already regarded as a shrewd move. It had in no way affected his work. To Eamonn, these were successful and productive years, among the best of his long career. Whatever he did, wherever he went, he was news.

On Monday mornings he travelled by car from The Quarry in Portmarnock to Dublin Airport where he boarded a plane for Heathrow. A car picked him up at the airport and he was driven directly to his flat in Chiswick. There, he had discussions with his secretary about his correspondence and forthcoming engagements. His mailbag alone from *This Is Your Life* was unfailingly large and he either answered letters himself or dictated them to his secretary. Throughout the morning he would talk with Malcolm Morris about *This Is Your Life* and try to iron out any problems, and before noon, with the producer of *Today* to enquire about the items for that evening's show. Shortly after lunch, a relaxed Eamonn arrived at the studios to study the programme script.

What made *Today* so satisfying for him was the contrasting nature of the items he presented. The programme was, for instance, used for the first time as a marriage bureau. Two lonely hearts told him why they could not find marriage partners. Viewers interested in either lonely heart were invited to write to the studio. Ten bachelors couldn't wait. They phoned in immediately, hoping for a date with the girl. There were two phone calls for the man. She was named as Bozena W., 24, from Purley, Surrey, who worked as a secretary for the Metropolitan Police. Her hobbies included opera, playing the piano, photography, dancing and 'going to discos'. Her ideal partner would be humorous and well-mannered.

Bozena said: 'Nothing's ever gone right for me. I am still looking. It has always been one-sided. I have never found anyone interested in the things I am interested in.'

She complained that the boys she met at the discotheques expected to be invited in for coffee.

Eamonn: 'Why don't you invite them in?'

Bozena: 'They expect too much. A cup of coffee means many things.'

He was introduced as Andy B., 22, an East Ender from Bethnal Green who worked in a West End men's wear shop. He was a Spurs fan and very keen on Elvis Presley. He told Eamonn that he lived in a rough district. 'The Kray brothers lived just a few streets away from me'.

Eamonn: 'I believe you've had a bit of trouble yourself?'

Andy: 'I had an incident with the law when I was fourteen through mixing with the wrong crowd.'

He said he had been courting a couple of girls, one for three months, but she ended the relationship, not him. 'I never tried to push it,' he explained. 'I never asked her once if I could come in for a cup of coffee....' Seemingly, the relationship ended on a tube train when Andy told his girlfriend that if they were still going out with each other at Christmas they could send joint Christmas cards.

Commented Eamonn: 'That frightened them off.'

After the programme, which was later screened in America, the two lonely hearts left the Thames TV studios at Euston and went home – separately. Paradoxically, Eamonn's approach to *Today* was very composed and he was seldom seen

[155]

to be flurried, despite the topicality of the material he was handling, which often included important running news stories of that day. In contrast, when one would have expected the opposite to be the case, he was often nervy in his attitude to *This Is Your Life*. Thames producers could find no easy explanation, other than the likelihood that he was too conscious of the prospect of failure at the pick-up point in *This Is Your Life*.

Once he used *Today* as a means to trap one of his favourite comedians, Bob Hope. Eamonn gave the impression to the comedian's Hollywood agent that he wanted to interview the star on the magazine programme when, in fact, he hoped to surprise him for *This Is Your Life*. To Eamonn, Hope was one of the all-time great comics; he loved his spontaneous one-liners; he happened also to like the man himself, which in Eamonn's case was always important. They had already met in Hollywood and privately Eamonn had vowed that one day he would hand him the red book.

Now, as he waited in his dressing room he was told that Hope was delayed. 'Sixty minutes seemed like sixty long days as we waited for Bob to walk unsuspectingly into our trap,' he recalled. Months before he had 'booked' him for the *Today* 'interview', and Bob Hope's wife, Dolores, had agreed to be an accomplice in the plot. Now she was in danger of losing her nerve. Eamonn offered her a drink and they chatted anxiously as the minutes ticked away. Another phone call came through to say that the comedian was held up in heavy traffic. Eamonn sighed and looked at his watch – there was only half an hour remaining to the start of the *Life* programme. Meanwhile, a warm-up comic was keeping the audience in happy mood. All the guests were locked in to avoid being spotted before the show. In there was Hope's daughter, Linda, who the previous day had met Frank Sinatra's daughter Tina at a hair-dressing salon in the West End and a short time afterwards they were spotted by a Fleet Street photographer who snapped them for an evening newspaper. As Eamonn recalled, 'If the picture was published and seen by Bob Hope he would want to know what Linda was doing in London when he thought she was at home in the States. There was only one thing to do: take the newspaper totally into our confidence by telling them the secret we had been setting up for so long. Sportingly they agreed not to publish the picture and risk spoiling the pleasure of millions of viewers.'

When Hope did eventually arrive an hour late he was immediately surprised in the foyer by Eamonn and guided directly into the studio. Although obviously amazed to be met by the applause of an enthusiastic audience, the famous comic took it all rather philosophically, smiling as Eamonn introduced a galaxy of stars, among them Tony Bennett and Dorothy Lamour.

Waiting in the wings was Lord Louis Mountbatten, who was eager to get on with the show as he had an urgent dinner engagement. Eamonn could almost hear him say that it was so late that if he wasn't soon called in to pay his tribute he would have to leave. It was his first time on the *Life* programme.

It would not be his last.

On Tuesdays Eamonn usually lunched with producer Malcolm Morris as they discussed amendments to the *This Is Your Life* scripts which sometimes arose out of certain suggestions from relatives of the subject. That evening, after completing *Today*, there was a final run through of the *Life* show. On Wednesday, Bill Grundy took over as presenter of *Today* while Eamonn was committed to making his 'pick-up' of the *Life* victim and immediately afterwards getting him back to the studio for the screening of the programme at seven o'clock. When a young reporter once asked him how he managed to present two such contrasting programmes during a single week, Eamonn replied modestly, 'It's simply a question of compartmentalising oneself; or devoting oneself entirely to the job on hand, otherwise there is a risk of confusion arising.'

[157]

Next morning, Thursday, there would be a meeting of the *Life* team to discuss the following week's show; afterwards Eamonn would continue with his work on *Today*, switching over to topical events without any apparent difficulty. That evening, at 9.20, he caught a plane from Heathrow to Dublin Airport where he was collected and driven to The Quarry. Grainne always noticed that her husband's face 'visibly brightened' the moment he stepped inside the door of the house. 'It must be the sea air,' she once joked. But it was true; he loved to be back, happy to relax with his wife and three children. It was a simple form of relaxation that he pursued. Often on Saturdays he cooked breakfast; that evening he and Grainne and friends might dine out together in Howth or elsewhere. On Sundays they sometimes took a drive in the country.

Over the weekend, Eamonn found time to talk with his business partners, Fred O'Donovan, Dermod Cafferky and Lorcan Bourke. Their Irish business empire was now reckoned to be worth £1 million. For the most part, the Gaiety Theatre, their biggest single venture, was paying its way. Although experts hinted of a likely economic recession on the way, such a grim prospect was scarcely touched on when the partners and friends met for drinks at Eamonn's luxurious home at midday on Sundays. He found some time also to talk to the press. Despite being cut off from his UK interests, he would take calls from Fleet Street journalists, particularly those he knew and trusted.

He was asked why he had turned down an offer to star in his own TV series in America. The invitation came from NBC, the American coast-to-coast network, after New Yorkers were given a recent taste of British TV talent on their screens. The question was nothing new to Eamonn. Always he felt that somehow he was expected at different stages of his career to accept one of the attractive offers dangled before him by the Americans. As he recalled, 'Some people got the impression that my accent – call it mid Atlantic if you like – would ensure for me success in the States. I didn't go along with that theory. I had to look deeper than that for security.'

On this occasion the shows had been sponsored by Thames Television and the only star they flew out to America was Eamonn who appeared live as host on a chat show. 'The NBC offer was one of several I had. They said I could do either the same kind of shows I do in Britain or star in a new idea. My answer was "No way". I love visiting America but joining the show-business migration to the States is not for me. The point of showing British programmes in New York was to give American viewers the chance to decide whether they wanted to see more. Judging by the mail we got the verdict seemed to be thumbs up.'

It struck him that Britain wasn't getting a fair deal out of the exchange of TV shows between the two countries and figures showed that they were buying more programmes than ever before. 'I think our television is the world's best and it's about time there were some exchanges. Some of our shows and series would be smash hits if they were shown over there. Adaptations like *Love Thy Neighbour* are hits already. So why shouldn't the originals be too?'

He answered questions about criticism of his US TV appearances in which he was compared unfavourably with Dick Cavett, who flew to Britain to act as his opposite number. Eamonn calmly explained, 'In America the host is the star of the show, and heaven help anybody who tries to upstage him. In Britain I try to make my guests the stars. I think that's what caused the reaction; critics were simply unprepared to accept a departure from the usual. But my mail shows the indications are that American viewers would welcome such a change.'

At fifty-four years of age, it was abundantly clear that he wasn't prepared to risk his future in America. That was only one reason; the other was of course that he was rich and famous, had a happy family life, and his future in Britain was assured. Instinctively, though, he was drawn to the States; he liked the financial rewards for painstaking work, yet he felt that it was perhaps a young man's country demanding lots of stamina to keep at the top. He didn't fear the prospect of working there; it was in his case a matter of choice. Nothing would uproot him now from his home in Ireland. He was strongly influenced by Grainne and the children. They liked the lifestyle he had provided for them, and the children were enjoying being educated in Ireland.

Summer in Portmarnock could be enchanting. With another series of *This Is Your Life* shows behind him, Eamonn was able to don his casual clothes and relax. Producer Malcolm Morris sometimes joined him for a while in those summer months and together they enjoyed some golf, walks, or a trip to the Abbey Theatre. 'I always look forward to my visits to Dublin,' Morris recalled. And Eamonn revelled in the privacy of his house and garden. The place exuded happiness as well as the laughter of his children who were growing up fast around him. Watching his children splash in the pool afforded Eamonn great pleasure; healthy children meant a lot to him.

No one in Dublin envied him his lifestyle. As his partner Fred O'Donovan would say, 'I think they realised he had worked tremendously hard for what he had achieved. I knew how hard he worked and because of that I wasn't surprised by his success. To Dubliners, he remained somewhat distant, probably out of his own sense of shyness, yet after Mass on Sundays, at which he sometimes read the lesson, he would have a friendly word with friends. To them, he hadn't changed, though Ireland itself had greatly changed. The middle-classes in the mid-seventies had money, a better life-style, a higher level of tolerance of the wealthy, and they came to regard Eamonn Andrews as 'one of their own'.

That he had returned to live in style was something to be admired in their eyes. But few looked up to him; that kind of Irish attitude was beginning to fade and die in the country. Eamonn preferred it that way. He wanted to go about his business without causing a public stir. Again it helped that so many Irish people saw him primarily as a businessman and not as a superstar in show-business terms. Dubliners were more inclined to stop the traffic for a glimpse of their favourite son, Gay Byrne, who continued to see Eamonn at weekends.

If Eamonn had not regretted his decision to live in Ireland, the same could not be said of Bill Nolan, who returned in the early seventies. Although he had become one of RTE's leading broadcasters, he still harboured some slight misgivings, yet at the same time he could be said to be happy.

Energetic and perceptive, he had followed Eamonn Andrews as the presenter of the BBC's *Sports Report* It was Eamonn who had given him his chance to become a broadcaster when he took him on the *This Is Your Life* team at the BBC. It was something that Nolan never forgot.

Now, in the 1970s, they had gone their own separate ways, mainly because each was so busy and much of Eamonn's week was spent in London. But Bill Nolan continued to watch *This Is Your Life* and was in no way surprised by its success. 'I felt right from the beginning it was a programme that had the ingredients to make it compulsive viewing. Essentially it is about people, and people are interested in other people. It has been criticised because it is sentimental but this hasn't affected the ratings.'

To Nolan, the show owed a lot of its success to Eamonn. 'There is no doubt about this. He was large, avuncular and self-effacing, as well as modest. All of these things came across to the viewer. Furthermore, he had the capacity to be embarrassed and to show his embarrassment.'

When Thames decided to revive the show, he was not surprised by their decision. 'I was surprised that it took so long for it to come back because *This Is Your Life* can run to the end of the century. They will never run out of subjects.'

Working closely with Eamonn on the *Life* show had, he says, given him insights that few others could hope to get. He came to admire his constant search for perfection. 'Leslie Jackson, or Jacko to us then, was the go-between between members of

[161]

Life and Eamonn. It was Jacko who accepted our scripts and passed them on to Eamonn. Days later they would be returned with certain comments and some of those comments might be surprising, or even blistering. You might say to yourself, "Eamonn's got the wrong drift," but on further examination you'd ask yourself perhaps, "Did I give him the wrong impression through my writing?"'

Gradually Bill Nolan got to know Eamonn as a friend, but never as a close friend. He remembered, 'Eamonn wasn't the kind of man who gathered friends around him. He tended to be reserved and shy and was distant from people. At Christmas time he would invite some of us over to his flat at Lancaster Gate for drinks. I can still see him standing shyly with a glass in his hand and that shy grin on his face as he listened to somebody or other. He wasn't a gregarious person who'd go into a room and hold court. He was never the centre of a party. He preferred to talk quietly on a one-to-one basis. I never saw him talk to more than two people at a time.'

Nolan was to see Eamonn in varying moods. He knew how disappointed he felt when Danny Blanchflower 'ran out' on the programme. 'I was personally involved as script writer in the programme and I think it would have been a very good one. In retrospect, I feel that Danny should have accepted the red book from Eamonn. Of course he was entitled to walk out, but I think the real loss was his. As Captain of Spurs he had a very high profile and the programme would have brought out a warmth in the man which, to my mind, has never surfaced.'

He sees *This Is Your Life* as an extension of Eamonn himself. Various people had believed that Eamonn wanted to be a writer, but to Nolan it was an actor that Eamonn really longed to be. As he explained, 'The actor in Eamonn got immense satisfaction dressing up to surprise subjects in the show, just as professional actors have to don costumes for period plays. He loved acting the part and the more outlandish the make-up he wore, the better he appeared to like it. It was the actor's disguise and to him it was part of the fun of the show. It probably also hid the tension he felt before the vital pick-up moment. I felt the show was becoming more and more a personal thing with Eamonn, totally different from *What's My Line?* which is a panel game and depends on the reaction of the panellists to inject in the show either fun or outrage. *Life* is about joy, tragedy, admiration, heroism, disappointment, human feelings. Eamonn understood the emotions he was bringing to the screen, just as an actor tries to understand the emotional range in Hamlet or James Tyrone. In time it became *his* show.'

Eamonn by now had almost lost count of the number of shows he had presented, yet after nearly twenty years he was able to say, 'I love *This Is Your Life*. It's so exciting and almost every time it's heartening for me, it's never boring.'

Malcolm Morris marvelled at Eamonn's enormous enthusiasm for *Life*. He knew this factor was part of the great success of the programme, for Eamonn's enthusiasm was transmitted to the viewer. There were people who Eamonn still wanted to surprise, among them Val Doonican. He admired Val's smooth style as an entertainer, his gentle way with songs, and how quickly he managed to win over audiences. 'Val's style is tailor-made for television,' Eamonn once confided to a show-business colleague. 'He can go on forever.'

Val's was one of the names he had pencilled into his notebook as a likely *Life* subject. He remembered he had been born in Waterford, worked in a factory for a paltry wage, and struggled in Ireland in the late forties to make it in show-business. It was only when he tried his luck in England that he eventually achieved success. From time to time, he had invited Val as a guest on the *Life* programmes and their friendship had endured.

For his part, Val Doonican never gave any thought to being the 'next victim'. But that was nothing unusual, for most people who had been surprised by Eamonn admitted afterwards, 'We never once thought it would happen to us.'

[163]

For Val, it all began on a mundane note. He was appearing at the Palladium and the publicity people wanted some new photographs of him and arranged that these would be taken on the South Herts golf course as he played a round of golf with famous professional, Dai Rees. The day fixed for the game was a Wednesday.

A few days before, Val was sitting at home when the phone rang. Picking up the receiver, a voice with an Irish accent said cheerfully, 'Val Doonican?'

'Yes,' replied the singer, thinking for a moment that it was his friend Jimmy Tarbuck playing another of his tricks on him. After a while he suspected it wasn't Jimmy.

'Who's speaking?' he asked impatiently.

'My name's Seamus O'Shaughnessy.'

'Who gave you my number?'

'I'm from the *Irish Times* in Dublin. Your number is in the office.'

'I'm sorry, but I don't think it is.'

Val got suspicious. He listened as the voice said, 'Tell me, what are you doing next Wednesday?'

After a slight pause, he replied, 'I'm playing a game of golf with Dai Rees and having some publicity pictures taken.'

'Well,' said the other, 'We've been tipped off that Eamonn Andrews is going to surprise Dai Rees for *This Is Your Life*.'

At that moment, Val's wife Lynn was sitting in the armchair opposite and heard him repeat the name of the programme. She inwardly winced, for she was sure the secret was out. But when her husband, who was still puzzled by the call, explained that it was Rees who was going to be the victim she made no remark.

On the Wednesday Val's touring manager drove him to the golf course and as they got out of the car at the clubhouse, Val said, 'Why don't you join us for a game?' The manager nodded: 'No, no, I'll walk around with you for a few holes.' With them also was a photographer. After playing the first and second holes, Dai Rees suggested that they cut across to the twelfth hole because workmen were digging up the fifth hole. Val thought: what a funny game of golf I'm having.

Next thing he knew he was coming up to the eighteenth hole. He hit the ball onto the green and as he strolled towards the hole with Rees he suddenly spied a tall individual standing on the green.

'Who the hell is that?' he said to Rees.

The golfer casually replied, 'I really don't know who it is. Probably one of the members.'

As he approached nearer, Val recognised Eamonn. He was wearing a golf cap and pullover. On the green he said to him 'What are you doing here, Eamonn?' At that moment something else crossed his mind. May be, after all, he was going to surprise Dai Rees for *This Is Your Life*. He chuckled at the thought. Then he heard Eamonn say beside him, 'That was a nice shot you played and I'm glad to say This Is Your Life, Val Doonican!'

Val smiled with astonishment. 'I don't believe it!'

Eamonn took his arm and led him towards the clubhouse. 'I still can't believe it, Eamonn,' muttered Val.

'Just enjoy yourself,' Eamonn told him.

He changed in the clubhouse and accompanied the *Life* members to Thames studios. After his feeling of disbelief had worn off, Val was thrilled with the show. As relatives and friends were paraded before him, he got the impression of being present at an old movie. Everything seemed to pass quickly before his eyes. They brought on his mother, his teacher, the musicians who used to perform with him. He found the experience very moving. Memories flooded back and all his yesterdays suddenly seemed to merge into one.

'It was lovely,' he would say later. 'I just sat there. Afterwards when people called to the house they wanted to see the book. They were fascinated that my life story had been condensed into such a number of pages.'

Eamonn, he remembered, handled the show expertly. 'He hardly projected himself once. He let the people be the stars. I began to think that is the reason why the show has enjoyed such a long run on television. I can't imagine anyone except Eamonn presenting the show.'

By now Eamonn was truly the master of disguise. It was becoming one of the real highlights of the *Life* show. He liked, as he said himself, to become 'invisible'. He dressed as a white-coated waiter to surprise Moira Lister in the bar of the Vaudeville Theatre. 'I got the feeling she was thinking the waiter was being slightly impertinent,' he recalled, 'but she passed it over graciously.'

He assumed the role of a Royal Highland Fusilier to surprise Andy Stewart, the Scots singer. He obviously derived a lot of fun out of breaking ranks – and getting away with it. 'As the order came to march,' he recalled. 'I clutched a bugle in one hand and the book, which was hidden under a specially made tartan wrap, in the other. We marched in formation up a flight of steps and on to the studio floor.'

Eamonn once joked that he was achieving an ambition by becoming a musician, spaceman, Father Christmas, waiter, pilot, even missionary. If that is only partly true, then, as Bill Nolan suggested, *This Is Your Life* was truly an extension of him; but perhaps it was even more. A realisation maybe of his childhood dreams when, like other boys, he imagined himself as a famous star, or singer, writer or pilot. It was an innocent thought but worth noting.

In the final analysis, maybe Eamonn found in disguise the simplest way to conceal his own innate shyness and, in the case of a pick-up, his nervous tension.

17 *'His Finest Hour'*

TERRY YARWOOD IS tall, lean and earnest. Quietly-spoken, he instantly strikes one as the kind of man capable of keeping a secret forever, so he was an invaluable asset to the *This Is Your Life* eighteen-strong team. For a number of years he had worked as director on *Today* and came to know Eamonn. 'We hit it off very well,' Yarwood remembers. 'I enjoyed my stint on the programme.'

On this September morning in 1976 he joined Malcolm Morris and Maurice Leonard, two of the *Life* team at the weekly production conference at the Thames TV studios in Teddington. As usual, Eamonn sat at the top of the table. The team were about to begin work on what was to be their eighth consecutive series.

Terry Yarwood had not long joined the programme, but he had already noted a number of celebrities he thought would make exciting *Life* subjects. Heading the list was Lord Louis Mountbatten. Although he had heard that Eamonn was anxious to surprise the Queen Mother he felt that was extremely unlikely to happen. It would be a Royal breakthrough if they could hand the red book to Lord Mountbatten.

For a while he listened as Eamonn suggested likely subjects. Then in a quiet voice, he said, 'What d'you say to Lord Mountbatten?'

The others in the room looked at Yarwood, then up the table to ascertain Eamonn's reaction. It wasn't enthusiastic. 'You'll never get him, Terry,' he said calmly.

'I think it's worth trying,' Yarwood persisted. 'It's a wonderful story.'

'I agree,' Eamonn said. 'It's clearcut. I mean we don't have to waste time in deciding who to contact. To me, the ideal person is Mountbatten's son-in-law, Lord Brabourne.'

He shrugged, as he added, 'I'd like to think we can get him but as I say I'm not so sure.'

Yarwood sensed that Eamonn was already showing slight enthusiasm. He reckoned the Mountbatten story would be ideal for the following year, Jubilee Year, and it would be nice to have a member of the Royal Family on the show.

The suggestion was discussed for a while at the table and before long Eamonn agreed with Yarwood that it was perhaps worth the effort. If anyone had cared to ask Brian Tesler, he would have said, 'Lord Mountbatten adores publicity. He would be only too delighted to accept the red book'.

Maurice Leonard was in agreement that the Mountbatten *Life* would be enormously exciting because of his involvement in two wars and his connection with India, and, of course, the *HMS Kelly* and its crew. But he also knew from experience that it was hard to influence Eamonn unless you presented a very convincing reason for doing something. As regards the choice of subjects for *Life*, he exercised a total veto. Therefore he was scarcely prepared when Eamonn said, 'Maybe Terry is right. If we can get Mountbatten I think we should go ahead.'

Yarwood was delighted. He saw the programme not only as the biggest challenge ever faced by the *Life* team, but also something fantastic for Eamonn. In subsequent weeks he kept Eamonn informed of his progress. 'I think we can set it up,' he told him. 'Lord Brabourne seems interested enough to consider the idea seriously. But he wants more time to make personal enquiries.'

Eamonn was prepared to wait. The team had noticed that he was becoming 'quite excited' about the prospect of surprising Lord Mountbatten. He was impressed by Terry Yarwood's

[168]

dedicated approach. Shortly before Christmas Lord Brabourne, who was married to Lord Mountbatten's elder daughter, Lady Patricia, asked for a meeting with a few of the *Life* team, including Terry Yarwood. 'It was rather hush hush,' remembers Yarwood. 'We met at a private address in Knightsbridge and Lord Brabourne put certain questions to us about the guests we planned to invite and when exactly it was proposed to do the programme. He was polite and helpful, but stressed that he hadn't told any of the family yet and again asked for more time to consider the matter. Before he left the room, another meeting was arranged.'

After Christmas, when Eamonn returned from a short holiday at home in Ireland, he learned that Lord Brabourne had broken the news to his family and they appeared 'quietly enthusiastic' about the plan to surprise Lord Mountbatten. However, Terry Yarwood knew that their biggest problem was finding a way to spring the surprise. It was common knowledge that Mountbatten spent a good deal of time abroad and it was up to them to find out when he would be home.

They had to wait until the New Year for an answer. As Eamonn recalled, 'Finally it was Lady Pamela Hicks who solved the problem for us with the revelation that one date she knew her father would certainly leave free was in April – her birthday. She would suggest that, instead of going to a play or show, they ask Howard Thomas, of Thames Television, and a friend of Lord Mountbatten, if he could arrange a private showing of selected episodes from the television series of *Lord Mountbatten's Life and Times*, which was made in 1967. Her father knew that some of the grandchildren were too young to have seen the series when it was originally shown and she and her sister had often suggested to him that it would be great fun for the younger children to see some of the episodes with him some time. He would therefore not think there was anything odd about the proposal.'

Terry Yarwood agreed with Eamonn that the plan could not be better. 'We all knew that it was hard to get Eamonn enthusiastic about some things,' he recalls, 'but he was now full of enthusiasm, though as usual somewhat cautious until he had finally sprung the surprise. There was a lot of work still to do, some more problems to be solved. We had to find the people who would piece together the story and make it exciting television.'

By now Maurice Leonard was busy on the project. It had been a lifelong ambition of his to be part of the *This Is Your Life* programme and he was now thrilled to be working on the biggest show yet. As Senior Researcher, he was faced with some painstaking work, but he was loving the challenge. 'We all knew we were onto something exciting and wanted to make the programme one of the best ever at Thames. It was my job to come up with the information so that the show could be properly shaped. I was helped by Lavinia Warner and both of us worked long hours, often at the Imperial War Museum in Hayes, Middlesex, looking at miles of archive film.'

It was Kay Bird's job to ensure that all the guests got to London and had an enjoyable stay. It was a mammoth task for her, as she planned for each of the 180 guests who would be arriving from all parts of the world. She was not helped by a threat of an overtime dispute at Heathrow Airport. Coming from Hollywood were Bob Hope, Jackie Coogan, Danny Kaye and Juliet Mills. Dame Vera Lynn had agreed to cut short a tour of Canada and the United States to fly back. Lord Mountbatten's own grand-daughter, Joanna, was to arrive from Sydney, Australia. Four thousand miles away in the Bahamas were the rest of the Mountbattens, including Lord Mountbatten.

Terry Yarwood admitted that even he had not visualised the true scale of this *Life* programme he had first suggested at the production conference six months before. 'Every day the story seemed to grow in dimension,' he recalls. 'It called for very strict security and secrecy to keep the secret intact. A last-minute newsleak would be a shattering blow to us all, especially for Eamonn who became involved in almost every aspect of the planning.'

Amazingly, Eamonn found time to think of his forthcoming new programme about money. *Time For Business* would be screened in the autumn, but already he was having discussions with his producer James Butler about the shape the programme would take. Few complained when he was named presenter. Being involved in business in the UK, and chairman of two companies in Dublin, made him ideal for the job.

'Eamonn Andrews,' said Thames Television chairman, Howard Thomas, 'had been chosen to present the new programme because he didn't have fixed beliefs and could meet The City as a professional, experienced television name, and someone with a very astute business mind.'

Eamonn saw the programme as a challenge to his own versatility and was satisfied that he could make it entertaining for ordinary viewers. He felt up to then there had been too much mystique surrounding financial programmes. Asked about his own views on money, he said, 'Money isn't the most important thing in the world, but everyone is now interested in it. We are all involved in business in some way. Our union is in business, and where the Government is a shareholder, we are a shareholder. I think the world of finance has now learned that television is not an intruder, but an explainer and reflector. People tend to think that secrecy is power, which of course it so often is ... which is how the barriers have grown up between the media and the money world.'

Eamonn was impressed by the care and thought Thames were putting into the launching of *Time For Business* using research from AGB, the people who compiled the Top Ten TV ratings. They planned to interview 10,000 people about the way they spent their money. He was aware that television was disliked by industry because it focused on management and unions, though he now felt that old attitudes were changing and industry recognised the value of informed television programmes.

"This Is Your Life". You were on the verge of saying something terribly rude.' But perhaps the most moving moment of all arrived when Lord Mountbatten met again his fellow survivors from the now legendary *HMS Kelly*. Reading from the red *Life* book, Eamonn recalled the days when Lord Louis was captain of the ship and how in a sea battle during the war it was almost shipwrecked by the enemy. 'But you refused,' he told Mountbatten, 'to abandon ship and this inspired Noel Coward to make *In Which We Serve*.'

For sustained effort, Terry Yarwood thought it was Eamonn's 'finest hour'. As he recalled, 'He was at the top of his form and the whole programme flowed almost effortlessly.' To Maurice Leonard, it was very exciting and demonstrated what one could do with an hour-long *Life* programme. Although people thought that we should be doing more long programmes this was only possible when the story was of epic quality.'

Eamonn would say, 'It was the best *This Is Your Life* we ever did.'

The programme pleased Mountbatten. He later requested Thames to send a copy of the *Life* to the Buckingham Palace archives for posterity. It was the first time such a request had been made.

Evidently the programme caught the imagination of viewers as well for the *Life* team received a number of congratulatory messages. Fleet Street devoted a good deal of space to the programme and praised Eamonn's deft handling of Lord Mountbatten and the numerous guests. As one paper pointed out, '*This Is Your Life* trapped its most illustrious victim last night ... Earl Mountbatten. And viewers were told of a new side to the seventy-six-year-old uncle of Prince Philip ... as the man who nearly became a film star. Veteran film star, Jackie Coogan, revealed how he had made a home movie with Lord and Lady Mountbatten and Charlie Chaplin in Hollywood in the twenties. The couple could easily have become film stars if they'd stayed in Hollywood, Coogan told the audience. After all, they had the looks and the glamour – that's the main thing.'

Later, Eamonn referred to this episode, when he wrote: 'We used a priceless clip of silent film in which Lord Louis appeared with his late wife, Edwina Ashly, on their honeymoon in Hollywood. Their co-stars were Charlie Chaplin and Jackie Coogan. Charlie sent a touching message for our *Life* show from his home in Switzerland and Jackie, having beaten the airport problems to fly in from Hollywood, told us how, when he joined the American Air Force, he served with Lord Louis in Burma.'

That July, Eamonn bowed out of *Today* and, never being the one to look back, was already thinking about his new money programme. After ten years he admitted privately that he had had enough of the evening show and looked forward to the new challenge. The *Sunday Times* commented, 'Eamonn Andrews is not, as malicious voices-off would have us believe, going through a mid-life crisis. This week, true, he bows out of Thames TV's *Today* programme after ten glorious years. But Eamonn, now in his 55th year, is moving on to greater things. No mean business man himself – as manoeuvering from a nightly to a weekly show within the same contract might seem to prove – he is to host a bright, yet gritty programme, about The City and big business. *This Is Your Life* will, of course, continue the while, as I've no doubt it always shall.'

The writer acknowledged that the *Today* show in losing Eamonn had lost its most articulate participant. 'Eamonn is more diplomatic,' he continued. 'He tells me that his going has nothing to do with whether the programme is good, bad or indifferent. The business show was just something that came up'.

Time For Business proved an ideal television vehicle for Eamonn's talents. As presenter, he handled the programme with conviction and seemed to be naturally at home with business people. Assigning this new role to him was, in the eyes of some Thames people, 'a masterly stroke by Howard Thomas'.

With the arrival of 1978, Eamonn's Irish business interests began to be affected by the Irish recession. Profits from some of his enterprises, such as the Television Club and hotels, were falling, and the golden days of the Gaiety Theatre seemed to be coming to an end. Eamonn continued to attend board meetings with his business partners and was reminded more than once that the future appeared somewhat gloomy. But at this stage he admitted he didn't see any cause for undue pessimism. In that year Jack O'Connor had joined the Andrews companies and remembered attending company meetings in a room in the Television Club: 'Eamonn always smoked a cigar and sometimes the room would be smoke-filled. I found him polite and courteous and he seemed to have a good grasp of how his business affairs stood in Ireland as a whole.' Friends wondered, though, if he really had the time to devote to his Irish companies and were inclined to ask if it would not be wiser on his part to opt out altogether. But Eamonn appeared to have a personal interest in the Gaiety Theatre and its future.

When Spike Milligan topped the bill at this Dublin theatre, Eamonn went along to see his friend whom he had first been introduced to in the late forties by Joe Loss. After the show, Eamonn and Spike dined out together and reminisced about old times. 'Spike didn't like to see Eamonn smoking large cigars,' says Jack O'Connor. 'I once heard him tell Eamonn, "Take that weed out of your mouth, can't you!" Eamonn laughed, but I think Spike was serious. They were good friends, and although they seemed to me very different characters Eamonn enjoyed Spike's zany sense of humour. He thought he had a lot of talent. He told me once that he used to enjoy the Goon Show enormously.'

The Thames *Life* team knew that Eamonn was anxious to surprise Spike, but how actually to do so posed a problem.

[176]

Spike's movements could be as unpredictable as the man himself. Yet Eamonn was determined to present him with the red book. But he had no illusions about the task before him. As he said, 'On reflection, *This Is Your Life*, Spike Milligan was probably the greatest gamble of all. We had waited for years for the right time and the right place to tell the incredible story of one of the world's most unpredictable characters.'

Now the place chosen to surprise him was Bexhill's De La Warr Pavilion, where Spike's former comrades in the 56th Regiment of the Royal Artillery were holding a reunion. Eamonn knew how fond Spike was of his old comrades and therefore would not miss the reunion. And they would love to hear his story and meet the others who had played their parts in it outside the Army.

The *Life* team experienced no problems with the organisers of the event. Full cooperation was promised. But Eamonn was still worried about the programme. Could they, for instance, find out exactly Spike's movements for that day? Would he actually turn up at the reunion? It was decided to put a man outside his house to spot him as he left and tail him, reporting to Eamonn and the *Life* production team in Bexhill – whenever he could.

'It did not take long for the drama to switch to farce,' recalled Eamonn. 'After following Spike for nearly 20 miles on an "away-from-it-all" route that even the AA wouldn't have recommended on a sunny Bank Holiday, our "private eye" could only presume he had been spotted and he gave up his pursuit.'

It was agreed at this stage to call in the police from two counties who kept watch for Spike's car. By now the planning had reached bizarre proportions. Eamonn and *Life* teams were in the TV lounge of the Granville Hotel anxiously awaiting news about Spike and if he had checked into his hotel some distance away, when one of the hotel staff said that the Granville was one of Spike's favourite meeting places before he was posted abroad during the war. Whenever he was in the

[177]

area, he never failed to make it his first stop.

Eamonn saw the amusing side: 'Never have so many doors been locked so quickly. Never have so many people changed to go out so fast as they did that night.'

Later, Spike looked shattered when Eamonn surprised him at the reunion with the words, 'This Is Your Life, Spike Milligan.' Eamonn, at that moment, reckoned that there was an air of vulnerability about the actor. 'When the show got going, he was obviously touched by the surprises, particularly by the arrival of his mother from her home in Australia. But of course, those who know Spike know that when he is moved he tries to disguise the fact with another touch of humour.'

There was a funny moment – the funniest of the show – when Peter Sellers arrived on set to greet Spike wearing his German uniform of helmet, dark glasses, and leather overcoat. Spike shook his hand – then dropped his trousers.

Eamonn summed up: 'It was a mad, mad but moving evening and I wouldn't have been at all surprised if, before the programme had ended, the De La Warr Pavilion had not itself taken off to sea with all of us on board and Spike at the helm'.

18 'Top Of The World'

THE 1980S... AND Eamonn's energy as well as his achievements continued to be a talking point in television circles. Soon he would be sixty, yet he still showed no visible signs of slowing, the hectic pace he set himself; if anything, he was becoming a total workaholic.

'Why does Eamonn insist, if he can, on doing everything live on TV, when it obviously means so much extra pressure on him?' asked Brian Tesler, his long-time friend at London Weekend Television. And he added thoughtfully, 'He could save himself the perspiration and the nervous laughter if he did not do programmes live. But it strikes me that Eamonn is prepared to risk it for the sake of the adrenal charge – and the audience love him for it.'

When Eamonn began to host ITV's late-night show in the previous year, he said, 'There are obvious dangers in doing the show live, but I enjoy them and so do the viewers. Live television is exciting and you have to accept that sometimes things go wrong. My old chat show faced its problems and once had to fade out Lord Boothby when he began talking about marijuana. It should be easier now. There are few subjects you can't talk about on television these days, and there is no kudos now in swearing on TV.'

He denied that he was ever as easily shocked as his critics used to claim. It was part of his professional duty to look shocked on behalf of the viewers. When he was asked about the accusation of 'gentle cosiness', he said, 'There is a danger in kowtowing but it is equally dangerous to be rude. You have to strike a balance. I'm not there to give people a grilling but to have a conversation to bring out whatever is there and to reveal new sides of people.'

It was plain that he was not prepared to change his screen image of 'nice guy'; nor did he believe that viewers now wanted to see an aggressive Eamonn Andrews who was ready to take on rude guests. Whether his gentle style was quite suited to the 1980s was another matter. Some of his detractors believed that it was dated, that Eamonn was more at home with shows like *This Is Your Life*.

Early in 1982 he got another opportunity to show his versatility when he was named presenter of a new international quiz show. *Top of the World* linked contestants in England, America and Australia by satellite. Eamonn said he was happy he did not have to answer the questions his contestants faced over the next thirteen weeks.

'They'll be around University Challenge level,' he explained, 'And while I can play a record of the London Symphony Orchestra, I cannot conduct them – so I don't have to be up to the standard of my contestants.' As one of its attractions, the quiz offered TV's richest prize, a 1924 Rolls-Royce Cabriolet worth more than £60,000.

There was an amusing aside prior to the screening of the first show, when a Fleet Street reporter quizzed Eamonn and found to his surprise that the quiz-master of *Top of the World* was fallible after all. When he asked Eamonn to name the first President of the United States, he was cautiously told 'Grant'.

Despite the hype, the quiz failed to catch the imagination of viewers to any great extent. Generally Eamonn's performance was classed as only 'moderate' and some critics thought he was experiencing difficulty with the world-wide link-up. 'Why does Eamonn have to shout so much?' asked one critic. Thames producer Malcolm Morris disagreed with the critics.

'As director of the show, I found that he handled the satellite link-ups beautifully and was always on cue. He was

Eamonn and Grainne in typically relaxed mood at their idyllic home by the sea near Dublin.

Eamonn purchased numerous art works for his home, 'The Quarry', and visitors came to admire them.

Eamonn and Grainne strolling by the waterfall tumbling from the rocks in their expansive garden.

Eamonn pictured by the swimming pool, which was built for the Andrews' children and designed by architect Sam Stephenson.

Family man Eamonn with Grainne, his mother Margaret, and the children, Fergal, Niamh and Emma.

Eamonn accompanied Grainne to Dublin's Gaiety Theatre for Bernard Shaw's *John Bull's Other Island*. Friends were surprised by his loss of weight.

Book-lover Eamonn was happy spending long hours in his study reading, correcting TV scripts and dealing with his copious correspondence.

Family grief at the graveside was depicted in the faces of Grainne Andrews and her children, Emma, Niamh and Fergal.

Among the many messages of sympathy was one from Paul and Linda McCartney. Paul was a long-time friend of Eamonn's.

The table at which Eamonn worked in his house in Portmarnock. Grainne wants it to remain untouched.

excited by new television technology and wanted to learn more about it. *Top of the World* was an international mastermind kind of show and I believe that Eamonn, as in the case of most things he did, carried off his role as presenter with aplomb.'

It struck Maurice Leonard, a producer on *This Is Your Life*, that Thames were looking around for another show for Eamonn. There had been rumours that it was intended to revive *What's My Line?*, so that in February 1984 he was not surprised when he learned from Philip Jones, Director of Light Entertainment, that the show would be screened in the following months. In announcing the series, Jones had remarked, '*What's My Line?* remains one of the best television panel games ever devised. Eamonn Andrews will be the chairman and the panellists are Eric Morecambe, Jilly Cooper, George Gale and Barbara Kelly. Miss Kelly and Eamonn Andrews both appeared on the first programme transmitted by the BBC in July 1951.'

Although the BBC had revived the show in the seventies without any significant success, Maurice Leonard felt it was worth reviving now. He agreed, though, that Thames were taking a gamble in doing so. It was intended to have a panel of four and a visiting celebrity slot. Leonard recalls, 'I could see that Eamonn was enthusiastic and wanted to get on with rehearsals. He was as painstaking as ever.'

Barbara Kelly was in no way surprised by the news that Thames planned reviving the show. 'I knew of Eamonn's enthusiasm for the show. He had never lost faith in its appeal for viewers.' She was flattered to be invited back on the panel. As she said, 'I was absolutely delighted. I had always enjoyed doing the programme because I was allowed to be myself. But I used to hate acting in the theatre. I'd never wanted to be an actress. I was no good with other people's lines.'

Barbara Kelly is an essentially warm, spontaneous person, straightforward and unpretentious. She married Bernard Braden in her native Canada when she was seventeen. In the early fifties when she was engaged as a panellist on *What's My Line?* she considered the programme fun but hard work. She adored Gilbert Harding on the panel, but she found it was hard to infuriate Eamonn. 'I used to try and pick an argument with him. It was futile – he wouldn't respond.' She recalled that the BBC show was broadcast live and consequently there were hazards.

'I remember one contestant, a portrait artist, had a huge handlebar moustache. After he had beaten the panel I casually asked him, "How do you kiss your wife under that moustache?" Next moment he strode across to our table, grabbed me in his arms and planted a real smacker right on my lips.'

A big talking point for the viewers was the different dangling earrings she wore each week. 'I didn't own any of them,' she says today. 'I used to borrow them from a jeweller the day before the show and return them on the Monday. One week the jeweller received a shock. There was a dear old lady contestant on the show whose job was an error spotter in a printing works. Her employers had promised to give her a pair of earrings as big as mine if she beat the panel. Unfortunately she didn't beat us and I could see she was very disappointed. It seemed natural for me to take off my earrings and give them to her. Next morning I went to the jeweller and paid him for the earrings. They cost one hundred pounds, which was a heck of a lot of money in those days.'

Eamonn had no doubts that *What's My Line?* – once described as the job-guessing panel game – would captivate a new generation of viewers. During its first thirteen-year run from 1951 to 1963 it had, he knew, become a national cult. It was compulsive viewing, attracting a ten million-strong audience, including the Queen Mother and her family. At eight o'clock on Sunday evenings whole families and neighbours gathered round their black-and-white TV sets to watch contestants first mime their unusual occupations and then answer the panel's questions with either yes or no. The show had the added bonus of a mystery celebrity. When this person came on, the panel were blindfolded. The celebrity would also disguise his or her voice.

What surprised Eamonn and the panel was that the game became popular despite the lack of fabulous prizes. The game show winner got just a signed certificate from Eamonn to prove that they had beaten the panel. Once, in an amazing sequel to a show, a contestant was jailed for fifteen months. A bank manager recognised the contestant, who gave his occupation as a frogman in the Orkneys, as the man who had previously been in and persuaded him he had a bank account in the Orkneys. But the sharp-eyed manager noticed the man was giving a different name to the one he had told the bank. Suspicious, he phoned the police. The contestant was questioned after the show. Five months later he was jailed after pleading guilty to obtaining money and a car with worthless cheques.

What's My Line? brought fame not only to Barbara Kelly, Gilbert Harding, Isobel Barnett, and magician David Nixon, but to Eamonn as well. He would say later, 'I've great affection for the show. I've no doubt at all that it launched me on my television career. I think it also made Gilbert Harding famous.'

When Leslie Jackson heard that Thames was reviving the show, he was amused at first. But, as in the case of the revival of *This Is Your Life*, he felt the show would succeed because of Eamonn's tremendous faith in it.

'When I produced the first series for the BBC in the early fifties,' he recalls, 'I had my reservations about Eamonn's ability to chair the programme, but of course he was a big success. Now, here he was back beginning a new series thirty years later. I could hardly believe it. However, I sensed it would be a success.'

The new series would begin on the same February evening as the first Wogan show was screened.

*

The risks involved in mixing business with show-business was at this time brought cruelly home to Eamonn as he watched his £1 million empire collapse in Ireland. He admitted he was embarrassed. He blamed the recession in Ireland and RTE's decision to dispense with sponsored radio programmes, which up to then had been a big source of income to his company. In addition, the burden of paying Value Added Tax had crippled the Gaiety Theatre, which was in urgent need of refurbishment.

By now the burly Fred O'Donovan, one of Eamonn's first business partners in Dublin, had left Eamonn's company after a disagreement over the appointment of impresario Noel Pearson into the company as artistic director. Eamonn would say that their decision was taken due to O'Donovan's ill-health, when a less strenuous role was planned for him. However, he decided to quit and was given a golden handshake of an undisclosed amount that included payment for his shares. These were re-distributed, leaving Eamonn and Dermod Cafferky holding thirty-eight per cent each while Lorcan Bourke had the other twenty-eight per cent.

The departure of Fred O'Donovan was a serious loss. He had been for years the driving force behind the companies, particularly the running of the Gaiety Theatre. Later, the decision to invest in the *MV Arran* proved disastrous. It had been Eamonn's idea to provide Dubliners with a floating nightclub but the time – and place – for the launching of such a project was wrong.

Eamonn flew to Dublin to consult with his partners and to help them provide answers for the receiver. It was reckoned that the companies owed £1 million. Overnight Eamonn's standing as an astute businessman took a tumble. With 200 people made redundant by the collapse he and his co-directors had to face tough criticism. It was clear, however, that it was now too late to save the companies.

Predictably, Eamonn's pride was hurt more than his personal finances, although he stated he had lost 'a substantial

[184]

amount'. He had failed to take the advice of friends who, years before, had advised him to resign as chairman of the companies and hand over to those with more time to run them. He refused. He said he wanted a business link with Dublin.

The collapse of his Irish enterprises was widely publicised in the British press, but in Thames Television no one dared to mention the subject to Eamonn save a few very close friends. To the majority of them, it was a complete surprise; they had long regarded him as the possessor of an outstanding business brain. Now they could only surmise that he hadn't had the time to devote to his companies. Curiously they wanted only to know him as a showman.

Eamonn appeared philosophical and hoped that time would heal the wounds. Nonetheless he found it hard to conceal his embarrassment. To forget the disastrous episode, he plunged into work. He was never the one to ponder for long over past mistakes.

The ratings for *What's My Line?* cheered him no end. He had first suggested to Philip Jones that the programme be revived and now he felt fully vindicated in his own judgment. Yet he hardly expected the reaction he got when at the end of the programme he paid a tribute to comedian Tommy Cooper who had died suddenly the previous Sunday. Eamonn had remarked, 'Good night... and sleep well Tommy Cooper.'

Hundreds of viewers bombarded Thames TV with complaints. They thought Eamonn was trying to be funny over the death on TV of Tommy. Later, he explained, 'It was meant as a sincere tribute. We wanted everyone to know the deep affection with which Tommy was held here. It was simply meant as that... a tribute from me and the panel.' Taking part in the show were comedian Ernie Wise, Patrick Mower, writers George Gale and Jilly Cooper and TV personality Barbara Kelly.

The sinewy Maurice Leonard worked with Eamonn on the show and found him a demanding performer. Usually he sent short biograpahies of the challengers on the programme to Eamonn's address in Chiswick. Soon he discovered that Eamonn liked to work on scripts until right up to the screening of the show.

'When he arrived from Dublin at his flat in Chiswick on Sunday night,' recalls Leonard, 'he would telephone me to discuss the scripts which I would have already mailed to him. If he disliked something, he might remark, "I can't believe what I'm seeing here." Then he'd ask to see me and I'd pop over to the flat.' The ground floor flat intrigued the producer. It was painted in an orange colour and looked spacious. Eamonn's desk was impressive, and conspicuous all around it were pictures of stage and film stars, most of whom he had interviewed in his shows, also cartoons of himself.

Leonard used to joke to Eamonn that he could not get away from him even in the toilet. 'There was this bronze bust of him in the toilet,' he remembers, 'and I'd tell him that his face was everywhere. He enjoyed that. At times he had a good sense of humour.'

It was his job to arrange mystery guests for *What's My Line?*, but he found it hard to please Eamonn. As he explained, 'When I thought I had a nice package for the show worked out and all in order Eamonn would still want to improve on it. This could be hard to take on occasions. It wasn't a question of lack of trust, rather his unending search for perfection. He used to say to me as we worked on the scripts together in Chiswick, "You should never put a show to bed. There is always something to do on a script".'

Working with him on *This Is Your Life* and on *What's My Line?*, Leonard reckoned he got to know Eamonn better than most television producers. 'It was always bigtime with Eamonn. You were conscious you were in a star's presence; and it wasn't only because he smoked Romeo and Juliet cigars. He had this aura of authority about him and one felt he fitted the glamorous world of show-business like a glove. After working on shows with him you needed a holiday afterwards, yet when you were not working on his shows, you missed the excitement.'

The only time he saw Eamonn emotional was when Thames screened his *This Is Your Life* 'I remember he said to me immediately after the show, "It's totally bloody shattering". There was another aspect to him which I know some producers found difficult to take. He withheld praise for fear you rested on your laurels. I suppose there was some logic in that. Eamonn adored his children. I used to welcome Grainne's visits from Dublin, for in her presence he tended to be more mellow. I could see he was very fond of her. Occasionally she sat in the green room and we'd have a word or two about the show. If Eamonn was giving me a hard time she'd dig me in the back, as though to say, "You know what he's like". All the time she kept a poker face. In my time with him he rarely swore before women; if he did, he apologised. In that way he was a perfect gentleman. He could enjoy a drink with us after shows. He was never boring company.'

Eamonn could be sensitive to press criticism, Leonard discovered. He was fond of reading newspapers and if he saw a reference to either *Life* or *Line* he would cut it out. 'If I came across anything in the papers about these shows,' recalls the producer, 'I'd ring him in Dublin to tell him. Whether it was good, bad or indifferent, he wanted to hear about it. If he found out that you withheld something on him he'd complain, "What are you doing by not telling me?" If someone wrote a snide piece about *What's My Line?*, he'd say to me, "What does he mean by that?" I think he could accept criticism but personal criticism tended to hurt him.'

Leonard felt that Eamonn tried to avoid too smooth a working relationship with a producer or programme director. 'The reason for this I felt was that in his view it might be bland and lack a professional edge or sharpness. Once, when I was working with him in Chiswick, Grainne joked, "I'm surprised you two are talking to each other." I think she knew we sometimes had friendly arguments. Eamonn at that moment

[187]

stared at Grainne and said, "What are you talking about, love? Maurice and I have never had a cross word." He meant it. We never really had a cross word over the *Line* series, but that didn't mean that we agreed on everything. We didn't.'

By 1985, Eamonn had got over the embarrassment created by the collapse of his Irish business empire. He was talking to the press and remarked that he was delighted to see the Gaiety Theatre, which was now being leased to a new company, beautifully refurbished. He admitted once more that his long-distance involvement in his Dublin companies had not worked satisfactorily. 'But it's yesterday's story,' he was quick to add.

He preferred to talk about television in general terms. Asked about the escalation of competition between the BBC and ITV, as shown in the recent drama over the purchase of the new series of *Dallas* by Thames TV, which some people had snidely suggested was executed because Thames was determined to prevent the BBC using *Dallas* as a competitor against *This Is Your Life*, thus keeping Eamonn's show out of the list of Top Ten programmes each week, he commented, 'Not true at all. I'm not privy to the secrets of the Boardroom and why they buy things but as I read the *Dallas* situation, *This Is Your Life* has been a thorn in the side of the BBC ever since we brought it back to ITV and it's driven my old friend Bill Cotton mad. It's been up in the Top Ten all the time and I've a hunch that he finally lost his patience this year and put *Dallas* head to head with *Life*, which is strictly pyrrhic battling because it meant *Dallas* could never get into the Top Ten itself and he topped *Life* down, except for two weeks ago when we got back again, against *Dallas*. We were Number Ten and *Dallas* was nowhere. True, it was the Bob Geldof story, but I regard that as irrelevant.'

That Eamonn was keeping a personal interest in the development of television on a global basis was evidenced when he was asked how he saw its future: 'I think there'll be fantastic changes but they're so bewildering that I don't foresee them at all. I just think the whole structure will change. The minute you cease to be able to control the airwaves – the mind boggles! Britain seems to be concentrating on cable television in the literal sense of the word, as opposed to over-air signals. I think it's because they feel there's maybe a better chance of controlling it!'

If satellite and cable programmes did multiply, what did he expect would happen to the viewing habits of those now restricted to BBC, ITV and RTE? Would the 'flagships' like his two programmes retain mass audiences, or would there be a complete fragmentation? Eamonn was frank: 'That's the bit I can't foresee. Obviously one would have to assume the possibility of such fragmentation and that kind of mass audience might not be available, certainly in ITV terms, then neither of my programmes, because they would not be affordable. You may ask if this would mean a flight to the lowest – or more populist – common denominator as in America? Well, public service broadcasting still exists in the United States, but they're always in financial trouble. I did a series that went through there, a one-off called *Top of the World* and they couldn't afford anything comparable. It's mostly sponsors and Foundations.'

Eamonn could be generous in his praise of fellow broadcasters. His admiration for Gay Byrne, the presenter of Ireland's most popular television programme *The Late Late Show* was unstinted. He could not, he said, think of anyone else who could sustain a two hour long programme like the *Late Late* as did Byrne. 'I don't think people realise how difficult it is. It's the very length of it. It would be a very courageous man or woman who'd take over from Gay Byrne – certainly I would not want it.'

Sometimes at weekends Eamonn and Gay enjoyed walks together. Gay made no secret of the fact that he had modelled his own career on Eamonn's. 'He is what I wanted to be when I was twelve years old.' It was by now the summer of 1985, and Eamonn looked well as he sat in the greenhouse, which he called Dig for Victory. He continued with his Sunday ritual of cooking pancakes and having them with syrup for breakfast. If a journalist wanted an interview he met him or her in his study.

When he returned to his old routine that autumn of commuting between Dublin and London, Grainne noticed for the first time the strain in his face. She decided to accompany him henceforth on his weekly trips. Her anxiety grew in subsequent months when he was hospitalised with severe bouts of bronchitis. His energy began to wane a little and he lost some weight. But he battled on. He was marvellous as usual with the children. As Grainne recalled, 'He was always drilling Niamh – telling her she must work to pass her exams.'

When he was advised by his doctor to slow down, he was reluctant to do so. He never wanted to miss a programme and no matter how bad he felt he was on the plane to begin another week of *This Is Your Life* and *What's My Line?* He signed a new contract at Thames Television which guaranteed him a significant increase of £60,000 a year. When he learned that Thames chiefs had given their go-ahead to the taking of *This Is Your Life* to Hollywood he regarded it as the realisation of a personal ambition. For years he had wanted to project the glamour of Hollywood across the *Life* screen.

Even now, producer Maurice Leonard noticed that Eamonn refused to take his programmes for granted. It was really the secret of his success. He approached each programme as though it was his first. He remained unruffled, urbane, and apparently unperturbed by any crisis. Yet he would admit, 'Doing the *Life* show I perspire a great deal, partly due to nerves and partly to the heat of the studio lights.'

Colleagues wondered how long more he could stand the pressure. Friends knew that he was worried about his health. At sixty-four, he appeared for the first time to be self-conscious about his lack of stamina. Maurice Leonard had come to recognise Eamonn as a workaholic who never spared himself. He had helped steer *What's My Line?* back to the sort of success it had enjoyed decades before. Now there were plans for another series.

Leonard was amused by Eamonn's fascination with titled people for the programme. 'He used to say that it was the business of stage and film stars to appear before the cameras, but titled people were different. They were less likely to be interviewed, so by getting them for *Line* they provoked interest. He used to mention the names of titled men and women I should try to get. It wasn't because he looked up to them, rather that they brought a unique freshness to the show. I never saw Eamonn overwhelmed by anyone, however famous. He tended to take them in his stride, mainly because he had interviewed so many legendary stars and notable personalities. Admittedly, he was nervous before both *Life* and *Line*, but this was always the case with him.'

Eamonn occasionally gave up cigarettes, especially for Lent. But Maurice Leonard noticed that with the start of a new *Life* series he was back on them again. When their conversation dried up, he used to switch the subject to boxing and found that Eamonn would talk about it 'until the cows came home'.

As the weeks passed, Eamonn tried to reassure his colleagues that he was feeling well, despite his attacks of bronchitis. Malcolm Morris knew how much he was looking forward to going to Hollywood and surprising stars like Dudley Moore. However, at the same time he was aware of Grainne's worries. She wondered if her husband would be really up to such a punishing schedule.

PART FOUR

The Final Round

Sadness strums our hearts
And lonely notes are playing.

Eamonn Andrews

19 'You're on Your Own'

WITH THE APPROACH of summer 1985 another *This Is Your Life* series was coming to a close, and holidays beckoned. Eamonn Andrews remarked casually to a few of the *Life* team 'D'you know, I'm putting on weight? I'm going to a health farm to work it off.'

Maurice Leonard was not convinced that Eamonn looked 'portly' or out of condition. Because he was tall, he thought some weight suited him. But more than once Eamonn confided that he reckoned he was overweight.

That September, when Maurice met him coming out of the lift in Thames Television in Teddington, he was taken aback. 'He must have lost two or three stones in weight. He looked terribly, terribly thin. I had got used to seeing him around Thames bronzed and handsome. Now his face was drawn and he appeared drained. The loss of weight simply didn't suit Eamonn.'

'I can't believe you've lost so much weight, Guv,' remarked Maurice. 'I presume it's by design?'

'Yes, yes' Eamonn replied with a smile. 'As you know, I've been to a health farm.'

'How do you feel now, Guv?'

Eamonn shrugged his broad shoulders. 'I feel just fine.'

Maurice Leonard later said to a friend, 'I think Eamonn has lost too much weight. I hope there's nothing wrong?' The friend laughed and assured him that 'Eamonn would quickly be back to himself, after a few good dinners'. However, as the weeks passed it was apparent to the *This Is Your Life* team that their star presenter wasn't looking nearly as vigorous as before. At times they were concerned, particularly Maurice Leonard, who worked with Eamonn on *What's My Line?*

As he recalls, 'I could see that his stamina wasn't the same as before; he was tiring easily, yet he never complained. Instead, he worked as hard as always, although I felt it was taking a good deal out of him'.

Working on *What's My Line?* could be demanding. Eamonn made it his business to meet the various contestants beforehand and, as he would say, 'get their measure'; he wanted to find out if any of them were nervous, if so, he would try to put them at their ease; he could be very charming and went out of his way to talk to the mystery celebrities. He was painstaking in his approach and would never accept anything but one hundred per cent from the production team.

Eventually, when Eamonn became aware that some people at Thames were showing concern for him, he tried to reassure them: 'I think a lot of people are frightened that I'm dying. If you lose weight in this business they say you have something bad. It's either cancer or AIDS.'

When he was admitted to a Dublin hospital early in 1987 for tests, it was reported in the newspapers that he had had a mild heart attack. But this was quickly denied and shortly afterwards Eamonn reappeared looking in somewhat better health, though his Irish friends were still anxious about his loss of weight.

He was back again in hospital in the April of that year with an attack of bronchitis. He had suffered for some years from this condition and 'took dozens of pills daily to keep himself alive'. As Grainne would confirm later, 'These pills had unfortunate side effects'.

For years she had tried to get him to slow down. 'All his friends know he was working too hard. But he loved his work and that's what he wanted to do.'

It was accepted that he was a workaholic. For years he had

worked long hours and was said to thrive on it. But now, at sixty-four, the strain, coupled with increasingly poor health, began to leave their mark. Furthermore, travelling backwards and forwards between London and his home in Dublin was taking its toll. Nonetheless, he was determined to carry on. London was where his work was – and he enjoyed it immensely. At the same time he loved catching a plane for Dublin and spending long weekends with Grainne and the children. Or golfing with his friends. Or merely strolling on the expansive beach at Portmarnock.

Sometimes now, after arriving from London, he looked tired and drawn. This worried Grainne. She felt that perhaps it was unwise after all for him to be commuting at his age. 'I saw the strain begin to tell. I felt a little guilty that he had to break his week to be with us. But I knew he liked it this way. He always insisted we made the right decision leaving London.'

Malcolm Morris, a frequent visitor to Eamonn's Portmarnock home, subscribed to the view that Eamonn would not change his weekly schedule for any money. 'I really think he loved this arrangement. He absolutely revelled in the family side, on the one hand in Dublin, and the professional side on the other hand in London. One acted as a stimulus to the other. I also think that he was both a family man as well as a loner secretly – I mean the way he continued to work such long, lonely hours in his flat in Chiswick.'

When Eamonn collapsed on the set of *What's My Line?* he returned to Dublin a little shaken. He was ordered by his doctor to rest. As he admitted, 'My doctor told me to go to bed for ten days but I told him I was booked on a flight to London. He shook his head and replied, "Well, in that case, you're on your own".'

Curiously, he was doing his best to conceal his ill-health. The reasons were not clear. Friends and working colleagues believed it was because Eamonn did not want to give up his commitments, or give any real hint that he was ill, as he

'On Tuesday we normally had lunch and went over some notes relating to a current or future *Life*. Later, I would leave him at the flat to attend to his own personal letters. *Life* viewers constantly wrote to him and he tried to reply to most of them – or his secretary did. In the evening he might visit friends or work alone, or do some small charitable work which he kept totally private and never wanted publicised.

'On Wednesday, Eamonn arrived at Thames about ten o'clock in the morning. He had a private dressing-room where we talked about any likely changes. On the previous evening I would have met the family and relatives of the subject of the *Life* show and certain amendments or deletions might have to be made to the script. A few hours later a timing for the show would be completed. Time was the essence. Since the show was taped live there would be no stop for any further changes.'

In the afternoon Malcolm Morris accompanied Eamonn in a chauffeur-driven car to the pick-up spot. On the way, Eamonn jotted down in green ink the words he would use to surprise the show's subject. Usually the pick-up was done around five o'clock and afterwards they dashed back to the Thames studio to be ready to go on the air at seven o'clock.

One thing was obvious to Morris – how nervous Eamonn always appeared to be – and he assumed the pick-up ordeal continued to take a great deal out of him. Puzzled that this should be so after more than thirty years as presenter of the show, he asked Eamonn, who did not hesitate to reply, 'It's simple. I don't think of myself doing twenty-six *Life* shows. I think only of the show on hand. No show is the same. Each one is different because the subject is a different person, so for me it's a new experience with fresh tensions. I'm never sure that a potential subject will actually agree to accept the red book.'

Malcolm Morris felt that *This Is Your Life* would continue to tax Eamonn's stamina. He soon saw that he was losing weight again and regrettably this was beginning to show up on the screen. His face was drawn and gaunt. Clearly, his loss of weight meant a loss of energy, yet Eamonn was making brave efforts to carry on. Obviously he was determined not to throw in the towel.

Eamonn's associates in Dublin could be said to share Thames chiefs' worries. When he attended the first night revival of Bernard Shaw's play, *John Bull's Other Island* at the Gaiety Theatre, he looked well in his finely tailored blue suit, yet when he took his seat beside Grainne in the front row of the Grand Circle a few friends could not help noticing his loss of weight. When he smiled, the smile was a little wan, and the renowned Andrews jaw, once described as 'lopsided' did not seem as granite-like as before.

In the carpeted corridor, off the main bar of the theatre, he was quietly greeted by his former business partner, Fred O'Donovan. Afterwards, Fred would tell a friend in the bar, 'I think Eamonn should retire now. He doesn't need the money. What he needs is a long rest.' His sentiments would be echoed by numerous old associates of Eamonn's in his native city.

But he didn't give up so easily. Those close to him knew of the stubborn streak in his make-up. In his boxing days he fought to the finish. One wondered now if he was coming to the final round and should retire before the referee stopped the fight. Perhaps Eamonn was remembering what Lord Mountbatten told him when he interviewed him in the late seventies, for when he asked him how long he intended to carry on at his then frenetic pace, the Earl replied, 'Anybody who has worked hard all their lives must never stop but go on working if they want to live, so I intend to go on working. I intend to die before I stop.'

But could Eamonn continue to defy the medical experts? In just one year he had lost nearly two stone as the illness left him a shadow of his former self. The former champion boxer was 6 ft 1in but he dropped to 12½ stone, looking gaunt and drained. Even Grainne, who had hoped and prayed for an improvement, had to admit that her husband was ill. On her advice he had eased up a little on his workrate. They had cut out a lot of socialising and Eamonn was anxious for his wife to start inviting friends to lunch again.

On a more cheerful note, they were planning to celebrate their thrity-sixth wedding anniversary in the sunshine of Lanzarote and both were looking forward tremendously to a break. 'We always went away somewhere for our anniversary,' Grainne said.

During that November weekend Eamonn complained of being unwell. He felt weaker than usual as he worked in his study in Chiswick. For some hours he had attended to his correspondence, writing replies as usual in green ink. Some days before he had been asked by a Dublin newspaperman for quotes for a media piece about leading Irish broadcaster Gay Byrne. As always, Eamonn was cautious about what he wanted to say and took his time. Byrne was, after all, a close friend over many years.

On Monday, 2 November, when the Dublin newsman rang the flat it was Eamonn's housekeeper who told him that he and Grainne had gone out on 'a little emergency'. That afternoon he spoke to Grainne on the telephone. She was cheerful and gave no hint about Eamonn's sudden hospitalisation. When he enquired if Eamonn had forgotten to write his piece for him, Grainne said, 'Oh, he remembered. He has left it here for you'. It read:

Gay Byrne is too original a broadcaster to have modelled himself on me or anyone else. If my presence on the radio scene, and my friendship with his amazing parents, helped shape him in that direction I would be happy to take the full credit for that. He must be one of the best radio broadcasters in the world and it just so happens that he was able to translate into television. I remember I had been Chairman of the RTE Authority for only a couple of weeks when one of the members wanted him off, and they were serious. He was already straying into subjects they felt should have been reserved for the greybeards. He was brash, he was cocky, but he was always clever enough to do his ground work in every detail. He was everything we needed to shake off the smothering blanket of the GPO. I fought my own battles on his behalf on the grounds that I knew more about broadcasting than I really did.

Gay has irritated me as often as my children do, but just as they do, he has charmed and delighted me more often. His biggest task in the next twenty-five years is to avoid becoming one of the Establishment.

It was a revealing tribute and underlined Eamonn's generous spirit towards a fellow broadcaster and his obvious admiration for Byrne for taking on the Irish Establishment when it was unpopular to do so, while at the same time recalling his own days as a young broadcaster in Dublin, when the GPO 'housed' Radio Eireann. Seemingly he had not forgotten those frustrating days.

That afternoon Eamonn had entered Cromwell Hospital for further tests and X-rays. Although Grainne knew that he hadn't been feeling well, she was scarcely prepared for the comment by at least one of the medical staff that in his present condition her husband should not be working. 'He should be in a wheel-chair,' the medico added.

Eamonn remained cheerful. Although Grainne had noticed a deterioration in his health over the previous few days, she was not alarmed. When the news broke that the Thames star presenter was admitted to hospital, a statement was issued by a spokesman who disclosed that Eamonn was being detained for tests. 'We hope he will be out in a few days, but it depends of course on the results of the tests.'

It now seemed certain that the following day's recording of *This Is Your Life* would be cancelled. It had been planned to make it at London's Hilton Hotel where the subject of the programme would be dining.

On Tuesday evening Malcolm Morris visited the hospital and joined Grainne Andrews at Eamonn's bedside. 'We had a glass of champagne together,' he recalls, 'and Eamonn appeared in fairly good spirits. He said he wanted to see a script of the next *Life* series. I tried to persuade him to relax and forget about scripts until later. Looking at him, I thought he was thinner than I had seen him before, yet he was as usual full of plans for the future.'

The medical staff insisted that Eamonn stay in hospital for some days. On Wednesday Grainne visited the hospital again and had a conversation with her husband. 'He said he expected to be discharged in a few days and he hoped we would be able to go on holiday together. He also asked me to bring in some scripts of *This Is Your Life*.'

They drank a glass of champagne and Eamonn was able to sit up in bed to watch *This Is Your Life*. He smiled as the cameras showed him surprising comedian Jimmy Cricket, the subject of the show. At 8.30 Grainne rose and kissed him on the cheek. As he returned the kiss on her cheek, he whispered, 'See you in the morning, darling.'

She returned to their flat in Chiswick feeling that Eamonn, though ill, was not in danger of death. On reflection, she remembered that in the past few years Eamonn had discussed death. 'He often said to me he wasn't afraid of dying. I told him I'd prefer to go first.'

It had been a trying day and she decided to retire early to bed. However, she was abruptly awakened after 2 a.m. by a phone call from the hospital. 'They said they were coming to collect me,' Grainne recalls. 'When they got here I asked them if Eamonn was dead – and they said yes.'

She arrived in a daze at the hospital. 'Your husband died peacefully in his sleep,' she was told. Grainne was in one sense relieved, for Eamonn had not known he was going to die. He had suffered no pain. Later, the cause of death was given as 'progressive deterioration of the muscle of the heart, a common enough disorder'.

Grainne, meanwhile, sent for her children to join her in London. She phoned Malcolm Morris with the news and he

told her he would come round as quickly as possible. Already
the news of his unexpected death was being flashed around the
world.

20　'Part of My Life'

IT WAS NEARLY three o'clock on Thursday morning, 5 November, when Malcolm Morris arrived at Cromwell Hospital. As he comforted Grainne Andrews, he was himself suddenly overwhelmed by a sense of shock and disbelief. It took a long time for the truth to sink in. He told himself that Eamonn had died in a dignified way and for a man who had devoted so much of his life to his profession, it was nice for him to go out while he was still at the top of that profession.

'I will miss Eamonn,' he told Grainne, 'but as far as I'm concerned he will always be part of my life anyway.'

He knew there were people who thought that Eamonn should have given up when he became ill, but he wasn't that kind of man. Eamonn was inspired by a fierce determination and was determined to carry on into the last round. *This Is Your Life* was the programme dearest to him and Morris privately felt that giving it up would perhaps have made Eamonn unliveable with because he would have been an extremely unhappy man.

Leslie Jackson was awakened at his home in Ealing by the jangle of the telephone by his bedside. Rubbing the sleep from his eyes, he looked at his watch: it was 6.45, and when he answered the call, it was the BBC on the line.

'Leslie Jackson?' a girl's voice enquired urgently.

'That's me,' he replied, puzzled.

'I'm told you worked with Eamonn Andrews?'

He smiled to himself.

'Of course I did... work with... Eamonn Andrews.'

A slight pause.

'Did you know that he died last night?'

'I'm sorry... I hadn't heard,' said Jackson, letting the news sink in slowly.

'Can you come over to the Television Centre to do a tribute?'

'I'd be delighted to. Can you send round a taxi, please?'

'Of course.'

They wanted him to go on breakfast television to talk to presenter Frank Bough. As he now shaved, he tried to collect his thoughts. It had been a shock to learn of Eamonn's death so early in the morning. He made himself a quick cup of tea and remembered that he had first set eyes on Eamonn in the St Andrew's Boxing Club in Dublin. It was so long ago he had almost forgotten.

After Eamonn left the BBC for ATV they lost touch for a while, but later he used to phone him at Chiswick about other matters, and he knew Eamonn's producer, Malcolm Morris. In recent months he had begun again to watch *This Is Your Life* and suspected that Eamonn was ill. Watching the strain in his face saddened Leslie Jackson, and he wondered how much longer he could continue with the show. The only reason he could think of was that Eamonn, with his boxer's instincts, was refusing to give up. He was saying to himself, 'I'll go the next round.'

To Jackson, it appeared an unwise attitude because some viewers were already commenting on Eamonn's gaunt appearance on the screen. Strain was something difficult to disguise, he knew, and soon Eamonn would have to face up to the reality. Some months before he had telephoned Malcolm Morris about an idea for *Life*. Morris had suggested that he offer the idea to Eamonn. 'Why don't you discuss with him what you have in mind? He's coming over from Dublin to start a new *Life* series soon.'

Jackson said, 'What's he coming back for?'

'To do another twenty-six shows.'

'He must be mad.'

He knew of Eamonn's obsessional interest in *This Is Your Life*, something he had first detected way back in the fifties at the BBC. It now seemed though that the show had become so much part of him that he couldn't live without it.

That morning, on the TV breakfast show, Leslie Jackson found he was calmer and less emotional than he ought to be, as though he had in some strange way been prepared for Eamonn's unexpected death. Allthough it had come as a shock to him, he wasn't in another way surprised. As he would explain, 'I knew he was pushing himself too hard and that the strain would inevitably kill him in the end. There is a time for quitting. Every boxer knows that.'

Bandleader Joe Loss was in bed that morning when he heard the news on radio. He was shattered. Although he knew that Eamonn had been ill during the past few months the thought of him dying at the age of sixty-four never once occurred to him. For a few moments he lay back too stunned to speak. Momentarily he awakened his wife, Mildred, who was sleeping beside him, and broke the news gently to her. She looked at him in disbelief.

Joe lifted himself out of bed and donned his dressing gown. He immediately telephoned Grainne Andrews at Chiswick. When she came to the phone, he expressed his sympathy and uttered a few words about Eamonn but at that moment he knew words alone could not convey all his feelings.

To Mildred Loss, Eamonn's death was like losing a brother. Since she first met him at the Theatre Royal in Dublin in the late forties, she had found his charm irresistible and his sincerity genuine. Over the years he had meant a lot to Joe and her. Now it seemed unbelievable that he would not call them again nor greet them with that warm, characteristic smile of his.

Though it was only a few minutes past eight o'clock, Joe Loss did not think of going back to bed. Over tea, he and

Mildred talked quietly about Eamonn and how for the past forty years he had been part of the British nation and innumerable families. To Joe, a veteran bandleader, it was an astonishing record. The nation would mourn his passing.

He rose and went into the adjacent room and returned presently with a locker full of letters which Eamonn had written to him since the fifties. Many of them were short, no more than notes, yet Joe could hardly comprehend how Eamonn had found the time and patience to write them. He looked across at Mildred, and said, 'I'm going to keep them. They are precious to me. I'll put them with the rest of my correspondence pack.'

Mildred picked out a few letters and notes. They were written in Eamonn's neat handwriting and green ink. A few evoked nostalgic memories. 'D'you know, Joe,' she remarked, 'Eamonn never changed in all the years we knew him. I can't think of a cross word to say about him.'

Joe was once asked why their friendship had endured. His answer was always the same: 'I'm fifty-seven years in the music business and count myself a good judge of character. What was Eamonn? He wasn't a comedian or a singer or an actor, he was a professional who worked hard to be a success. He never did things with disregard for others; he was a gentleman as well as a gentle man'.

Frankie Vaughan was in Hong Kong when he heard the news of Eamonn's death. He was instantly saddened. He always maintained that anyone who had been surprised by Eamonn for *This Is Your Life* had a special affection for him.

He could not see any performer taking his place. Eamonn's style was unique and he brought to the show an extra dimension. He would be a grave loss to Thames. Like his wife Stella, who was with him in Hong Kong, he had hoped that Eamonn would pull through his illness. Now he would be missed. He had long regarded him as 'a nice man, a man one could trust'. Frankie felt he knew him as well as anyone else in the entertainment business. There was the loner side to him and that he understood, for he, like Eamonn, did his own thing.

Terry Yarwood was in bed when colleague Brian Klein called him to break the news. It was five in the morning and he listened in silence as Klein mentioned a few details. To Yarwood, who had been close to Eamonn, first on the Thames TV programme *Today*, and later on *This Is Your Life*, his death now at the age of sixty-four seemed unreal and unwarranted. They had already been looking forward together to many more *Life* series.

With his head on the pillow, he remembered little things that might otherwise have escaped him in more normal circumstances. One was that Eamonn, despite his obvious pain, seldom if ever complained or looked for sympathy. There was the single occasion, though, a few weeks before in Manchester, when they were visiting the Granada Television studios, that he had noticed how tired Eamonn looked. He was seated in the dressing room and suddenly, and with a faint smile, took his hand and said, 'Terry, we've been together for a long time. I hope we can go on working together.' Yarwood had been taken by surprise, for Eamonn was never the one to betray emotion if he could help it. Now he seemed to be relying on his friends to support him, as though he needed them desperately. He looked more exhausted than he had ever seen him during their years together.

They had been happy years. Eamonn valued loyalty above all else and knew he could always depend on the *Life* team. Terry Yarwood's own most unforgettable moment – and he remembered it vividly now – was when he told Eamonn at the programme conference, 'I think we can go ahead with the *Life* of Lord Mountbatten.'

Barbara Kelly, who had first made Eamonn Andrews' acquaintance when she was chosen as a panellist on *What's My Line?* in the early fifties, was at home when she heard the news of his death. She received it with a sense of 'great shock and

[210]

utter disbelief'.

For years she had regarded him as a glamour personality and a television presenter with great charisma. It saddened her deeply when she first heard of his illness, and seeing him in more recent *Life* programmes confirmed her fears. Working with him on *What's My Line?* had always been fun. Eamonn handled the most difficult people with a mixture of charm and firmness, never rudeness. Thames' decision to drop the programme had not surprised her. It was obvious that it was taking a lot out of Eamonn and he was not really up to it at the end. Nonetheless, she admired his courage. As host he was, in her view, irreplaceable. The programme would not be the same with someone else in the chair.

In the sixties she had been surprised by Eamonn when he presented her with the famous red book. Barbara Kelly recalls that she 'sobbed through the entire programme'. At the same time, she found *Life* an unique experience. She would remember Eamonn with love, 'simply with love'. As far as she was concerned, he combined integrity and humour, loyalty and fair play.

Brian Tesler, of London Weekend Television, was at home when he first heard the news. 'My wife and I were sitting down to breakfast when the phone rang. It was Philip Jones, Head of Light Entertainment at Thames, who was on the line, and he told me sadly of Eamonn's death. I couldn't believe it. Only two weeks before I had talked to him at a reception and although he looked thin and somewhat drawn, he was in good spirits. We shared an interest in American crime fiction and I remember we got talking about some new novels. He told me he and Grainne were planning a holiday abroad. Normally we sent each other postcards when on holidays. I don't ever remember Eamonn complaining about ill-health, except maybe once when he talked about a bug he had picked up and how it had affected his chest. My immediate feeling after hearing of his death was "What a waste at such an age," and my second was concern for Grainne and the children. How would they cope without him? Over breakfast, Audrey and I began to remember things in our life regarding Eamonn, little events that spanned many years.'

Lady Ryder of Warsaw was at her Foundation headquarters in the Suffolk village of Cavendish when she heard the news on the radio. Even she, who had lived with death in the war years, was instantly saddened by the realisation that Eamonn had passed away. Although she had met him only on a few occasions, he had made an impression on her. 'He was such a sincere man, you see. He wanted to help the Foundation in any way he could, but as I said before I really didn't want to bother him. His life was a hectic one. I used to watch *This Is Your Life* and continued to admire the way he presented the programme. I could not imagine anyone else do it.'

To Henry Cooper, the news of Eamonn's death came as a shock. He was attending to company business in Hendon when a colleague said to him, 'Henry, did you hear that Eamonn Andrews died last night?' Immediately he recalled how well Eamonn had looked at his son's wedding months before. Admittedly, he hadn't looked well on television in more recent weeks, but Henry attributed this to Eamonn's dieting.

'I didn't dream there was anything seriously wrong with him,' he recalls. 'I told myself that boxing had lost a sincere friend with Eamonn's death, and the best radio commentator it ever had.'

Bill Nolan is today Director General of the Olympic Council of Ireland. Although he rarely, if ever, met Eamonn Andrews after the 1970s, he still continued to look at *This Is Your Life* and marvelled at the durability of Eamonn as presenter. As he recalled, 'Since I scripted many *Life* shows I know everything about the programme's format, yet I found myself watching it. It is exciting television – that was the reason.'

Bill was at home when he heard the news of Eamonn's passing. The previous evening he had watched *This Is Your*

Life and though he thought Eamonn's face looked drawn he never reckoned he was so near death. Now, as he sat in an armchair, he cried. 'The reason I cried,' he says, 'was because Eamonn had always remained the most admirable of men. He never got involved in the murky side of television. He was a monument to how to get to the top in television – and stay there.'

To Bill Nolan, Eamonn was a BBC man. 'He loved radio and nothing gave him more pleasure than presenting *Sports Report* on Saturdays. Nothing compensated him for the loss of that.'

That morning when James Gilbert, Head of Comedy at Thames, was told the news by his colleagues he knew that they had lost a legendary figure. A few weeks before, when he had met him, they had talked briefly and he remembered Eamonn saying, 'Why Jim, we've been working here for years and have never dined together. Let's fix a date for dinner.' Gilbert knew that Eamonn was enormously dedicated to *This Is Your Life*, and was by now totally identified with the show. Despite his fame, he found the star presenter self-effacing and rather modest. He had a passion for *Life* and this was accepted in Thames. He brought to it a tremendous degree of integrity.

Everywhere in Thames that morning James Gilbert found an almost stunned silence, a place in a state of shock. As he explained to a friend, 'Why not? Eamonn was truly popular here, an institution'.

Maurice Leonard was on holidays in the Canary Islands when he heard the news. 'I remember it was Thursday morning and my telephone rang. It was the office calling me to tell me about Eamonn. They didn't want me to read first about his death. I'll never forget the impact on me. For a few moments I was distraught, as though a close relative had died unexpectedly. It was only at that moment that I realised how much I cared about Eamonn. Admittedly he could be tetchy as well as charming, yet at the end of the day you forgave him and you wanted to go on working with him. He was that kind of man.'

[213]

To ease the pain, Leonard knocked back two brandies and decided to walk the beach alone in the hot sunshine. Occasionally he stopped in his tracks, stared out to sea and let memories of Eamonn flood back. For a long time he had considered him unique, totally different from anyone else he worked with in television. Eamonn's work methods were often different. A few weeks before he himself had been asked to assist on the *Life* programme of conductor Georg Solti. Later, at the playback, he found to his surprise that Eamonn was sitting down, which was rare for him; normally he liked to be one of the party.

To Leonard, Eamonn looked very tired and dispirited. Going over to him, he asked, 'How are you doing, Guv?'

'I'm fine, I'm fine,' said Eamonn, trying to look cheerful.

'You look a little tired. Are you alright, Guv?'

'I'm feeling okay. Don't worry about me.'

'As you say, Guv.'

Leonard wondered at that moment whether after all *This Is Your Life* was proving too taxing for Eamonn. He no longer seemed the restless and energetic presenter who strove for perfection and expected the team to give every ounce. This first became apparent to him during the recording of *What's My Line?* He recalled Eamonn saying to him, 'I am not well. What is the latest possible time I can be at the studios?'

It was obvious to him then that the double workload of *Line* and *Life* was proving too much for Eamonn, yet he managed to complete the series. Like everyone else at Thames, Maurice Leonard admired Eamonn's brave efforts to carry on but it was putting a great strain on him.

After a telephone call from the BBC, Lynn Doonican rushed upstairs to wake her husband Val, who had been asleep. He had gone to bed very late the previous night.

'I'm sorry to wake you, love,' Lynn said, 'but there's been a phone call from the BBC... Eamonn has died.'

Val stared at his wife in disbelief.

[214]

'What . . .? I don't believe it!'

Lynn said, 'They want a quick word on the phone with you. Frank Bough will speak to you.'

Val lifted the receiver beside the bed and waited for Frank's voice.

'How long have you known Eamonn?'

In a tired voice, Val recounted their first meeting in Dublin in the late forties and how their show business paths had crossed on numerous occasions in Britain. After a pause, he told Frank, 'As far as the Irish contingent of show-business in Britain is concerned we have definitely lost our general now. That is my honest opinion. He's gone. Eamonn blazed the trail for us. He was the pacemaker, a gentleman and so respected in the business.'

For a long time afterwards Val could not believe Eamonn was dead. Like everyone else, he had known he wasn't looking well and that *What's My Line?* had been cancelled, but no one seemed to know for sure what was really wrong. His own admiration for Eamonn stemmed from the way he ran his career. Everyone agreed he ran it brilliantly. He seldom, if ever, took the wrong options. On a more personal note, he avoided scandals and gossip. To Val, he had never changed in forty years – 'absolutely never'. A year before when he himself was topping the bill at a Dublin theatre he got a call from Eamonn inviting him to join him in a round of golf next morning.

'There he was on the phone, the same Eamonn,' recalls Val. 'I had been introduced to his daughter in an hotel and Eamonn heard about it. I remember he planned to have a car pick me up, but unfortunately I contracted severe laryngitis and had to cancel it. He was so disappointed. That was Eamonn.'

Terry Wogan was asleep in his secluded house in Buckinghamshire when he was awakened by his wife, Helen. It was nearly eight o'clock in the morning.

'What is it, darling?' he asked wearily.

Helen said, 'Radio 4 wants to talk to you.'

Terry listened in silence as he was told the news of Eamonn Andrews' death. He wasn't expecting it, although he had suspected he was seriously ill. Later, Thames Television telephoned to say they wanted him to present the special tribute to Eamonn. 'We have cleared it with the BBC,' said a spokesman.

Terry made no secret of the fact that he and Eamonn were never close friends. Despite the age gap between them – fourteen years – they were very different personalities: Wogan, outgoing and loquacious; Eamonn, shy and possessing an uncharacteristic Irish reserve. Nonetheless, Terry was the first to acknowledge Eamonn's considerable achievements as a broadcaster.

'I admired him because he broke the ice for people like myself to try our luck in radio and television in Britain. He made the Irish voice acceptable; for years he had been doing programmes that commanded top ratings. I've been doing the same thing for only eighteen years, but that hardly compares with Eamonn's record, which in my view will never be broken – certainly not by me. True, there was only the BBC when he first made it in British broadcasting, but that hadn't made it any the easier, for everyone was trying their utmost to compete for top place.'

To Terry Wogan, Eamonn brought to his professional work the qualities of dignity, decency and good humour, not forgetting humanity. These were the reasons for his continued success. Nor was he ever artificial – you saw what you got. People tended, he knew, to compare them as performers, but Terry would go to pains to explain, 'We were entirely different. Eamonn was brought up in the tradition of radio scripts; I disliked them. In my breakfast radio programme for the BBC I was encouraged to ad lib. In my television programmes I try to make them look spontaneous. Eamonn was able to handle scripts – he liked that kind of approach. I consider that both Eamonn and myself were lucky because we got the programmes that suited our talents. Eamonn went on

[216]

to excel in *What's My Line?* and *This Is Your Life*. I think that if I had been around the BBC in those days I would not have achieved as much as Eamonn achieved, or succeeded in the same way that he did. I am a less disciplined person, for one thing, and I don't want to work off a script. In a way his approach was tougher than mine is today.'

That Thursday afternoon, when Terry arrived at Thames Television, he found the place 'shell shocked'. It was understandable, he knew, for Eamonn Andrews was regarded as a legend by his colleagues. He got down to work quickly preparing the programme's script. Thames chiefs, he was told, wanted 'a decent tribute' to their most outstanding broadcaster. Terry reckoned he could give them that.

He was in sympathy with the subject.

One newspaper headline that day summed up the whole story: EAMONN – THIS WAS YOUR LIFE. Tributes poured in for the legendary broadcaster and the world of broadcasting itself was in mourning. The host of *This Is Your Life* and *What's My Line?* was universally popular, though it was probably true to say that he had been unaware how popular he really was with his colleagues – and with television viewers.

People responded in the previous weeks to the fighter in Eamonn, and to the fact that, in boxing parlance, he bravely 'went the distance'. Jimmy Savile, whom Eamonn had once surprised on *This Is Your Life*, echoed the sentiments of many when he said, 'Eamonn was one of the nicest guys in show-business'. Hughie Green, as others would inevitably do, recalled his own experience on the *Life* programme: 'It came within an ace of disaster because I didn't recognise him at first and – well, let's just say we had to put a few bleeps in the sound track'.

Comic Roy Kinnear was more perceptive than most because he realised the nerve-racking ordeal Eamonn went through when he sprung a surprise with his big red book.

Eamonn once told him that he had nothing to eat for a day before the show went on air. Roy said, 'He told me he was so nervous that he probably wouldn't bother with a snack the next day. It must have taken so much out of him. Now he is gone and no one will be able to replace him.'

Irish comedian Jimmy Cricket, who was the last celebrity 'target' on *This Is Your Life*, considered Eamonn 'a good Irish ambassador and yet he was just like the man next door'. Showbusiness legend Max Bygraves had lunch with Eamonn and Tommy Cooper just days before funnyman Cooper died. Max said, 'It's ironic now but Eamonn looked at us and joked, "We must be the three most impersonated men in Britain. When we go half the acts in the country will be finished."'

Bob Hope had become friendly with Eamonn over a number of years and liked his sense of humour. 'We were always kidding each other. In fact he still has some of my money since we played golf last time and I was hoping to get it back from him soon, but I suppose I never will now. Seriously, though, I'll miss Eamonn. We had great fun together, the two of us.'

The Times, in a lengthy obituary notice, made the important point:

It was possible to watch Eamonn Andrews carefully for a long time without noticing the professional skill with which he worked, guiding a conversation, drawing none of the limelight to himself. It is not to do him justice simply to say that he had 'the gift of the gab'; what he did was to imbue his guests with a confidence which allowed them to shine through. In this he showed an unobtrusive professionalism which seemed to belong to his character and to the world of television, so that it would be entirely meaningless in any other world.

The remarkable affection which television viewers felt for Eamonn Andrews was based however, not only on the skill of his work. It grew, too, from his genuine interest in, and friendliness for, people. These qualities made it easy for his audience to identify with him and to feel that he had taken them with him to meet and share the world of gorgeous actresses, brilliant comedians and cheerfully ebullient politicians.

If, in his native land, Eamonn was on occasions taken somewhat for granted because his face seemed to be on television screens for ages; or, if he was reckoned by some begrudgers to be more businessman than showman, his death now reminded old and young generations of Irish people how versatile a talent he had possessed. Not only was he a brilliant boxing commentator but a most effective host of *This Is Your Life* and *What's My Line?*

Irish broadcaster John Skehan saw Eamonn's success in psychological terms: 'It was important to all of us in broadcasting in Ireland. There was a feeling of reflected glory. A feeling, too, that if Eamonn could do it, so could others. He gave us a pride in our standards, a first realisation that we were as good as the next. When he sprang to the top of the ladder, we all felt we had a foot on a rung'.

Eamonn had the sharp eye of the born journalist, which as we know he once wanted to be in Fleet Street. Returning to Dublin after his work for Thames Television, he would sometimes ask a close show-business friend whom he could trust, 'Is there any likely subject around for *This Is Your Life?*' He was ever on the lookout.

Over the years he had presented the red book to Irish subjects such as Stephen Behan, rugby star Bill McBride, actor Noel Purcell, Terry Wogan, and Bob Geldof. Surprising 'one of his own' gave him special pleasure. He loved doing unknown people whenever he could. This afforded him special satisfaction. One thing tended to puzzle Eamonn – he was never sure of the extent of his popularity in Ireland. In Britain, he knew it was considerable. Years ago an Irish journalist accompanied Eamonn to a Butlin's Holiday Camp some miles from Dublin and saw the true popularity of the broadcaster; 'Eamonn drove me to the camp on a Sunday in his Ford Thunderbird. At the time he had become a director of Butlin's Holidays and was taking a look at his Mosney property. He hadn't reckoned on the camp being crammed with English holiday-makers who recognised him instantly. With Lorcan Bourke, his father-in-law, we made a beeline from the bar to the Thunderbird. The campers pursued us, hammering on the car windows and scrawling their names in lipstick on the white roof. That was indeed celebrity status – even the Irish onlookers had to admit.'

By now the Andrews children, Niamh, Fergal and Emma, had arrived at the flat in Chiswick where they had a tearful reunion with their mother. Being close to Eamonn, it was a deeply distressing moment for all three. In the corner of the sitting room stood two cases. As Grainne would say later, 'Although I had packed them for our wedding anniversary in Lanzarote two days previously, I think I knew we wouldn't be going away. I hated the job of unpacking them.'

Instead, Grainne and the children would accompany Eamonn's remains by plane back to Dublin for burial.

21 *The Homecoming*

IT WAS A quiet homecoming for Eamonn Andrews on that bleak November evening in 1987.

Heavy fog had delayed the flight into Dublin airport for more than half an hour. The waiting party of close relations and friends were allowed to make their way across the tarmac to greet Mrs Andrews and her children. There was an emotional scene when Noel Andrews, Eamonn's brother, stepped forward to embrace Grainne and then Emma, Niamh and Fergal. They were then taken through the VIP lounge.

It was the final air trip for Eamonn, who for twenty-five years had slipped unobtrusively in and out of Dublin. He had become popular with the airport staff, who liked to greet him with a smile, or a simple 'Hello, Eamonn'.

Now his remains were taken from the Aer Lingus jet to a funeral parlour in the city's northside where they would remain over the weekend. Because of the flight's delay, there was no service at the funeral parlour and the family was immediately taken to their home in Portmarnock by a waiting car.

Suddenly, a Dublin that wasn't prepared for Eamonn's death was now getting ready to give him a traditional farewell. It promised to be the biggest show-business funeral since Brendan Behan's – and that 'theatrical event' was still being talked about twenty years afterwards by Dubliners. For on that chill March morning, Behan's people, consisting of women with bags, publicans, writers, taxi-drivers, actors, boxers, bookies and whores, had lined the city's streets in mourning as they watched the cortege make its way slowly to Glasnevin cemetery.

Eamonn's funeral would be a shade more dignified, though no less colourful. Unlike Eamonn, Brendan Behan laughed in the face of death. Once he told his wife, Beatrice, 'I'd love to see my own funeral. It's a pity I won't be there.'

Eamonn, who avoided the subject where possible, nonetheless regarded Brendan as a writer of talent and a Dublin man with a big heart. He had enjoyed *The Hostage* when it was the rage of London.

Micheal MacLiammoir had called Dublin 'a city of derision'. But in Dubliners' eyes, death is a great leveller – and an occasion for forgiving. Even those workers who had lost jobs after the collapse of the Andrews empire would in all probability attend the final ritual and see it as the event it was – the death of Ireland's greatest broadcaster. That he was a businessman – and a failed one in Irish eyes – did not now seem to matter any more. They were prepared, like the British people, to regard Eamonn as the supreme showman and superstar.

The Irish media, like its counterpart in the UK, gave Eamonn's passing blanket coverage. They concentrated for the most part on his virtues, particularly as a family man. And on radio Gay Byrne told his listeners he was 'just too sad' that day to bring himself to present an item on Eamonn's death. Listeners had been ringing up to ask why he had made no mention of the event and he explained, 'I'm just too sad to bring myself to do it. Maybe tomorrow I'll be in better form'.

In the country's biggest daily newspaper the *Irish Independent* columnist Desmond Rushe echoed what many Irish thought of Eamonn:

He was a supremely polished professional who knew his job and did his homework. He looked well – a big, handsome, well-built man to whom smiles and laughter came with

[222]

natural ease, and he had an inbuilt dignity. He was intelligent, and he had a winning sense of humour. He had a softly reassuring voice which he could use with formidable articulateness.

But, above all, there was a great depth to his humanity. His charm was not skin-deep; his sincerity was not a mask. On stage and off, he was a warm and immensely likeable human being. He had a markedly sympathetic personality and, no matter what his medium, he displayed a remarkable capacity to establish a meaningful rapport.

But how well had the ordinary man known the star broadcaster? It is true to say that to the majority he was but a face on the box, for in Dublin he lived a very private life, as though he deliberately wanted to shun the limelight. However, *This Is Your Life* had continued to attract thousands of viewers and as long as that was so his popularity and status remained unblemished. In Irish eyes, it was a feather in his cap that he and the family had decided to make Dublin their home, when other Irish stars had decided otherwise.

Veteran evening paper journalist John Finegan, who had once seen Eamonn carry props for his own theatrical production across the Dublin streets to the little Peacock Theatre, recalled now that when he first knew him he was working in an insurance company. 'We both then lived in the same area, Dolphin's Barn, and frequently caught the same unauthorised single-decker bus at 9.20 each morning (that "pirate" bus, taking short cuts through the "Tentars" was much faster than the trams).' According to Finegan, 'Fame meant little to Eamonn; he was, as a star of television, the same outgoing, friendly person he had known on the "pirate" bus in the 1930s.'

Typical of the times, the British media was already speculating as to who might take over from Eamonn as presenter of *This Is Your Life*. Star names were mentioned, even Terry Wogan's and Henry Kelly's – but somehow in

Dublin the exercise seemed not only irrelevant but almost irreverent, since the burial was still to come.

First, the remains were brought on that grey November evening to Eamonn's old parish church in Portmarnock, where he had often read the Lessons during Sunday Mass. Politicians, actors, journalists, boxers, nuns, television personalities and the ordinary folk of the area packed the church. To the local people, Eamonn's death had come as a shock, despite their remarking among themselves in recent months on his loss of weight. Yet he invariably contrived to be friendly and cheerful. Sometimes they recognised his tall figure as he strode the nearby seashore, or glimpsed him at the wheel of his Mercedes as he drove past. They regarded him as an integral part of the district, although few had ever seen inside his 'big house'.

To the media, Eamonn's death remained *the* story. Television bulbs flashed outside and inside the church, picking out leading politicians, churchmen and show-business stars. Gay Byrne, in a brief tribute, remarked to a young reporter: 'Eamonn really set the pace for all of us in the business, both in England and in Ireland. He was what I wanted to be when I was twelve years old. It is very sad.'

The priest's words, though, seemed to sum up the feelings of most of the congregation: 'He was a friend of many but an entertainer of millions.'

There to hear the tributes, was Mrs Andrews and her children. It was by now four days since Eamonn had died unexpectedly and the strain tended to show in Grainne's sad expression, though it was obvious to those who knew her that her children were an enormous source of strength to her.

Next morning, Wednesday, 10 November, was bright with a fresh wind blowing in from the sea. Soon the church would be filled for the Requiem Mass, attracting once more scores of celebrities. Already the floral tributes had arrived from Terry Wogan, Bob Monkhouse, Jimmy Tarbuck, Mike Yarwood and Alex Higgins, whose wreath read, 'Fond Remembrance'.

[224]

The wreath from Paul and Linda McCartney was of carnations and fresias shaped into a Celtic cross, and worded, 'With deepest regret'.

For some people in the congregation it was difficult to accept that Eamonn, who had been for so many years preoccupied with his *Life* programme, was now gone. Or as the bishop put it a moment later, 'It is very hard to really believe that Eamonn, who seemed larger than life, has been taken from us.'

In a way there was a slight hint of unreality about the occasion, as if at any moment Eamonn, red book clutched firmly under his elbow, might descend on someone and utter the immortal words, 'This is your life...'. Brendan Behan would have loved the sense of occasion about the ceremony, the genuine grief. His had been a city funeral, Eamonn's was beside the sea, some miles from the city. But from all sides they had come that morning for the final ritual.

Eamonn's people in a way were only a little different from Brendan's, and Eamonn, who never recognised class distinctions, would have been the first to agree. Apart from holidays abroad with Grainne, his had been an ordinary lifestyle, and that was the way he liked it.

At the ceremony that morning were many journalists who had known Eamonn for years. As one newspaper would put it, 'Half of what used to be Fleet Street was at the funeral to record the final act of a successful life which had brought him fame and family love.'

Grainne Andrews was accompanied by her children and the chief mourners were Noel Andrews and Eamonn's sister, Mrs Treasa Durkan. There was a moving moment as Fergal Andrews read the first reading during the Mass and his daughter Emma read the second. Niamh, his second daughter, read one of the prayers of the faithful.

Once more the Andrews listened silently to tributes: Eamonn would be remembered as a very gifted broadcaster and television presenter over many years, as a fine ambassador for Ireland, and as a man who was proud of his native city of Dublin and brought credit to it.

That morning the hearse stopped for two minutes near the Andrews' home, a custom that belongs to older and simpler times. It was fitting, for this was the house he loved, it was a monument to his life's work, and the shelves of his study reflected his interest in broadcasting as well as boxing. It was, as he never tired of telling friends, his only real luxury. After the sweat of the television recording studios, it was heaven. His dream house.

He liked to retail the story how he once caught a young Dublin chisler of four burrowing through the fence in the garden. He admonished him for doing damage to the fence and advised him in future to use the gate if he ever wanted to visit the house. Fifteen minutes later the boy was back – through the gate – requesting an interview with Eamonn. He got it.

A few miles away Eamonn would be buried. Autumn provided him with a striking backdrop against which to make that final exit. It was an afternoon of blue skies and bright sunlight that burnished the copper leaves falling in nearby lanes in the old hillside graveyard. Birds sang as a bishop intoned the farewell.

Missing among the onlookers gathered round the grave was a number of the 'London brigade' they were expected to attend the memorial Mass in Westminster Cathedral. Joe Loss and his wife Mildred had intended to come to Dublin for the funeral but, as Joe would say, 'A last minute hitch meant I had to cancel arrangements.'

After the burial, relatives and friends returned to the Andrews home in Portmarnock. Leslie Jackson, the man Eamonn called Jacko, joined them. As he watched people line up awaiting their turn to sympathise with Grainne, he suddenly thought how alone she appeared in the big house.

'She stood there, dressed in black, listening to the same words from everyone. I felt for her – and admired her courage. How she would miss Eamonn! From the first time I had met

[226]

them together, I knew theirs was a great love. Afterwards, I saw it when Grainne became ill and Eamonn worried himself sick about her. Now I could hardly bring myself to go up to her.'

22   'A True Ambassador'

'MAYBE EAMONN WOULD have been embarrassed by the sheer splendour of the tribute.'

Val Doonican expressed the view lightly after the memorial Mass in Westminster Cathedral, which was attended on that December morning by 2,000 people.

To Val, who had become accustomed to show-business spectaculars, it was like a big, Royal occasion, awesome in its dimension and beauty. 'I've never been so impressed by anything in my life. It seemed everyone in television was there. I did not realise that Eamonn was held in such universal esteem.'

Earlier, he had been asked by the memorial organisers to sing at the Mass, and agreed, but there was a late change of plan and instead he carried the altar gifts with Henry Cooper, Katie Boyle, Barbara Kelly and Derek Guyler.

To Leslie Jackson, it was a moving occasion but in no way soppy or sentimental. He agreed the liturgical ceremony was magnificent, and nothing was too drawn out. 'I think it was just as Eamonn would have liked.'

Bernadette Greevy sang Mozart's 'Laudate Dominum' with the Cathedral choir, and afterwards said she only wished it had been a happier occasion. Since childhood, she had known Eamonn Andrews and the Bourke family and counted it an honour to be invited. It was, however, the unique atmosphere that impressed her: 'Although it was in essence a show-business tribute, I felt that the occasion in itself transcended that aspect and, in fact, was much bigger. How Eamonn would have loved to mingle with all the stars present!'

Grainne Andrews sat calmly through the pageantry, surrounded by her children. Her face reflected pride as well as sorrow as she watched Fergal – so similar in face and build to the young Eamonn – read the psalm. Later, she would say, 'I'm sure Eamonn would have been flattered and honoured by the number of people who attended the Mass. I found the ceremony very touching.'

In nearly every row was seated a friend – or a star – who, either at one time or other, Eamonn must have met on or off screen. For Eamonn it was like the last and most lavish version of *This Is Your Life*. Stars he surprised with the famous red book – such as Terry Wogan, Danny La Rue, Leslie Crowther and Sir John Mills – all were somewhere among the huge congregation.

Entering the Cathedral that morning a veteran Thames producer had remarked to a colleague, 'It's a bit like the passing of Royalty to have a Cardinal Archbishop deliver the homily and have so many people indicates the affection Eamonn was held in.'

It was no secret that Eamonn admired Cardinal Hume, and the Cardinal now joined in the dignified farewell, assisted at the Mass by twenty-five priests. He spoke gently to the congregation of Eamonn's professionalism which he combined with such obvious goodness. His supreme and certainly unconscious achievement was to let the world see the mind and generous face of one of Ireland's finest sons: open, smiling, sympathetic. His faith made him see the other people as members with him of the family of God.

For years, Eamonn was regarded as an unofficial Irish ambassador in London. He was connected for a period with the development of the Irish Club in Eaton Square, and was known to be disappointed that it never achieved the status intended. Differences among committees had not helped, but Eamonn took no sides.

[229]

Eamonn's trouble was that he couldn't find time for all he wanted to achieve. It was as simple as that. Friends knew it; his colleagues often reminded him of it. Years ago he had said he wanted to do less work, yet inwardly he had realised he could not hope to write seriously while at the same time running around the world surprising people for *This Is Your Life*. Later, he was inclined to settle for television in the hope that he would earn enough money to settle down later to write.

To the end Eamonn remained an optimist. Despite racial strife and threat of wars, he preferred to look at a brighter world. He could still say after twenty-five years, 'I'm not at all worried about it.' It was the faith in Eamonn talking. His children understood. True, he worried like any responsible parent worries, but it wasn't in a black or despairing way. To Leslie Jackson, one of his oldest friends, Eamonn never lost his sparkle on the screen – or his marvellous zest for life. 'Eamonn,' he would tell his friends, 'has still the enthusiasm of a television apprentice. It's amazing.'

After the memorial Mass, Grainne and her children mixed with the guests at the special reception. It was, as she liked to recall, the biggest reunion in years. 'I met Barbara Kelly and she said to me, "Do you realise we are the only two left now? The others are dead."' Barbara was recalling the old days of *What's My Line?* when she came to know Grainne, Gilbert Harding and the others. Leslie Jackson shook Grainne's hand and recalled the years when Harding used to visit the Andrews' home. Jackson loved the man. Malcolm Morris, who spent many happy days in Eamonn's Dublin home, recalled more recent memories for her of Eamonn.

There was a poignant moment as Cardinal Hume took her hand and whispered, 'He was loved by all. I adored him too.'

At a brief press conference later, Philip Jones of Thames Television said that three *This Is Your Life* programmes made shortly before Eamonn's death would be shown in January. Five of the 'classics' from the series would also be shown. The family would have a say in choosing them. Emma Andrews

[232]

mentioned the Bob Geldof programme. Inevitably, the question of a replacement was discussed. Philip Jones said that Eamonn 'cannot be replaced' but a new presenter would have to be found for the series. Fergal Andrews suggested Mike Yarwood and Niamh commented, amid laughter, 'Dad's working on it now'.

It was a tired Grainne Andrews who returned to Dublin with her children to begin a new life without the man she was married to for almost thirty-six years. A pile of letters awaited her – and every morning for days the postman was to deliver more.

'It's incredible the number of letters I've received,' she told friends. 'Thousands of them, many from total strangers. People have sent me copies of letters Eamonn wrote to them over the years. I never realised he was writing to them. Seemingly, he would write back to anyone who wrote to him asking for advice or help. He kept up correspondences for years. And here are these letters coming back to me in the green ink he always used with the familiar squiggle of his signature at the end of them.'

Even after a lifetime, she had to admit that she hadn't realised how popular her husband was. It was now some weeks after his death and she was still in 'a trance'. 'Sometimes I get angry that he was taken away from me. There are times that I'm thankful. Doctors have told me that had he lived he would have been very restricted. I know how Eamonn would have hated that kind of life; I mean he was always so active and never idle for a moment.'

One thing she and the family would miss was Eamonn's home cooking. He always cooked the Christmas turkey. Like everything else he did, he was, as Grainne would say, 'a perfectionist even when cooking. He had to have everything at his fingertips. If I put them out of his reach, he'd go spare.'

People in Portmarnock came to know Eamonn as a regular jogger. He rose at seven, donned his tracksuit, and went for a run. Other times he would slip up to the local convent to hear morning Mass. 'When he came back,' recalls Grainne, 'He'd get me fresh orange juice and give me a kiss. I'd ask, Was it body or soul this morning, darling? We'd laugh a lot at that.' On sunny days Eamonn had liked to spend time in the garden. He was a gardening lover, though on his own admission 'not very good at it'. Grainne remembers, 'He was always trying out new-fangled things at the end of the garden. But the marrows and cucumbers which emerged were invariably crooked or warped in some way. Myself and the children called him The Squire Andrews when he went for the spade.'

One morning, going through his papers and documents, she came across 'lots of poetry' he used to write when he was in his twenties before they met. Some day she hoped to have it published in book form. In more reflective moments, Grainne accepted that their marriage had been a partnership with no question of her being in the background. 'Eamonn had his life as a television personality and I looked after the house and children. But neither of us thought of him as being the front figure and me being in the background.'

She recalled with pride how he telephoned her from the studio after every show. It was, she knew, Eamonn's way of placing value on her judgment. It was the show-business link between them. They had at the same time remained friends and lovers. When she first met him he was a very romantic person and in the intervening years had not changed. She still had in her possession every letter he wrote. 'Eamonn hates me to read them,' she used to say.

Some of their happiest moments together were on holidays abroad. They had come to love the Algarve and generally rented a villa there. Normally they ate out in small restaurants for lunch and then went to the market to get the ingredients for dinner, which Eamonn always cooked.

She would miss *This Is Your Life* with Eamonn as presenter. It was her favourite programme and she rarely, if ever, missed it. Visitors to The Quarry invariably asked her now who she thought should take over from Eamonn. She wasn't sure,

[234]

although the first name that came to her mind was Mike Yarwood's.

'We used to roll around with laughter at his impersonation of Eamonn. It was wickedly cruel, but I remember Eamonn couldn't stop laughing at it.'

Whoever it was took over as presenter, she knew, *This Is Your Life* would never be the same again for her. It was Eamonn's show.

It was *his* life.

Index

Glendenning, Raymond, 49
Goodman, Mark, 106
Gordon, Richard, 14, 136
Grant, Cary, 106
Greevy, Bernadette, 228
Gregory, Dick, 122
Green, Hughie, 217
Green, Syd, 85
Gruenberg, Axel, 65–6
Grundy, Bill, 157
Guinness, Sir Alec, 6, 157
Gutteridge, Reg, 16
Guthrie, Duncan, 75
Guyler, Derek, 228

Harding, Gilbert, 45–7, 52–5, 58, 80, 83, 93–4, 113, 124, 182–3, 232
Harris, Dermot, 3, 4
Harris, Elizabeth, 4
Harris, Richard, 3–5, 11, 14, 140
Harris, Rolf, 134
Harnett, Noel, 33
Harvey, Laurence, 122, 124
Hay, Gladys, 48
Herschen, Otto, 230
Hicks, Lady Pamela, 169, 173
Higgins, Alex, 224
Hill, Benny, 198
Hill, Dick, 85
Hill, Lord, 123
Hillery, President, 20
Hillery, Mrs Maeve, 20
Hoby, Alan, 49
Hope, Bob, 106, 146, 156–7, 170, 173, 218
Hope, Dolores, 156
Hope, Linda, 156–7
Housego, Fred, 7
Hume, Cardinal Basil, 229, 232

Ingle, Jimmy, 26

Irving, Henry, 24
Iturbi, Jose, 33, 44

Jackson, T Leslie, 9, 51–4, 57–8, 60, 63–6, 68–70, 72, 74, 79, 84, 88, 90, 92, 97–9, 103, 105, 107, 109–10, 112–14, 116, 127, 133, 161–2, 183, 207–8, 226, 228, 231–2
Jameson, Derek, 7
Johannson, Ingmar, 16, 80
Johnson, Jack, 145
Jones, Audrey, 212
Jones, Philip, 181, 185, 211, 232–3

Karloff, Boris, 68
Kavanagh, Ted, 53
Kearns, Joe, 20
Kelly, Barbara, 7, 53, 84, 93, 181, 183, 185, 210–11, 228, 232
Kelly, Henry, 223
Kinnear, Roy, 217–18
Klein, Brian, 6, 210
Kunz, Charlie, 34
Kydd, Sam, 136

Lamour, Dorothy, 157
La Rue, Danny, 229
Laski, Marghanita, 53
Law, Denis, 102
Leonard, Maurice, 167–8, 170, 173–4, 181, 185–8, 190–1, 195–6, 213–14
Lister, Moira, 166
Little, P.J., 33
Loss, Joe, 9, 41–4, 59, 82, 89, 134, 143, 176, 208–9, 226
Loss, Mildred, 9, 41–3, 59–60, 89–90, 143, 208–9, 226
Louis, Joe, 145

Reed, Robert, 149
Rees, Dai, 164–5
Riddington, Ken, 48
Riddington, Mrs, 48
Robinson, Eric, 85
Roche, Dominic, 51
Rushe, Desmond, 222
Rushton, William, 120
Ryder, Sue, 71–5, 212

Savile, Jimmy, 12–13, 140, 217
Schweitzer, Albert, 150
Seddon, Professor Herbert, 58–60
Sellers, Peter, 178
Shakespeare, William, 27
Shaw, Bernard, 23, 27, 201
Shrimpton, Jean, 126
Sinatra, Frank, 86, 156
Sinatra, Tina, 156
Skehan, John, 219
Sloan, Tom, 112–13
Solti, Sir Georg, 214
Sommerfield, Teddy, 49, 65, 85, 108–9, 112–15
Spinks, Leon, 147
Stephenson, Sam, 14, 139
Stewart, Andy, 166
Stewart, Michael, 137
Sutherland, Joan, 20

Tarbuck, Jimmy, 136, 164, 224
Terry-Thomas, 120
Tesler, Brian, 108–9, 112–16, 122, 127–8, 131–134, 139, 168, 179, 211
Thomson, Kenneth, 141
Thomson, Lord, 141

Thomas, Howard, 123, 169, 171, 173, 176
Thomas, James, 134
Todman, Bill, 106
Trueman, Freddie, 121
Tunney, Gene, 34

Ustinov, Peter, 20

Vaughan, Frankie, 81–3, 85, 135, 198, 209
Vaughan, Stella, 135, 209
Vernon Girls, 85

Waldman, Ronnie, 52–3, 63–5, 83, 90
Walker, Billy, 145
Warner, Lavinia, 170
Wayne, John, 6, 106
West, Mae, 106
Wiggin, Maurice, 120, 123
Wilcox, Herbert, 82
Wilde, Oscar, 27
Winnick, Maurice, 46–7, 49
Wise, Ernie, 185
Wogan, Helen, 215–16
Wogan, Terry, 9–10, 119, 183, 215–17, 219, 223–4, 229
Wogan Towers, 14
Wood, Dr Michael, 150–52
Worth, Harry, 81

Yana, 85
Yarwood, Terry, 167–70, 173–4, 210
Yarwood, Mike, 224, 235
Yeats, Jack, 34